A
GUIDE
TO
JEWISH
THEMES IN
AMERICAN
FICTION
1940-1980

by

MURRAY BLACKMAN

The Scarecrow Press, Inc.
Metuchen, N.J., & London
1981

Z
1231
F4
B52

Library of Congress Cataloging in Publication Data

Blackman, Murray, 1920-
    A guide to Jewish themes in American fiction,
1940-1980.

    Includes indexes.
    1.   American fiction--20th century--Bibliography.
2.   Jews--Fiction--Bibliography.   I.   Title.
Z1231.F4B52   [PS374.J48]   016.813'54'0935203924
ISBN 0-8108-1380-7   80-24953

Dedicated

to

Martha

for

her

unflagging

faith

in

me.

May I acknowledge with deep gratitude:

the opportunity afforded to me through Walden University to complete a journey begun twenty years ago;

the personal friendship and the magnificent guidance given me by Dr. Sylvan D. Schwartzman of the Hebrew Union College - Jewish Institute of Religion;

the untiring dedication and personal interest of my secretary, Mrs. J. Wesley (Mary) Stewart.

TABLE OF CONTENTS

I. INTRODUCTION:
JEWISH FICTION AND ADULT JEWISH EDUCATION

The Jewish historical experience has been marked by a commitment to the concept of continuous learning. That dedication by the "People of the Book" was understood to be a response to Divine commandments. In his retelling and sum-
mary of the unique covenant relationship between the Hebrew
people and God, Moses spoke these words: "Hear, O Israel,
the statutes and judgements which I speak in your ears this
day, that ye may learn them, and keep, and do them" (31:
219; numbers refer to the List of References at the end of
this Introduction). He then enjoined his listeners: "And
these words, which I command thee this day, shall be in
thine heart: And thou shalt teach them diligently unto thy
children, and shalt talk of them when thou sittest in thine
house, and when thou walkest by the way, and when thou
liest down, and when thou risest up" (31:221). To this day,
Jews affix to the doorposts of their homes a cylinder con-
taining a parchment bearing these words. Learning and teaching, teaching and learning, are life experiences continuously
alluded to in Scripture and in subsequent Jewish literature.
To the Jew,

> Education is important as a means to living the
> full, the good, the desirable life. It is essentially
> life-centered, though it is more interested in the
> ideal life than in the practical realities of what is

1

> now being done.   Education has its high value in
> Judaism because together with prayer and faith
> (though Judaism talks little about the latter, pre-
> ferring actions to talk) it is considered a primary
> means of achieving proper action.   Education is
> then the key to which the Jews have built the ethics
> of living for God [8:75].

Unlike other revealed religions, Judaism developed
means by which sacred writings were to become the common
inheritance of all the people.

> ... the endeavor to educate the whole people in its
> religion created a unique system of universal educa-
> tion, whose very elements comprised not only reading
> and writing, but an ancient language and its classic
> literature [47:322].

Though the origins of the methods and practices of the
educational system are lost in the obscurity of the past, a
dramatic incident recorded in the Book of Nehemiah described
a practice that became the foundation for that system.   With
the return of the Jewish exiles to their homeland following
the Babylonian exile in the sixth century B. C. E. , Ezra as-
sembled the people in Jerusalem.

> And Ezra the priest brought the Law before the
> congregation, both men and women, and all that
> could hear with understanding.... And Ezra opened
> the book in the sight of all the people ... even the
> Levites caused the people to understand the Law
> ... and they read in the book, in the Law of God,
> distinctly, and they gave the sense, and caused them
> to understand the reading [31:1048].

Ezra determined that

> education is to be the primary instrument for the
> fulfillment of the Jewish religion.   He has begun the
> practice of the systematic study of the basic re-
> ligious books with the broad masses of the people.
> He has begun the longest unbroken tradition of study
> by a whole people known to Western man, and per-
> haps all mankind [8:71].

One of the great historians of the post-Biblical age in
Judaism, George Foote Moore, regarded the endeavor to edu-

cate the whole people in its religion as an "undertaking with
no parallel in the ancient Mediterranean world" (47:281).
The radical innovation by Ezra of public reading and inter-
pretation of Torah became the foundation of the synagogue
practice of reading sections on Mondays and Thursdays, these
being market days, as well as on the Sabbath. Moore observed that

> for the education of the whole people in the princi-
> ples and practice of its religion Judaism had two
> institutions ... the synagogue and the school ...
> and these two ... worked together in a harmony
> which resulted in substantive unity of instruction
> [47:281].

Thus, by the fifth century before the Common Era,
educational structures had been created in Palestine that allowed the total community to study basic source materials.
Within the three centuries following, a free-public-school
system had been developed so that, at least, all males would
be literate. Beyond the class of sages, the full-time scholars, the Jewish community could boast of an adult student
population concerned with learning.

> Adult education was widespread and popular among
> the Jews. Every Jew knew that he was obligated
> by sacred Law to study Torah every day of his
> life. Consequently, many men, even artisans and
> industrial workers, reserved part of every day for
> study [15:76].

Biblical readings formed the foundation of the adult-
education curriculum. Three times weekly, these readings
were given in the synagogues, in addition to every holiday
and fast day and the first day of every month. Each verse
was read in Hebrew, ten verses being the minimum require-
ment, and then interpreted into the vernacular of the time,
Aramaic. Such translation was accompanied by discourses.
While academies for higher learning came into existence to
develop and perpetuate a learned "professional" scholar group,
these very academies were open to other adults so that they
might benefit from the discussions.

Following the dispersion caused by the Romans in the
first century of our era, the thriving centers of Jewish life
in Babylonia soon surpassed their Palestinian counterparts in
the excellence of their educational institutions. That vast

"treasure trove of law, history, morals, ethics and folklore, known as the Babylonian Talmud" (27:940) is regarded as superior to and more authoritative than the Palestinian Talmud. The Babylonian academies created a unique mass-adult-education enterprise, the "Kallah," study assemblies.

> Twice a year during the month of Ellul, the month preceding Rosh Hashanah, and the High Holy Day season, and during the month of Adar, preceding the Passover festival, thousands of students and scholars would come to the academies from all parts of the Diaspora and spend the month, in study and discussion. The talmudic tractate analyzed during the month's session of the Kalla was one which had been announced at the end of the previous Kalla gathering and had thus been studied by the participants during the preceding five months [27:940].

These sessions gave men an opportunity to desist from their occupational pursuits and to engage in an expansion of their knowledge.

The period of the Middle Ages were not "Dark Ages" in the European Jewish communities. In every country in which Jews resided, an educational structure was reared for both formal and informal learning. Every synagogue harbored within its walls a room set aside for daily study.

> In this environment there grew and developed the chevro, the regular group of men who would meet to study even briefly some text that fitted their capacity. Early in the morning before the daily toil, or late in the Sabbath afternoon, the simplest would be reading the Book of Psalms. Others might be studying the basic code of Jewish law or the legends and folklore of the Talmud. Whatever the subject, this was a free association of adults, continuing their study, without professional guidance, in a give and take of knowledge or opinion, for no other reason than that to be a man meant to continue to learn [8:77].

Moses Maimonides, a towering figure in Jewish intellectual history, gave utterance to the Jewish concern for continuing learning in his great work of the twelfth century, Mishneh Torah:

> Every man in Israel is obliged to devote himself to

study, be he rich or poor, of good health or af-
flicted by diseases, a youngster or a doddering eld-
er; even if he be a beggar living on charity or a
father burdened with a family, he ought to set aside
time for study by day and night.... Among the
greatest scholars of Israel there were wood-pickers
and water-carriers, even blind men, and they never-
theless studied the Torah by day and night.... Up
to what age is one obliged to study the Torah? Unto the day of death ... [8:94].

The Age of the Enlightenment, paired with political
emancipation in the eighteenth century, fomented a radical innovation for the majority of Jews in Western Europe. When
the ghetto walls came tumbling down, education was split into
two disciplines, religious and secular. This did not hold
true for Jews in Eastern Europe, where political reformation
was to arrive later, if at all.

The Jew, emigrating to the New World from Western
Europe, maintained the synagogue as the center of Jewish
learning. The pattern had been established by the small
number of earlier arrivals from Sephardic (Spanish-Portu-
guese) backgrounds. However, the need to develop new roots,
the intense desire to become Americanized, the pressures of
livelihood--all these contributed to a truncated Jewish educational system. Secular and religious learning were pursued
in different institutions; the former removed from the aegis
of the Jewish community. Formal education became child-
centered. Adult Jewish studies were reduced to a leisure-
time activity, intermittently pursued by an alarmingly dimin-
ishing number of devotees.

Contemporary Adult Jewish Education

The American Jewish synagogue, in its self-image and historic role, continued to fulfill one of its tasks as a lifelong
continuing-education center. Traditional patterns of curricula
content for adults had dictated the use of classic sources:
Bible, Rabbinic, and post-Rabbinic writings. Now faced by
the weakened loyalties of American Jews, Rabbinic leaders
became aware of the need to organize teaching materials
around subject matter they considered to be basic for the in-
formed Jew.

In 1928, Dr. Jacob Singer, in a paper prepared for

the thirty-sixth annual convention of the Central Conference
of American Rabbis, called for the creation of a commission
"for the furtherance of Adult Education in Judaism, so that
much of the waste and misdirection of energy might be guided
into more effective channels with inevitable improvements in
results" (54:368). His challenge was accompanied by "Outlines for Adult Education in Judaism" (55:428-464). Singer
developed three areas of study, each with twenty lessons accompanied by bibliographies. "Jewish History" spanned the
millennia from beginnings through the American experience.
"Judaism" encompassed theology, prayer, festivals, and
modern Jewish denominationalism. "Bible Study" introduced
the students to an awareness of Biblical literature, its development and significance, and specific books within the collection known as Scriptures.

        The materials, used as sources for suggested read-
ings, included most standard works in print at the time.
Classic histories, like the five-volume History of the Jews,
by Heinrich Graetz; Abraham L. Sachar's A History of the
Jews; History of the Jewish People, by Margolis and Marx;
and selected articles in Funk & Wagnalls' Jewish Encyclo-
pedia provided the foundation for the "Jewish History for
Adults" lessons. Similar standard works, many used in
graduate studies in the rabbinic seminaries, were listed in
the remaining categories of lessons. For many years, the
"curriculum" for adult Jewish studies in most synagogues re-
flected Singer's outlines. The method most commonly employed was the lecture approach with reading assignments by
the students.

        However, responding to new knowledge from the field
of secular education, synagogue leadership began to create
varied materials and methods to convey information, to
strengthen individual commitment to Judaism and to assist in
the development of self-awareness and self-enrichment.

                By the end of World War II, it was apparent that
                a major upheaval had taken place in American
                Jewish life. This period marked a turning point
                in the whole pattern of American Jewish life. . . .
                By the early 1950's, it was obvious that adult
                Jewish education was coming to the fore as an
                important new development in the American Jewish
                community [11:101].

        The major national Jewish congregational bodies cre-

ated central agencies for adult Jewish studies.   They provided
guidance to member congregations in the enunciation of goals
and in the creation of suggested courses and study materials.
The National Federation of Temple Brotherhoods created a
kit to stimulate study activities in men's clubs (49:1-24).   It
reviewed various programs in existence throughout the country and demonstrated the wide variety of existing adult education offerings.   They ranged from single lectures to ten-
session courses.   They covered such subjects as "Historic
Controversies in Jewish Life, " "The Religions of the Western
World, " and "Prayerbook Hebrew. "   Filmstrips, breakfast
meetings, and weekend camp retreats were among the techniques employed to attract students.   In some communities,
several congregations joined to create "Academies of Jewish
Studies, " with a four-year course of study culminating in the
awarding of certificates of achievement.

        B'nai B'rith, Hadassah, and the National Federation
of Temple Sisterhoods were among the many national service
and fraternal groups to create study-guide materials for local
member groups.   Such guides were usually for discussion
leaders, the subjects being single themes.   Studies under-
taken by some of the national Jewish organizations have revealed an extensive array of materials and methods employed
in the pursuit of a wide variety of objectives (13:1-24).

        The materials in adult Jewish education are as varied
as the objectives.   Television kinescopic films have been
used in courses ranging from "Adventures in Jewish Religious
Thought in the U. S. " to "Jews in Israel and Other Lands. "
Filmstrips illustrate "Modern Jewish Personalities. "   The
workshop technique takes advantage of cooking skills to teach
some aspects of "Festivals of the Jewish Year. "   For introducing various communal agencies, field trips are employed
widely.   Recordings, tape cassettes, and innovative types of
transliterated materials provide beginnings for students in a
study of the Hebrew language.   Lectures, forums, and panels
are basic approaches, too.

        However, heavy reliance is placed on traditional clas-
sic literary sources, befitting the People of the Book.   The
lack of Hebrew-language facility among the majority of American Jews gave rise to the production and use of translations,
abridgments, and anthologies.   The problem-centered approach
seized upon works in the fields of history, sociology, philoso-
phies of Judaism, ritual and ceremonial practices, and human
relations.   All too often, books designed for the religious

education of preadults found their way into adult programs. Homer Kempfer's observation that "the voluntary nature of adult education forces every program director to be his own curriculum expert" (34:61) could be enlarged to the areas of collecting, analyzing, and even creating materials for study. Present-day adult Jewish education can best be characterized by comparing the congregational rabbi to Kempfer's "program director." He is his own curriculum expert, responding to the felt needs of his congregants and guided by that ancient dictum: "The world rests upon three foundations-- study, worship and good deeds" (30:15).

The creation of adult Jewish education programs and materials has continued to be the responsibility of national organizations, rabbis of local congregations, and program directors of secular Jewish institutions. Although there have appeared some creative and innovative approaches to content, little attention has been paid to the educative process of adults.

Knowledge of the psychology of adulthood, motivation, developmental tasks, the adult learning process, and methods of teaching adults are elements conspicuous by their absence in adult Jewish education endeavors. In 1957, the Hebrew Union College - Jewish Institute of Religion in Cincinnati introduced the first graduate elective course offered in the country on "Methods and Materials in Adult Jewish Education" (6: A1- B2). Adult Jewish education had finally come of age.

The Nature of Informal Adult Education

Education has been defined as "essentially a process involving the acquisition of (1) new facts and (2) new attitudes and methods, and permitting a new and more confident approach to the problems of everyday living" (34:17). Leaders in the adult-education movement emphasized that the learning experience could not be limited to the preadult. "Real education comes after we leave school ... there is no reason it should stop before death" (14:10).

For the purposes of this study, adult education is conceived of as

> an experience of maturing, voluntarily selected by people whose major occupation is no longer that of going to school or college in which these individuals

> or groups plan meaningful tasks and apply sustained inquiry to them [17:15].

Informal adult education occurs when

> a group of people come together in a number of meetings for the purpose of learning something simply because they want to know about it. ... It would not be an informal course if the purpose was to grant credits towards a degree or diploma; it would then be an academic course. At the other extreme, it would not be an informal course if it had no educational objective at all; it would then be a recreational activity [37:84].

The motivation behind the adult student was expressed succinctly almost fifty years ago by Dr. Eduard C. Lindeman.

> What they want is ... intelligence, power, self expression, freedom, creativity, enjoyment, fellowship. ... They want to count for something; they want their talents to be utilized; they want to know beauty and joy; and they want all these realizations of their total personalities to be shared in communities of fellowship. Briefly they want to improve themselves; this is their realistic and primary aim [39:13-14].

The adult-education movement developed to a level where postgraduate training for educators in that field became a recognized academic discipline in many universities. Dr. Paul L. Essert served as executive director of such a department at Columbia University. In his pioneer text in the field of adult education, he pointed out that

> when men and women seek adult education, they are collectively trying to bring an interplay of five experiences into a state of equilibrium with cultural change. These experiences are (1) occupational achievement; (2) understanding, or search for truths and beauty; (3) self-government; (4) close fellowship; and (5) intermittent solitude [17:17].

The goals of the adult Jewish student are categorized aptly in the last four rubrics.

More specifically, the goals of the adult Jewish educational program have been delineated as

> 1.   The acquisition by our adults of authoritative knowledge and information concerning every area of Jewish learning.
>
> 2.   The formation of an attitude of great appreciation and respect for our spiritual and cultural heritage as it continues to grow.
>
> 3.   To enable mature men and women to make the ideals of Judaism ... operative in their day-to-day living by providing a yardstick for ethical conduct in home, business, community, national and international life.
>
> 4.   To provide our people with the emotional strength of our faith in times of personal, family, or community stress [38:13].

Characteristics of the Adult Student

Adult students, whether in planned learning settings or pursuing independent study, possess mind-sets that differ from those of children.   Their skills in living, responses to environmental challenges, success or failure in performing life tasks, and wisdom derived from experience differentiate them from younger students.   They possess greater continuing power in the use of mathematical symbols (35:90).   They find more meaningful a problem-centered or situation-centered learning experience (5:167), whose program "must be fashioned to solve the peculiar problems at hand in terms of the particular adults involved" (5:125).   Such programs must start "where the learners are environmentally as well as intellectually" (5:125).   "Such factors as nationalistic backgrounds, urban or rural areas, education, religion, geographical location, ... to a significant degree ... will determine the nature of the program, its direction, and its extent" (5:169).

Recent demographic studies provide a description for us of the American Jew.

> Third generation American Jews are largely concentrated in the college-educated groups and in high white-collar occupations [26:19].

87% of all Jews in the United States 14 years old
and over lived in the large urbanized areas of
250,000 population or more, in contrast to only one
of every three persons in the general population
[26:38].

As of 1957, 17% of the adult Jews were college
graduates, compared to only 7% of the general
population. If those who attended college without
graduating are included, the percentage of Jews was
30, or exactly twice the 15% of the general population [26:62].

With residence and education controlled, 70% of
the Jewish males were white-collar workers, compared to 41% of the general male population [26:75].

With other studies confirming much of these statistics, the
average adult Jew may be described as literate; upper- and
middle-class rather than lower; professional and in business
rather than hard-hat and blue-collar worker; an urbanite who
is a patron of cultural activities and a high consumer of reading materials, including fiction.

Those adults most motivated to read are "the ones
with the most education ... in the upper [rather] than in the
lower income groups.... We know that the readers are the
ones with the most education" (11:9).

Criteria of Materials for Adult Education

Many educators in fields other than that of English literature
have found great value in the use of fiction for collateral
readings.

The novel or drama that is accurate in its historic
atmosphere and historic setting contributes much to
history teaching. It gives a picture of the times
and of the people. A knowledge of the customs,
the prevailing ideas and prejudices, the mode of
living, the controlling values of life--these are a
few of the by-products of collateral reading of historical fiction and drama [36:233].

In a voluntary-education setting, the mature reader tends to
read

> (a) a wide variety of materials that contribute
> pleasure, widen horizons, and stimulate creative
> thinking; (b) serious materials which promote a
> growing understanding of one's self, of others, and
> of problems of a social, moral, and ethical nature;
> and (c) intensively in a particular field or materi-
> als relating to a central core [35:44].

Within that variety of materials read by the mature reader,
no single type exemplifies the above criteria better than fiction. Through fiction, the writer may define "one of the universal human types, ... represent a whole phase of the history of a nation and a civilization, ... and reveal a passion
for the realities of human nature..." (9:36).

One of the most gifted of American rabbis, Dr. Solomon B. Freehof, attracted "thousands of Pittsburghers, people of all faiths ... to hear him in sessions called the
'largest adult literary class in Pittsburgh'" (32:122). His
annual series of book reviews showed the response of his
listeners to the special gifts of writers of fiction. In one of
his public reviews, Dr. Freehof described the novel as an
"art form which uses the individual as the mirror to concen-
trate the rays of many great ideas" (23:7-8). He saw the
novelist as serving a "great function in helping towards the
redemption of the modern age" (25:12). Centered upon human beings, the novel develops an awareness of the

> uniqueness of personality, and when you read the
> novel, if it is a successful novel, a new personality
> has been created in whom you find yourself as a
> unique personality, and with whom, through the
> pages of the novel, you live an additional or a
> parallel life [23:7].

Use of Fiction in Adult Jewish Education

The years 1940-1980 were a traumatic period for American
Jews. The achievement of status and affluence at home
coupled with the Holocaust, World War II, the establishment
of the State of Israel, and the several wars in the Mideast
created an identity crisis. American fiction is a mirror of
that period, created largely by Jews who represent "one
third to one half of the new generation of major American
writers" (7:24). Saul Bellow, in describing the writer's role,
maintained that

> we do not make up history and culture.... We
> make what we can of our condition with the means
> available. We must accept the mixture as we find
> it ... the impurity of it, the tragedy of it, the hope
> of it [3:2].

Knowledge of the past, wrestling with the present, and pro-
jections of the future are essential to the learning process.
Fiction reflects these conditions.

Particularly for American Jews, Jewish writers of
fiction have special importance.

> ... they, insofar as they are Jewish, have at pres-
> ent wide appeal; the more Jewish they are the more
> universal their appeal seems to be. It is in this
> sense that Jewish writers are in the position of
> creating for all Americans--Jew and Gentile alike--
> the most useful, the most livable, the most viable
> images of what it means to be an American in the
> 60's [21:5].

Harold U. Ribalow, who has among his credentials a number
of anthologies of works by Jewish writers, observed that "the
constant seeking for human values in American life is nowhere more compulsive than among Jewish writers" (52:25).

A prominent literary critic suggested that "we live
in an age of rootlessness, alienation and terror, in which the
exiled condition thought peculiar to the Jew comes to seem
the common human lot" (20:258). Time Magazine, in a special essay, tried to probe the reasons behind the seeming
domination of American fiction by Jews. It concluded that in

> an age of "alienation" the Jew is looked to as an
> expert in estrangement--the perpetual outsider who
> somehow knows how to keep warm out there. At
> the same time, in a homogenizing society, the
> Jewish tradition is increasingly valued as rich and
> deep; Gentile readers seem to be finding themselves
> in Jewish fictional characters [59:1].

For Jewish readers, the universal appeal of the Jewish writer is transformed into a particular meaning. In his
sweeping study of the Jew in the American novel, Leslie
Fiedler characterized the beginnings of the Jewish-American
novel; as a problem novel, "its essential problems must be

those of identity and assimilation" (19:16).   Forty years later,
the problem is the same.   "The question that links all Jews
today is the question of continuation.   Subterraneously or
overtly this question faces every Jew: Continuation or assimilation?" (2:16).

Fiction, when successful, provides an illuminating
personal experience for readers.   It reflects their human
condition and may respond to their quests for personal worth
and meaning.   The Jewish writer is "in the final analysis a
Jew who has chosen the art of writing to extol or condemn a
certain way of living, believing, fighting, or in one word:
being" (28:xiii).   The Jewish novel may assist readers in
their search for identity, for being.

Statement of the Problem

Churches and synagogues have "constituted the largest cate-
gory of participation in the field of adult education" (56:353).
A review of synagogue programs has revealed an awesome
array of courses, programs, and techniques (13:1-24).   Conspicuous by its absence in most programs and sources of
materials for adult Jewish education is the body of literature
that expresses "who we are ... our own self conception and
the ideas others have developed about us" (45:3), namely fiction.   Dr. Jacob Singer, who outlined one of the first syl-
labi of adult Jewish education courses in 1928 observed that

> the best approach to an epoch in the past is through
> the historical novel.   The impression gained of the
> early Christian period in Kingsley's Hypatia, or of
> the French Revolution in Dickens' A Tale of Two
> Cities is immeasurably greater for the general
> reader than any learned treatise could possibly
> afford [54:371].

Yet, nowhere in his lists of readings did he recommend a
novel.   Educators have concluded that

> since adults came voluntarily to our classes, we
> need attractive and enticing materials.   The adult
> sees quickly the link between what he is reading,
> seeing or hearing and his own life interests ...
> [12:112].

In terms of subject matter, they have urged that books "be

selected with a sensitivity to ... current developments in
human affairs ... " (37:92).

Jewish writers of fiction reflect and intepret their essential human condition, experience, and values.

> The author's Jewishness works itself into the heart
> of ... books, and it does so in two identifiable
> ways; first, Jewish history and the values of Jew-
> ish experience comprise the basic life standard for
> taking the measure of life in the modern secular
> world in general; and second, the central character
> is a man involved in a spiritual quest which in-
> cludes, as one of its ultimate desires, reattach-
> ment to the kinds of truths in the covenant which
> Abraham made with God [53:120-121].

Fiction meets the many criteria for the selection of materials
to be used in adult education. It would seem appropriate to
review hundreds of adult-education programs sponsored by Reform Jewish congregations and national Jewish secular organizations since 1958 (6:A1-Z8). Rarely have there been references to novels or short stories in lists of recommended
books or texts. Even in a ten-session course on Modern
Jewish Life in Literature, no work of fiction was named in
suggested readings (50:16). The popularity of book reviews
has continued unabated. They seem, however, to be mere
responses to the most current best-seller lists. B'nai
B'rith has published one discussion guide for a six-session
course revolving around four modern Jewish writers and the
themes of their novels (16:1-23).

A singular example of the use of fiction for adult stu-
dents was a course offered at the State University of Iowa by
Leo W. Schwarz in 1962. "Man and Meaning in Contemporary
Jewish Literature"

> attempted to offer a critical analysis of 20th cen-
> tury Jewish writing, with the aim of determining
> the dominant views of contemporary Jewish writers
> regarding the nature of man and the meaning of
> life [51:11-15].

Dr. Schwarz's themes included "The Question of Identity and
Alienation, " "The Problem of Suffering, " "The Search for
Faith, " "The Conflict of Race, " and "The Gulf Between the
Generations. " Each theme was accompanied by a bibliography

that included such Jewish writers of fiction as Bellow, Roth, Asch, Wouk, Salinger, Levin, Angoff, and countless others. Obviously, a college course for credit cannot be compared with informal adult learning experiences. However, the possibility is present that such an approach can be transposed to meet the needs of the voluntary adult student.

The Purpose of This Book

The primary purpose of this book is to provide a taxonomy of themes relating to Jews and Judaism, as adumbrated in adult fiction published in the United States from 1940 to 1980. No such bibliography or guide exists.

A secondary purpose relates to the use of the bibliography. Administrators of adult Jewish education programs will find an organized source of materials helpful in the planning of curricula. Some suggested programs are to be found in Section IV. In addition, adults motivated to self-study approaches can refer to the subject categories for reading materials. Works of fiction of this period may be found in public libraries and in Jewish institutional libraries. Many have been on best-seller lists and have been issued in paperback. The use of contemporary fiction responds both to motivational and accessibility criteria.

Beyond these goals, which are based upon the use of fiction in adult Jewish education, a derivative use may be discerned. Researchers who seek to understand and to interpret the American Jewish experience will find in the bibliography entries the perceptions of literary craftsmen. Specific areas of concern and appreciation; developmental analyses of themes within time periods; hypotheses based upon the interactions of one human being and another; people relating to personal, social, political, and economic forces--these are but a few of the possibilities in which such a taxonomy will be necessary.

Creating the Thematic Index

To create the Thematic Index, it was necessary first to compile a bibliography of all works of fiction in English, relating to Jews and Judaism, published in the United States from 1940 to 1980.

The primary sources used for the bibliography were
The Jewish Book Annual, published by the American Jewish
Book Council, and the American Jewish Yearbook, published
by the American Jewish Committee.   Each annual edition
contained bibliographies of American Jewish fiction.

In 1940, Fanny Goldstein, Librarian of the West End
Branch of the Boston Public Library, created a list of Jewish fiction in English covering the prior forty years.   It was
a list of selected titles.   Goldstein described her rule for
selection as including

> books of real fiction dealing with Jewish life ...
> that she can conscientiously recommend to the gen-
> eral reader....   Books which, in the compiler's
> judgment, are unwholesome in content or treatment,
> or present Jewish life in a distorted way, or Jew-
> ish caricatures rather than characters have been
> omitted....   On the whole, only such works have
> been included as ... present themselves as good,
> wholesome, well-written ... [25:500-501].

The two primary sources referred to above suffered
from a similar selection process, although the compilers did
not indicate that their lists were not complete.   Omissions
became apparent when other reference works were employed.
Publishers Weekly, Library Journal, and the annual Book Review Digest cumulation revealed many other works of fiction
relating to Jews and Judaism.   One large class of novels,
written by non-Jews, depicted the birth and development of
Christianity.   These books covered a historical period cru-
cial to a complete picture of Judaism.   They had been omitted
in the "Jewish" bibliographies even though other novels by
non-Jews were present and works by Jewish authors on those
same themes had been included.   Although some of the
omitted novels might have been considered biased in their
attitudes toward Judaism, they did reveal insights into the
Jewish community of that time.   Another group of novels included here were those in which Jews were minor characters or in
which Jewish themes were incidental to the main plot.   The only
criterion, therefore, used to develop the bibliography was whether or not the works related to Jews and Judaism.

No one of the bibliographic sources represented a complete listing of works of fiction relating to Jews and Judaism.
A Guide to Jewish Themes in American Fiction 1940-1980 repre-
sents the only comprehensive bibliography of such works.

The Thematic Index is an alphabetical ordering of sub-
ject headings representing themes relating to Jews and Judaism in American fiction from 1940 to 1980. The entries in
the Thematic Index are based upon several sources: The
General Inquirer (57:170-190); the Index to Jewish Periodicals;
Weine Classification Scheme for Jewish Libraries; Relative
Index to the Weine Classification Scheme for Judaica Libraries; Subject Headings for a Judaica Library; Joseph L.
Baron's A Treasury of Jewish Quotations; and Articles of
Interest in Current Periodicals. In addition, the books
themselves dictated their own themes and subject headings,
the reader acting like a "literary critic (who analyzes) ...
the contents of the text, seeking out patterns, categorizing
them ..." (57:629).

As noted earlier, a secondary purpose to be served
is the use of the Thematic Index for adult-education purposes.
To illustrate this objective, several programs already in existence were chosen and works of fiction were substituted for
the standard reference books suggested to the student. This
approach to curriculum planning is represented in Section IV.

REFERENCES

1. American Jewish Committee. American Jewish Year-
       book. Vols. 44 (1942/43)--79 (1979). Philadelphia:
       Jewish Publication Society of America.

2. Angoff, Charles, and Levin, Meyer, eds. The Rise of
       American Jewish Literature, An Anthology of Selec-
       tions from the Major Novels. New York: Simon &
       Schuster, 1970.

3. Bellow, Saul, cited by Lily Edelman, Jewish Best
       Sellers. Washington, D. C.: B'nai B'rith, [n. d.].

4. _____, ed. Great Jewish Short Stories. New
       York: Laurel Edition, Dell, 1963.

5. Bergevin, Paul. A Philosophy for Adult Education.
       New York: Seabury, 1967.

6. Blackman, Murray. "Education E-4, The Philosophy and
       Content of Adult Jewish Education." Cincinnati,
       [n. d.]. (Mimeographed.)

7.   Boroff, David.   "Questing."   Jewish Heritage, Spring
      1965.

8.   Borowitz, Eugene B.   "Judaic Roots of Modern Educa-
      tion."   Heritage of American Education.   Edited by
      Richard E. Gross.   Boston: Allyn and Bacon, 1962.

9.   Brooks, Van Wyck.   The Writer in America.   New
      York: Avon, 1953.

10.   Clift, David H.   "Introduction."   Adult Reading.   Fifty-
      fifth Yearbook of the National Society for the Study
      of Education, Part II.   Chicago: University of Chi-
      cago, 1956.

11.   Cohen, Samuel L.   "American Jewish Education."   Vol.
      66 of the American Jewish Yearbook.   Philadelphia:
      Jewish Publication Society, 1965.

12.   Dale, Edgar.   "Reading and Related Media."   Adult
      Reading.   Fifty-fifth Yearbook of the National Society
      for the Study of Education, Part II.   Chicago: Uni-
      versity of Chicago, 1956.

13.   Davis, David.   Adult Jewish Education Programs in Re-
      form Congregations, 1959-1962.   New York: Union
      of American Hebrew Congregations, 1962.

14.   Dewey, John, cited by J. R. Kidd.   How Adults Learn.
      New York: Association Press, 1959.

15.   Drazin, Nathan.   History of Jewish Education From 515
      B. C. E. to 220 C. E.   Baltimore: Johns Hopkins
      Press, 1940.

16.   Edelman, Lily.   Living Room Learning Packet #1, Jew-
      ish Best-Sellers, From Frampol, Lithuania to Sub-
      urbia, U. S. A.   Washington, D. C.:   B'nai B'rith,
      [n. d.].

17.   Essert, Paul L.   Creative Leadership of Adult Educa-
      tion.   New York: Prentice-Hall, 1951.

18.   Fiedler, Leslie A.   No! In Thunder.   Essays on Myth
      and Literature.   Boston: Beacon, 1960.

19.   _____.   The Jew in the American Novel.   New
      York: Herzl Institute Pamphlet No. 10, 1959.

20. _____ . Love and Death in the American Novel.
     New York: Stein and Day, 1966.

21. _____ . "The New Jewish Writer in America,"
     Jewish Heritage, Winter 1961.

22. _____ . Waiting for the End, The American Liter-
     ary Scene from Hemingway to Baldwin. London: Jon-
     athan Cape, 1965.

23. Freehof, Solomon B. Review of Alexandra by Gladys
     Schmitt. December 3, 1947. (Typewritten.)

24. Gamoran, Emanuel. Changing Conceptions in Jewish Ed-
     ucation. New York: Macmillan, 1924.

25. Goldstein, Fanny. "Jewish Fiction in English, 1900-
     1940." The American Jewish Yearbook, 5702, Vol-
     ume 43. Philadelphia: Jewish Publication Society of
     America, 1941-5702.

26. Goldstein, Sidney. "American Jewry, 1970: A Demo-
     graphic Profile." American Jewish Yearbook 1971.
     Edited by Morris Fine and Milton Himmelfarb. New
     York: American Jewish Committee, 1971.

27. Greenberg, Simon. "Jewish Educational Institutions."
     The Jews: Their History and Religion. Vol. III.
     Edited by Louis Finkelstein. Philadelphia: Jewish
     Publication Society, 1949.

28. Gross, Theodore L., ed. The Literature of American
     Jews. New York: Free Press, 1973.

29. Guttmann, Allen. The Jewish Writer in America, As-
     similation and the Crisis of Identity. New York: Ox-
     ford University Press, 1971.

30. Hertz, Joseph H. Sayings of the Fathers. New York:
     Behrman House, 1945.

31. The Holy Scriptures. Philadelphia: Jewish Publication
     Society of America, 1917.

32. Jacob, Walter; Schwartz, Frederick C.; and Kaveler,
     Vigdor W., eds. Essays in Honor of Solomon B.
     Freehof. Pittsburgh: Rodef Shalom Congregation,
     1964.

33. Jewish Book Council. Jewish Book Annual. Vols. 1
    (1942)--37 (1979/80). New York: Jewish Book Coun-
    cil of the National Jewish Welfare Board.

34. Kempfer, Homer. Adult Education. New York: Mc-
    Graw-Hill, 1955.

35. Kidd, J. R. How Adults Learn. New York: Associa-
    tion Press, 1959.

36. Klapper, Paul. The Teaching of History. New York:
    Appleton, 1926.

37. Knowles, Malcolm S. Informal Adult Education, A
    Guide for Administrators, Leaders, and Teachers.
    New York: Association Press, 1950.

38. Kranston, Harold I. Your Congregation's Adult Jewish
    Education Committee: A Manual. New York: Union
    of American Hebrew Congregations, 1962.

39. Lindeman, Eduard C. The Meaning of Adult Education.
    New York: New Republic, 1962.

40. Lindhorst, Frank A. Teaching Adults. New York:
    Abingdon, 1951.

41. Liveright, A. A. A Study of Adult Education in the
    United States. Brookline: Center for the Study of
    Liberal Education for Adults at Boston University, 1968.

42. Malin, Irving. Jews and Americans. Carbondale:
    Southern Illinois University Press, 1965.

43. _____, ed. Contemporary American-Jewish Liter-
    ature. Bloomington: Indiana University Press, 1973.

44. _____, and Stark, Irving, eds. Breakthrough, A
    Treasury of Contemporary American-Jewish Litera-
    ture. New York: McGraw-Hill, 1964.

45. Marcus, Alfred. "The Making of a New Jewish Liter-
    ature." Response, Spring 1973.

46. Messbarger, Paul R. Fiction With a Parochial Pur-
    pose, Social Uses of American Catholic Literature,
    1884-1900. Boston: Boston University Press, 1971.

47. Moore, George Foot. Judaism, in the First Centuries
     of the Christian Era, The Age of the Tannaim. 3
     vols. Cambridge: Harvard University Press, 1966.

48. Morris, Nathan. The Jewish School, An Introduction to
     the History of Jewish Education. London: Eyre and
     Spottiswoode, 1937.

49. National Federation of Temple Brotherhoods. A Kit to
     Stimulate Jewish Adult Education. New York: Na-
     tional Federation of Temple Brotherhoods, 1958.

50. Noveck, Simon. Adult Study Groups. Washington,
     D.C.: B'nai B'rith, [n.d.].

51. "Program Notes and Suggestion." Clearing House, A
     Professional Bulletin for Hillel Directors & Counsel-
     ors. Washington, D.C.: B'nai B'rith Hillel Founda-
     tion, December 1963.

52. Ribalow, Harold U. "Reflections of a Jewish Writer."
     Jewish Heritage, Winter 1961.

53. Rosenfeld, Alvin H. "The Progress of the American
     Jewish Novel." Response, Spring 1973.

54. Singer, Jacob. "Adult Education and Judaism." Vol.
     XXXVIII of the Central Conference of American Rab-
     bis Yearbook. Edited by Isaac E. Marcuson, [n.a.].
     Central Conference of American Rabbis, 1928.

55. _____. "Outlines for Adult Education in Judaism."
     Vol. XL of the Central Conference of American Rab-
     bis Yearbook. Edited by Isaac E. Marcuson, [n.a.].
     Central Conference of American Rabbis, 1930.

56. Stokes, Kenneth. "Religious Institutions." Handbook
     of Adult Education. Edited by Robert M. Smith. New
     York: Macmillan, 1970.

57. Stone, Philip J.; Dunphy, Dexter C.; Ogilvie, Daniel
     M.; and Smith, Marshall S.; with associates. The
     General Inquirer: A Computer Approach to Content
     Analysis. Cambridge: MIT Press, 1966.

58. Swift, Fletcher H. Education in Ancient Israel. Chi-
     cago and London: Open Court, 1919.

59. Time Magazine. Time Essay: The New American
     Jew. June 25, 1965.

60. Weinberg, Helen. The New Novel in America, the
     Kafkan Mode in Contemporary Fiction. Ithaca: Cor-
     nell University Press, 1970.

61. Wilson, H. W. (firm). Fiction Catalog. 1941 Edition,
     1942-1979 Supplement to the Ninth Edition. New York:
     H. W. Wilson.

1. Aaron, Chester. About Us. New York: McGraw-Hill, 1967.
    Life in a mining town in Pennsylvania, 1929-1944, with emphasis on adolescence.

2. Aaronsohn, Michael. Broken Lights. Cincinnati: Johnson & Hardin, 1946.
    Autobiographical novel of Reform rabbi blinded in World War I.

3. Abbe, George. Mr. Quill's Crusade. New York: Island Press, 1948.
    Jewish psychologist and refugees confront prejudice in complex plot of an artist and his idealist neighbor.

4. Abel, Hilde. The Guests of Summer. Indianapolis and New York: Bobbs-Merrill, 1951.
    Adolescent Jew lead into maturity after she rejects European Jews encountered in Adirondacks hotel.

5. Abele, Rudolph Von. The Party. Boston: Houghton Mifflin, 1963.
    German officer's liaison with Jewish mistress, now in a concentration camp, provokes tension with commanding officer.

6. Abrahams, Peter. The Path of Thunder. New York:
   Harper, 1948.
      Tragic novel of South African racial tensions il-
   lustrated in love between colored school teacher and
   white Jewish woman.

7. _____. Tell Freedom. New York: Knopf, 1954.
      South African setting of influence of Jewish girl
   in introducing a young non-Jew to wonders of literature.

8. Abzug, Martin. Seventh Avenue Story. New York:
   Dial, 1947.
      Garment industry in New York provides backdrop
   to competition between small manufacturer and big
   business.

9. Adams, Nathan M. The Fifth Horseman. New York:
   Random House, 1967.
      Spy story of search for a Nazi war criminal by
   an Israeli intelligence officer.

10. Ader, Paul. The Leaf Against the Sky. New York:
    Crown, 1947.
       Inter-dating theme of collegians, a Jew and a
    young conservative Southerner.

11. Adler, Warren. The Sunset Game. New York: Vik-
    ing, 1977.
       Senior citizens in retirement village in Florida
    prove themselves to be experts in the game of living.

12. _____. Trans-Siberian Express. New York: Put-
    nam, 1977.
       American cancer specialist attempts to prolong the
    life of Soviet politician and is drawn into a conspir-
    acy, which unfolds on the spectacular railroad.

13. Agnon, S. Y. A Guest for the Night. Translated by
    Misha Louvish. New York: Schocken, 1968.
       Symbolic journey from Palestine to home village
    in Eastern Europe and return to new life in the Holy
    Land.

14. _____. In the Heart of the Seas. New York:
    Schocken, 1967.
       Folktale replete with Hasidic symbolism of journey
    of pious Jews from Middle Europe to Israel.

15. _____. Twenty-one Stories. New York: Schocken,
     1970.
          Agnon's themes include loss of home, exile from
     family, Diaspora, loss of faith, generally reflecting
     pre-World War I life in the small Polish Jewish
     community.

16. _____. Two Tales. New York: Schocken, 1966.
          The first story, set in Jaffa before World War II,
     is about a biologist whose preoccupation makes him
     forget a childhood marriage vow; the second is about
     a Jerusalem bookseller after World War II and his
     involvement with the supernatural.

17. Aichinger, Ilse. Herod's Children. Translated by
     Cornelia Schaeffer. New York: Atheneum, 1963.
          War-time Vienna setting of child refugees who ac-
     cept the aimlessness of their boat journey.

18. Ajar, Emile. Momo. Translated by Ralph Manheim.
     New York: Doubleday, 1978.
          Arab boy in Paris is mothered by an aging Jew-
     ish ex-whore who runs an illegal nursery for chil-
     dren of prostitutes.

19. Albrand, Martha. A Call from Austria. New York:
     Random House, 1963.
          Suspense tale about Nazi treasure in Austria to
     be used to finance a new political party.

20. Alexander, Sidney. Michelangelo, the Florentine: A
     Novel. New York: Random House, 1957.
          Jewish friends of Michelangelo reflect plight of
     Jews in Rome and Florence.

21. Algren, Nelson. The Man with the Golden Arm. New
     York: Doubleday, 1949.
          Chicago slum setting portrays victims of poverty
     environment and drugs.

22. Allmen, Rick. Stanley: The 2nd Avenue Don Juan.
     New York: Harper & Row, 1974.
          Stanley seeks to lose his virginity in New York
     setting during the late 1930s.

23. Alloway, Lawrence. Moses, the Man. New York:
     Vantage, 1951.
          List of Moses emphasizing early years in Egypt.

24. Alman, David. Generations. Chicago: Regnery, 1971.
East Side setting of peddler and his children and
wife, a victim of the Holocaust.

25. Alpert, Hollis. The Claimant. New York: Dial, 1968.
American Jewish lawyer tracks down Nazi war
criminals while involved in restitution claims.

26. Ambler, Eric. The Levanter. New York: Atheneum,
1972.
Palestinian Arab guerrilla group seeks to attack
Tel Aviv in a fast-paced postwar thriller.

27. Amichai, Yehuda. Not of This Time, Not of This
Place. New York: Harper & Row, 1968.
German émigré, now an Israeli archaeologist, con-
fronts Israeli sabras and postwar Germany at a cross-
road in his life.

28. Andersch, Alfred. Efraim's Book. Translated by
Ralph Manheim. New York: Doubleday, 1970.
A German Jew, now a London journalist, searches
in Berlin in 1962 for colleague's daughter and self-
identity.

29. _____. Flight to Afar. Translated by Michael Bul-
lock. New York: Coward-McCann, 1958.
Victims of Nazi terror, including Communist and
Jewish girl, seek to escape oncoming German army.

30. Anderson, Elliot, ed. Contemporary Israeli Literature.
Philadelphia: Jewish Publication Society, 1977.
Prose and poetry are featured in this anthology con-
taining works by major Israeli writers.

31. Andler, Marjorie Duhan. A Sign upon My Hand. Garden City: Doubleday, 1964.
Wealthy New York Jewish girl experiences insecur-
ity in a gentile world.

32. Andrzejewski, Jerzy. The Inquisitors. Translated by
Conrad Syrop. New York: Knopf, 1960.
A tale of Torquemada, the Spanish Inquisitor-
General, in the period prior to the Expulsion from
Spain.

33. Angoff, Charles. Between Day and Dark. New York:
Yoseloff, 1959.

Second-generation Boston student, Harvard graduate, and adjustment to New York life.

34. _____. The Bitter Spring. New York: Yoseloff,
1961.
Emancipated intellectuals in literary world of New
York.

35. _____. In the Morning Light. New York: Beech-
hurst, 1953.
Americanization process of immigrant family in
Boston milieu in early twentieth century.

36. _____. Journey to the Dawn. New York: Beechhurst, 1951.
Adjustment of Eastern European immigrant family
at turn of the century in New England.

37. _____. Memory of Autumn. New York: Yoseloff,
1968.
Editor of magazine in New York during rise of
Nazi power in Europe in early 1940s.

38. _____. Mid-Century. New York: Barnes, 1974.
David Polansky in the 50s is covered in this tenth
novel of the series.

39. _____, and Levin, Meyer. The Rise of American
Jewish Literature. New York: Simon & Schuster,
1970.
Anthology of selections from twenty-two novels by
American-Jewish writers.

40. _____. Season of Mists. New York: Yoseloff, 1971.
The Polansky family continues in this ninth volume
in the series, which carries David past the creation
of the State of Israel into its first war.

41. _____. Something About My Father, and Other People. New York: Yoseloff, 1956.
Thirty-five short stories, most of them interpret-
ing Jewish life in the United States.

42. _____. Summer Storm. New York: Yoseloff, 1963.
The Depression years and their effect on Jewish
family life.

43. _____. The Sun at Noon. New York: Beechhurst, 1955.

Effect of college experience on young second-generation Jew at Harvard, 1919-1923.

44. _____. Toward the Horizon. Barnes, 1979.
The eleventh volume in David Polansky's saga finds him appointed as college department chairman, but he returns to teaching position.

45. _____. Winter Twilight. New York: Yoseloff, 1970.
Portrayal of Jewish and Christian characters in America during years immediately preceding the establishment of the State of Israel.

46. Ansell, Jack. His Brother, the Bear. New York: Doubleday, 1960.
Intermarriage in Louisiana setting portraying frustrations of the relationship surfacing during religious holiday.

47. _____. Dynasty of Air. New York: Arbor House, 1974.
A history of the radio industry from 1920 to 1948, headed by Jewish cast of network mogul.

48. _____. Giants. New York: Arbor House, 1975.
This detailed description of the growth of the television industry features the Jewish giant who was the pioneer.

49. _____. Jelly. New York: Arbor House, 1971.
New Orleans cabaret singer is revealed as former rabbi who left wife and pulpit for liaison with non-Jew.

50. _____. The Shermans of Mannerville. New York: Arbor House, 1971.
Louisiana is the scene of dramatic confrontation of prominent Jewish merchant with blacks and Christians of the area.

51. _____. Summer. New York: Arbor House, 1973.
Fifteen short stories of Jews in the South, one dealing with small boy facing death by cancer, awaiting Elijah.

52. Appel, Benjamin. Life and Death of a Tough Guy. New York: Avon, 1955.

New York immigrant setting of conflict between generations, self-hatred.

53. _____. A Time of Fortune. New York: Morrow, 1963.
    Story of two families, Jewish and non-Jewish, and capitalist and anarchist personalities.

54. Apple, Lewis T. Some Are Friends. New York: Crown, 1951.
    Intermarriage theme with attendant conflicts and misunderstandings.

55. Apple, Max. Zip: A Novel of The Left and The Right. New York: Viking, 1978.
    Nice Jewish boy teams up with junkyard king and student radical to promote Puerto Rican boxer in Cuba.

56. Arcone, Sonya. The Golden Hammer. New York: Atheneum, 1963.
    New York garment-industry setting, drive for success and effect on personal relationships.

57. Arent, Arthur. Gravedigger's Funeral. New York: Grossman, 1967.
    International suspense thriller set in New York and Germany with neo-Nazi characters.

58. Ariss, Jean. The Quick Years. New York: Harper, 1958.
    A happy intermarriage in California rural setting with return to Judaism by nonobservant Jew.

59. Arnold, Elliott. Forests of the Night. New York: Scribner's, 1971.
    World War II novel of Jewish RAF bomber who discovers neo-Nazi revival in Germany.

60. _____. A Night of Watching. New York: Scribner's, 1967.
    Danish Jews smuggled to Sweden in 1943 to escape German capture.

61. Arnothy, Christine. Shalom, Aviva! New York: McKay, 1970.
    Relationship of French photographer and Israeli

sweetheart and his realization of the meaning of the
land of Israel.

62.   Aronowitz, Erwin. <u>Of Blood and Oil: With an Israel
Background: A Novel</u>. New York: Exposition, 1951.
Adventures of American physician fighting with
Jewish underground in Palestine prior to independence.

63.   Arvay, Harvey. <u>The Piraeus Plot</u>. New York: Bantam, 1975.
The Israeli secret service is given an assignment
to prevent Arafat's assassination by more-militant
Arab terrorists in plot hatched in Athens.

64.   Asch, Sholem. <u>The Apostle</u>. Translated by Maurice
Samuel. New York: Putnam, 1943.
Portrayal of Saul of Tarsus and early years of
Christianity.

65.   _____. <u>Children of Abraham; Short Stories</u>. Translated by Maurice Samuel. New York: Putnam, 1942.
The twenty-nine short stories reflect Jewish life
from Rome in the Middle Ages to Germany in Nazi
times.

66.   _____. <u>East River, A Novel</u>. Translated by A. H.
Gross. New York: Putnam, 1946.
Turn-of-the-century life of immigrants in New
York's East Side with interreligious conflicts.

67.   _____. <u>Mary</u>. Translated by Leo Steinberg. New
York: Putnam, 1949.
Reverent portrayal of Mary, Mother of Jesus, and
events in the development of Christianity.

68.   _____. <u>Moses</u>. Translated by Maurice Samuel.
New York: Putnam, 1951.
Recreation of life of Moses using non-Biblical leg-
endary sources.

69.   _____. <u>A Passage in the Night</u>. Translated by
Maurice Samuel. New York: Putnam, 1953.
Prosperous real-estate magnate seeks to make
amends for theft in his youth.

70.   _____. <u>The Prophet</u>. Translated by Arthur Saul
Super. New York: Putnam, 1955.

Novel on Second-Isaiah with major setting in Babylonia.

71. _____. Salvation. Translated by Willa and Edwin Muir. New York: Putnam, 1951.
Nineteenth-century Polish Jewish life in small village; highlights role of folk religion.

72. _____. Tales of My People. Translated by Meyer Levin. New York: Putnam, 1948.
Short stories mainly depicting Jewish life in Eastern Europe prior to and following Nazi period.

73. Ashton, Helen. Tadpole Hall. New York: Macmillan, 1941.
Austrian refugees and evacuated British children and their relationships to English family.

74. Asimov, Isaac. Pebble in the Sky. Garden City: Doubleday, 1950.
Science-fiction novel in which Jewish tailor is transplanted into different era.

75. Astrachan, Sam. An End to Dying. New York: Farrar, Straus & Cudahy, 1956.
Quest for identity of immigrants to America from Eastern Europe and their rise up economic ladder.

76. _____. Katz-Cohen. New York: Macmillan, 1978.
Two American-Jewish families are witnesses to assimilation, insanity, while creating doctors, ambassadors, magnates, and psychiatrists.

77. _____. The Game of Dostoevsky. New York: Farrar, Straus and Giroux, 1965.
Through a game, similar to Monopoly, players try to corner the market in spiritual grace by confessing to one or more of the seven deadly sins.

78. Auchincloss, Louis. The Dark Lady. Boston: Houghton Mifflin, 1977.
Fashionable, upper-class Jew of New York is married to ambitious non-Jew who dominates family relationships.

79. _____. A World of Profit. Boston: Houghton Mifflin, 1968.

New York high-society setting with ambitious Jew
seeking to be accepted.

80. Ausubel, Nathan, ed. A Treasury of Jewish Humor.
Garden City: Doubleday, 1951.
Anthology of short stories illustrating Jewish hu-
mor by prominent authors.

81. Axelrod, George. Where Am I Now--When I Need Me?
New York: Viking, 1971.
Hollywood cast of characters includes writing instructor attempting his great novel, a black house-
keeper, movie stars, and call girls.

82. Ayalti, Hanan J. No Escape from Brooklyn. New
York: Twayne, 1966.
Unhappily married Brooklyn Jewish candy-store
owner, his affair with an Irish girl and return to
his family.

83. Ayme, Marcel. The Transient Hour. New York:
Wyn, 1948.
Jewish refugee from Poland is enmeshed in moral
decline of Paris during the German occupation.

84. Babel, Isaac. The Collected Stories of Isaac Babel.
Translated by Walter Morison. New York: Criter-
ion, 1955.
Short stories and vignettes of Odessa Jewish mid-
dle-class life in Czarist Russia during the Russian
Civil War.

85. _____. The Forgotten Prose. Edited and translated by Nicholas Stroud. Ann Arbor: Ardis, 1978.
Seventeen of his stories and excerpts from his
diary for 1920 comprise a portrait of Babel and life
in the Soviet Union.

86. _____. You Must Know Everything: Stories, 1915-
1937. Translated by Max Hayward. New York: Farrar, Straus and Giroux, 1969.
Stories deal with Odessa and Leningrad during
World War I, the Russian Civil War, and the after-
math of blood-baths of vengeance.

87. Baker, Nina Brown. Next Year in Jerusalem. New
York: Harcourt, Brace, 1950.

Fictionalized but authentic biography of Theodor
Herzl, founder of modern Zionist movement.

88. Balchin, Nigel. The Fall of a Sparrow. New York:
Rinehart, 1956.
Love story of Jewish girl and son of a distinguished British soldier, a rebel from the social establishment.

89. Bankowsky, Richard. The Barbarians at the Gate.
Boston: Atlantic/Little, Brown, 1972.
An SS official in a small Polish town has troubles
with shipments of deported Jews, local religious cult,
and his marriage.

90. _____. The Glass Rose. New York: Random
House, 1958.
Polish girl, ravished by immigrant father, finds
understanding in a New York Jewish manufacturer.

91. Banks, Lynne Reid. Children at the Gate. New York:
Simon & Schuster, 1968.
Israeli kibbutz setting for a Canadian Jewish woman creates sympathetic link between Arab children
and Jews.

92. _____. House of Hope. New York: Simon & Schuster, 1962.
Interfaith love affair between London Jewish playwright and secretary who seek life together on Israeli kibbutz.

93. Barakat, Halim. Days of Dust. Translated by Trevor
LeGassick. Wilmette, Ill.: Medina University Press,
1974.
An Arab novelist recreates the 1967 Arab-Israeli
War with scenes in Amman, Beirut, Jericho, and
Jerusalem.

94. Barash, Asher. Pictures from a Brewery. Translated by Katie Kaplan. Indianapolis: Bobbs-Merrill,
1974.
Turn-of-the-century Jewish matriarch runs a
brewery in a small Polish town.

95. Barber, Rowland. The Midnighters: A Documentary
Novel. New York: Crown, 1970.

The memoirs of a 1948 Israel war hero are used
to recreate arms smuggling and creation of the Israeli air force.

96. Bargellini, Piero. David. Translated by Elizabeth
Abbott. New York: Kennedy, 1954.
Life of King David from boyhood through his ma-
ture years.

97. Barker, Shirley Frances. Strange Wives. New York:
Crown, 1963.
Spanish Jews settle in Newport, Rhode Island, seek-
ing freedom in American colonies.

98. Barmash, Isadore. Net Net. New York: Macmillan,
1970.
Merchandising empire built by Jewish discount
chain-store owner and effect on business world.

99. Baron, Alexander. From the City, from the Plough.
New York: Washburn, 1949.
Jewish member of British infantry battalion butt
of anti-Semitic attitudes and practices.

100.   . The Lowlife. New York: Yoseloff, 1964.
English Jewish gambler copes with family and
neighbors in lower-class economic environment.

101.   . Strip Jack Naked. New York: Yoseloff,
1967.
English Jewish gambler of The Lowlife and his
love affair with younger American girl.

102.   . With Hope, Farewell. New York: Washburn, 1952.
London-ghetto background of rise to manhood prior
to World War II.

103. Baron, Joseph L., ed. Candles in the Night. Phila-
delphia: Jewish Publication Society, 1940.
Stories by non-Jewish authors include settings in
Tiberias, Colonial America, and Poland.

104. Barrett, Laurence. The Mayor of New York. New
York: Doubleday, 1965.
Jewish mayor of New York City and his struggle
with political forces and machines.

105. Bartholomew, Cecilia. The Risk. New York: Doub-
      leday, 1958.
          Effect on esteemed chemist, his family, and
      neighbors of security-risk investigation and job sus-
      pension.

106. Bartov, Hanoch. The Brigade. New York: Holt,
      Rinehart and Winston, 1968.
          World War II setting of Jewish soldiers in British
      brigade and assignment to Germany at end of war.

107. _____ . Whose Little Boy Are You? Translated
      by Hillel Halkin. Philadelphia: Jewish Publication
      Society, 1978.
          The pioneer period of the 1930s in Palestine is
      seen through the growing up of a boy in a small
      village.

108. Bartram, George. The Aelian Fragment. New York:
      Putnam, 1976.
          Israelis, CIA, PLO, and Turks on trail of a
      manuscript fragment of interest to Russians and an
      American professor.

109. Bassani, Giorgio. Behind the Door. New York:
      Harcourt Brace Jovanovich, 1972.
          Jewish high-school student in Ferrara, Italy, re-
      mains "behind the door," an outsider within his non-
      Jewish age group.

110. _____ . Five Stories of Ferrara. Translated by
      William Weaver. New York: Harcourt Brace Jo-
      vanovich, 1971.
          Occupation of northern Italy by German Nazis
      and Italian Fascists and deportation of Jews.

111. _____ . The Garden of the Finzi-Continis. Trans-
      lated by Isabel Quigley. New York: Atheneum,
      1965.
          Upper-class Italian-Jewish family swept up in
      anti-Semitic developments prior to World War II.

112. _____ . The Gold-Rimmed Spectacles. Translated
      by Isabel Quigley. New York: Atheneum, 1960.
          Suicide by prominent Italian-Jewish doctor victim
      of rumors of homosexuality in atmosphere of pre-
      World War II anti-Semitism.

113. _____. The Heron. New York: Harcourt, Brace
   & World, 1970.
      Middle-age reminiscences by Italian Jew who sur-
      vived World War II by hiding in Switzerland.

114. _____. The Smell of Hay. New York: Harcourt
   Brace Jovanovich, 1975.
      Several stories of Italian Jews faced by Fascist
      repression, one of whom is a homosexual physician
      who is driven to suicide.

115. Bassing, Eileen. Home Before Dark. New York:
   Random House, 1927.
      Only Jewish faculty member in New England
      school assists girl suffering emotional breakdown.

116. Bauer, Florence Anne Marvyne. Abram, Son of Ter-
   ah. Indianapolis: Bobbs-Merrill, 1948.
      Biblical novel of Abraham, the "founder" of Juda-
      ism.

117. _____. Behold Your King. Indianapolis: Bobbs-
   Merrill, 1945.
      Young Jew follows Jesus to Golgotha.

118. Baum, Camille. A Member of the Tribe. New York:
   Lyle Stuart, 1971.
      Nice Jewish girl grows up to be a talented pian-
      ist, marries too early, and maintains close bond
      with mother.

119. Baumbach, Jonathan. What Comes Next. New York:
   Harper & Row, 1968.
      Jewish college student reacts to problems caused
      by aftermath of World War II.

120. Beagle, Peter S. A Fine and Private Place. New:
   York: Viking, 1960.
      Fantasy set in cemetery features Bronx widow
      who visits her husband's grave.

121. Becker, Jurek. Jacob the Liar. New York: Harcourt Brace Jovanovich, 1975.
      Jew in Nazi-controlled ghetto pretends to have a
      radio with news of approaching Russian liberators
      but cannot save the town from deportation.

122. Bedford, Syville. *A Legacy*. New York: Simon & Schuster, 1957.
Age of Bismarck and union through marriage of wealthy Jewish Berliners and south German aristocracy.

123. Behrman, S. N. *The Burning Glass*. Boston: Little, Brown, 1968.
Playwright returns to Jewish identity under impact of Hitler period.

124. BeKessy, E. *Barabbas*. New York: Prentice-Hall, 1946.
Role of Barabbas in intrigues between Pilate, Herod, and High Priest.

125. Bellow, Saul. *Dangling Man*. New York: Vanguard, 1944.
Emotional conflict of young man prior to induction into army.

126. _____. *Adventures of Augie March: A Novel*. New York: Viking, 1953.
Picaresque tale of West-Side Chicago boy of Depression years moving to manhood.

127. _____. *Herzog*. New York: Viking, 1964.
Spiritual quest of intellectual, failure in life, who gropes for meaning and substance.

128. _____. *Humboldt's Gift*. New York: Viking, 1975.
A prize-winning writer learns from his deceased friend, a Jewish poet, of the need to temper idealism.

129. _____, ed. *Great Jewish Short Stories*. New York: Dell, 1963.
Short stories including works by Buber, Peretz, Agnon, and Sholom Aleichem.

130. _____. *Mr. Sammler's Planet*. New York: Viking, 1970.
Elderly Polish survivor of Holocaust and his relationship with family and varied gentile characters in New York.

131. _____. *Mosby's Memoirs and Other Stories*. New York: Viking, 1968.

Stories of people who try to make it alone, including a wasted intellectual, an old lady dying in the Utah desert, an educated man forced to work for the Welfare Department during the Depression.

132. _____. The Victim. New York: Vanguard, 1947.
Subtle relationship of Jew and gentile, brought together by a seeming harm to the latter, a classic study of anti-Semitism.

133. Ben Amotz, Dahn. To Remember, To Forget. Translated by Zeva Shapiro. Philadelphia: Jewish Publication Society, 1974.
Israeli sets out from Jerusalem to claim German reparations and returns with gentile wife, Mercedes Benz, and son.

134. Benaya, M. The Levelling Wind. New York: Pantheon, 1958.
Tensions caused by life on Israel's borders and impact on emotions of soldiers.

135. Benedictus, David. The Rabbi's Wife. New York: Evans, 1976.
English rabbi's wife is caught in an Arab terrorist attack on his synagogue and abducted to Lebanon.

136. Ben-Gavriel, M. Y. Mahaschavi in Peace and War. New York: Citadel, 1960.
Israeli chicken farmer caught in adventures caused by war and his civilian responsibilities.

137. Bennett, Hal. The Black Wine. New York: Doubleday, 1968.
Growing up of Negro boy whose life is touched by Jews, one of them his mother's lover.

138. Bercovici, Konrad. The Exodus. New York: Beechhurst, 1947.
Effective Biblical-style novel of life of Moses, with emphasis on his personal qualities of humaneness and courage.

139. Bergelson, David. When All Is Said and Done. Translated by Bernard Martin. Athens: Ohio University Press, 1978.
Jewish girl in pre-Revolutionary Russian shtetl

experiences fruitless rebellion against the monotony
of women's lives.

140. Berger, Thomas. Crazy in Berlin. New York:
      Scribner's, 1958.
         Emotional breakdown suffered by German-Amer-
      ican GI obsessed by guilt for Nazi crimes against
      Jews.

141. Berger, Zdena. Tell Me Another Morning. New
      York: Harper, 1961.
         Vignettes narrated by adolescent inmate of Ger-
      man concentration camp depicting self-reliance and
      ultimate survival.

142. Bergner, Herz. Light and Shadow. Translated by
      Alec Braizblatt. New York: Yoseloff, 1963.
         Eastern European immigrants to Australia who
      win acceptance and whose son intermarries.

143. Berkovitch, Reuben. Hasen. New York: Knopf,
      1978.
         Two preteen boys hiding near concentration camp
      fail in plan to free brother.

144. Berliner, Ross. The Manhood Ceremony. New York:
      Simon & Schuster, 1978.
         A middle-class twelve-year-old Jewish boy from
      Fairfax, Virginia, is kidnapped and raped by a men-
      tal defective and survives to celebrate his Bar Mitz-
      vah.

145. Bermant, Chaim. Ben Preserve Us. New York:
      Holt, Rinehart and Winston, 1967.
         Rabbi in Scottish town and his problems with con-
      gregation and community.

146. _____. Jericho Sleep Alone and Berl Make Tea.
      New York: Holt, Rinehart and Winston, 1966.
         Two humorous novels about Jewish life in Eng-
      land.

147. _____. The Last Supper. New York: St. Martin's,
      1973.
         Through device of "sitting shiva," a London fam-
      ily chronicle unfolds from prerevolutionary St. Pe-
      tersburg to English status.

148. _____. Now Newman Was Old. New York: St.
      Martin's, 1978.
           A retired Jew travels from England to Los An-
      geles and becomes involved in his children's lives.

149. _____. The Second Mrs. Whitberg. New York:
      St. Martin's, 1976.
           Pakistanis move into changing neighborhood in
      Glasgow while Jewish widower attempts to avoid a
      remarriage.

150. _____. The Squire of Bor Schachar. New York:
      St. Martin's, 1977.
           Elderly Jewish couple from England retire to Is-
      raeli town, seek British licorice franchise while sis-
      ter elopes with young Moroccan.

151. Bern, Ronald L. The Legacy. Boston: Mason/Char-
      ter, 1975.
           The Jewish-black-Southern interactions are mir-
      rored in the tale of the Southern Jewish college stu-
      dent who marries a gentile girl.

152. Bernays, Anne. Growing Up Rich. Boston: Little,
      Brown, 1975.
           Following the death of her parents, the daughter
      of a socialite Jewish family takes up residence with
      suburban guardians whom she considers too Jewish
      and too vulgar.

153. Bernhard, Robert. The Ullman Code. New York:
      Putnam, 1975.
           Israeli agents seek to probe the past where lead-
      er of revolt in a concentration camp may have been
      involved.

154. Bernstein, Abraham. Home Is the Hunted. New York:
      Dial, 1947.
           Frustrations of Jew in advertising field who con-
      cealed his origins and finally returns to Jewish way
      of life.

155. Berri, Claude. Marry Me! Marry Me! New York:
      William Morrow, 1969.
           Two French lovers who are engaged to be mar-
      ried while girl is pregnant and the final happy re-
      solution of their problems.

156. _____. The Two of Us. New York: Morrow,
      1968.
           Relationship between Jewish boy and elderly anti-
      Semite during Petain regime in France.

157. Berstl, J. The Tentmaker: A Novel Based on the
      Life of St. Paul. New York: Rinehart, 1952.
           Saul's early life as student and weaver in Jerusa-
      lem through his return from Tarsus as interpreter
      of Jesus' role.

158. Biderman, Sol. Bring Me to the Banqueting House.
      New York: Viking, 1969.
           Adventures of orphan in foundling home in Denver
      and his constant search for his father.

159. Bieler, Manfred. The Three Daughters. Translated
      by Katherine Talbot. New York: St Martin's, 1978.
           Upper-middle-class German family in Prague in
      the 30s and 40s involved with Jewish banking house
      and are victims in Russian takeover from the Ger-
      mans.

160. Bilenkiss, Gaston. Beggar's Paradise. New York:
      Pageant, 1958.
           Nineteenth-century setting of panoramic view of
      Jewish life in Russia.

161. Birstein, Ann. Dickie's List. New York: Coward,
      McCann & Geoghegan, 1973.
           The New York literary establishment is revealed
      through the eyes of the wife of an editor, using his
      list of writers.

162. _____. Star of Glass. New York: Dodd, Mead,
      1950.
           Young secretary's view of life of a rabbi and the
      intrigues within synagogue activities.

163. _____. Summer Situations. New York: Coward,
      McCann & Geoghegan, 1972.
           Three novellas of middle-class women trapped in
      their society.

164. _____. The Sweet Birds of Gorham. New York:
      McKay, 1966.
           Teacher at New England college and her affair
      with the poet-in-residence.

165. _____ . The Troublemaker. New York: Dodd,
     Mead, 1955.
          Generational conflict between mother who is ill-
     adjusted to her environment and bright adolescent
     daughter.

166. Bishop, Leonard. Days of My Love. New York:
     Dial, 1953.
          Charity racket provides solution for insecure
     group on New York's East Side.

167. _____ . Down All Your Streets. New York: Dial,
     1952.
          Grim novel of drug addict and his family during
     Depression in New York's East Side.

168. Bissell, Richard Pike. $7\frac{1}{2}$ Cents. Boston: Little, Brown,
     1953.
          Comic novel of factory superintendent involved in
     strike and vagaries of girlfriend.

169. Black, Campbell. Death's Head. Philadelphia: Lip-
     pincott, 1972.
          Nazi doctor returns to Berlin in 1945 to escape
     American reprisal and finally kills Jew who had
     helped in his medical experiments and recognizes
     him.

170. Black, Kathy. Riches and Fame and the Pleasures
     of Sense. New York: Knopf, 1971.
          A middle-class Jew, active in student riots at
     Columbia University, seeks to write a book based
     on tape-recordings of her friends.

171. Blacker, Irwin I. and Ethel H., eds. The Book of
     Books: A Treasury of Great Bible Fiction. New
     York: Holt, Rinehart and Winston, 1965.
          Anthology of fiction based upon Biblical person-
     alities and themes, including Moses, David, Sol-
     omon.

172. _____ . The Middle of the Fire. New York:
     Scribner's, 1971.
          Israel, in the period between the 1948 and 1967
     wars, is the setting for brave men and beautiful
     women and anti-Semitism.

173. Blake, Patrick. <u>Escape to Athena</u>. New York:
      Berkley/Putnam, 1979.
          American-Jewish comedian involved with Ger-
      mans and their prisoners on Greek island at the
      close of World War II digging for artifacts.

174. Blankfort, Michael. <u>Behold the Fire</u>. New York:
      New American Library, 1965.
          World War I Palestinian Jews aiding British
      Army against the Turks.

175. _____. <u>I Didn't Know I Would Live So Long</u>. New
      York: Scribner's, 1973.
          An artist in eclipse, faced with news of father's
      impending death, retraces his emotional life.

176. _____. <u>The Juggler</u>. Boston: Little, Brown,
      1952.
          Adjustment to Israel by former inmate of con-
      centration camp who was a famous juggler.

177. _____. <u>The Strong Hand</u>. Boston: Little, Brown,
      1956.
          Love of orthodox rabbi and journalist whose mar-
      riage is forbidden because of Jewish law relating
      to presumed widows.

178. Blaustein, Esther. <u>When Momma Was the Landlord</u>.
      New York: Harper & Row, 1972.
          Daughter describes her growing up in Newark,
      New Jersey, with mother managing apartment house.

179. Blicker, Seymour. <u>The Last Collection</u>. New York:
      Morrow, 1977.
          Moneylender in Montreal hires two musclemen
      to collect bad debts from an inveterate buyer of
      unneeded things.

180. _____. <u>Shmucks</u>. New York: Morrow, 1977.
          Rumanian immigrant taxi driver and junior busi-
      nessman in Montreal meet in alley and share swing-
      ing adventures.

181. Bloch, Lucienne. <u>On the Great-Circle Route</u>. New
      York: Simon & Schuster, 1979.
          A first-person reminiscence of upper-middle-

class life during and after World War II in New York.

182. Block, William A. The Remarkable Cure of Solomon
      Sunshine. Englewood Cliffs, N. J.: Prentice-Hall,
      1974.
          The son of a Russian-Jewish quack and an Indian
      princess searches for a medical remedy which will
      assure immortality.

183. Blocker, Joel, ed. Israel Stories: A Selection of
      the Best Contemporary Hebrew Writing. New York:
      Schocken, 1962.
          Anthology of short stories by contemporary Is-
      raeli writers touching upon current problems.

184. Blond, Anthony. Family Business. New York: Har-
      per & Row, 1978.
          Wealthy eccentric in Anglo-Jewish society, and
      an anti-Zionist, Lord Sterling (born Steimatsky)
      changes after death of son in the Palmach.

185. Bloom, Harry. Sorrow Laughs. New York: Abelard-
      Schuman, 1959.
          Effects of arson case on Jewish family during
      Depression years.

186. Blum-Alquit, Eliezer. Revolt of the Apprentices:
      and Other Stories. Translated by Etta Blum. New
      York: Yoseloff, 1970.
          Twenty-seven tales, originally in Yiddish, cover
      life in Polish shtetl and New York's East Side Jew-
      ish ghetto.

187. Blumenfeld, David. Greed for Power. New York:
      Comet, 1956.
          Russian-Jewish immigrant turned financier loses
      self-respect in drive for power and fame.

188. Blunden, Godfrey. The Time of the Assassins: A
      Novel. Philadelphia: Lippincott, 1952.
          Destruction of Jewish community of Kharkov by
      deliberate campaign of Nazis.

189. Blyth, Myrna. Cousin Suzanne. New York: Mason/
      Charter, 1975.
          A chronicle of New York Jew married to a Greek
      tycoon: her loves, her babies, and her baubles.

190.   Blythe, Le Gette. <u>Bold Galilean</u>. Chapel Hill: Uni-
       versity of North Carolina Press, 1948.
            Romans accept Jewish monotheism and then be-
       come followers of Jesus.

191.   Bobker, Lee. <u>The Unicorn Group</u>. New York: Mor-
       row, 1979.
            A Jewish chess-playing accountant, an investiga-
       tor of corruption, is engaged by U.S. President to
       unmask killers of top American agents.

192.   Bogner, Norman. <u>Arena</u>. New York: Delacorte,
       1979.
            Two Jewish and two Italian families escape from
       Nazi Munich in 1938 after a bank robbery and es-
       tablish new lives in America, including the creation
       of a rival to Madison Square Garden.

193.   _____. <u>The Hunting Animal</u>. New York: Morrow,
       1974.
            A wealthy Jew is followed through his numerous
       sexual adventures and business deals.

194.   _____. <u>Seventh Avenue</u>. New York: Coward-Mc-
       Cann, 1967.
            Intrigues within garment industry in New York
       centered on rise from Brooklyn slum setting of
       ruthless businessman.

195.   Bolt, David. <u>Adam</u>. New York: John Day, 1961.
            Recreation of Biblical account of Adam and Eve
       and Genesis legends.

196.   Bor, Joseph. <u>The Terezin Requiem</u>. Translated by
       Edith Pargeter. New York: Knopf, 1963.
            Czech conductor arranges concert by musicians
       within concentration camp.

197.   Boris, Martin. <u>Two + Two</u>. New York: Times/
       Harper & Row, 1979.
            Jewish doctor in his 40s is attracted to married
       Italian patient, and their affair changes the lives of
       both families.

198.   Borowski, Tadeusz. <u>This Way for the Gas, Ladies
       and Gentlemen</u>. New York: Viking, 1967.
            Short stories illuminating terror and horror of
       Auschwitz concentration camp.

199. Bottome, Phyllis. Survival. Boston: Little, Brown, 1943.
   Viennese psychiatrist refugee and his experiences during days of air blitz in Great Britain.

200. Bourjaily, Vance. The End of My Life. New York: Scribner's, 1947.
   World War II experiences of American ambulance drivers in North Africa and Italy and ultimate settlement of one in Palestine.

201. Bowles, Paul. The Sheltering Sky. New York: New Directions, 1950.

202. Boyle, Kay. His Human Majesty. New York: Whittlesey, 1949.
   Isolation of Jewish soldier whose family was killed in concentration camp from buddies in army camp.

203. _____. The Smoking Mountain: Stories of Postwar Germany. New York: McGraw-Hill, 1951.
   Anti-Semitism still evident in postwar Germany recovering from trauma of defeat.

204. Bradbury, Bianca. The Curious Wine. New York: Beechhurst, 1948.
   Intermarriage of Jewish doctor and Christian wife threatened by bigotry in small Connecticut town.

205. Bradford, Ina. Queen of Barefoot. Philadelphia: Dorrance, 1958.
   Rural Illinois backdrop to pressure by Jewish husband upon Christian wife to change her religion.

206. Brady, Leo. The Edge of Doom. New York: Dutton, 1949.
   Philosophical Jewish detective investigates murder of priest by a Catholic.

207. Brandow, Theo. Close to Saturday. Philadelphia: Whitmore, 1971.
   Big-city setting of trials of growing up in anti-Semitic environment.

208. Brandwein, Chaim. In the Courtyards of Jerusalem. Philadelphia: Jewish Publication Society, 1967.

Short stories of impact of 1948 war on residents
of the Meah Shearim quarter of Jerusalem.

209. Breggin, Peter Roger. After the Good War: A Love
      Story. New York: Stein and Day, 1973.
      A political satire based upon a future time when
      the U. S. has delivered the world from the dreaded
      "Hebrew disease," the anguish and joy of specula-
      tive thought, and rebellious attempts to spread it.

210. Brelis, Dean. Shalom. Boston: Atlantic/Little,
      Brown, 1959.
      Blind patriarch leads refugees from a DP camp
      on ship from Marseilles to Israel in 1948.

211. Brenner, Marie. Tell Me Everything. New York:
      Dutton, 1976.
      Syndicated gossip columnist, a Jewish-American
      princess from Texas, and her friend, a plant-shop
      proprietor, try to find men in media and TV world
      of New York.

212. Brenner, Yosel Haim. Breakdown and Bereavement.
      Translated by Hillel Halkin. New York: Cornell
      University Press, 1971.
      Old-World Orthodox Jews in Jerusalem, their un-
      fulfilled desires, and human struggles, are por-
      trayed on the eve of World War I.

213. Brickner, Richard P. The Broken Year. New York:
      Doubleday, 1962.
      Convalescence from injury and its impact on New
      York Jewish boy who gains understanding of family
      and friends.

214. Brinig, Myron. Footsteps on the Stair. New York:
      Rinehart, 1950.
      Relationship between immigrant Jewish family
      and Irish family in Middle West town.

215. _____. The Looking Glass Heart. New York:
      Sagamore, 1958.
      Self-centeredness results in deprivation in a wom-
      an of mature responsibilities and love.

216. _____. The Sadness of Lexington Avenue. New
      York: Rinehart, 1951.
      Child of intermarriage raised by Christian grand-

parents, becomes member of Yorkville bund and attacks Jewish grandparents.

217. Briskin, Jacqueline. Rich Friends. New York: Delacorte Press, 1976.
　　　Southern California setting of Jewish woman's friendship with prominent family, her affairs, and her family.

218. Brod, Max. The Master. New York: Philosophical Library, 1951.
　　　Scribe of Pontius Pilate recounts events at time of Roman occupation of Judea and birth of Christianity.

219. _____. Unambo: A Novel of the War in Israel. Philadelphia: Jewish Publication Society; New York: Farrar, Straus and Young, 1952.
　　　Birth of the State of Israel through war and its effects upon movie star and film director.

220. Brodkey, Harold. First Love and Other Sorrows. New York: Dial, 1958.
　　　Nine short stories written as autobiographical narratives of youthful love, dating, and marriage and the trials of young people.

221. Brodsky, Michael. Detour. New York: Urizen/Dutton, 1977.
　　　Jewish medical student attempts to define himself in analyzing his past, which includes an obsessive mother, and in suffering through a relationship with a girl.

222. Broner, E. M. Journal Nocturnal and Seven Stories. New York: Harcourt, Brace & World, 1968.
　　　The title piece and other stories contrast tradition-bound Jews with enlightened contemporaries and reflects Jewish-Negro-Arab conflicts.

223. _____. A Weave of Women. New York: Holt, Rinehart and Winston, 1978.
　　　Twelve women and three wayward girls gather in Old City of Jerusalem and seek identity through traditional ritual while moved by feminist ferment.

224. Brooke, Dinah. The Love Life of a Cheltenham Lady. New York: Coward, McCann & Geoghegan, 1971.

American-Jewish actor "seduces" an Oxford graduate, marries her, and their baby girl is killed in
accident in Tuscany while mother is having love affair.

225.   Brooks, Richard.   The Boiling Point.   New York:
       Harper, 1948.
       Involvement of Jewish merchant in election in
       Southern town with highlights of struggle for union and
       Negro rights.

226.   Brophy, Brigid.   Flesh.   New York: World, 1963.
       British setting of shy Jew transformed by wife
       from rigid middle-class background to appreciation
       of sensuous world of love and the arts.

227.   Brown, Rosellen.   The Autobiography of My Mother.
       New York: Doubleday, 1976.
       After an estrangement of several years, the
       daughter of a brilliant lawyer moves back with her
       child, born out of wedlock, and precipitates a con-
       flict between them.

228.   Browne, Gerald A.   Hazard.   New York: Arbor
       House, 1973.
       Middle East thriller in which a sexy superman
       foils Arab plot to destroy Israel with bacteriological
       weapon.

229.   Browne, Lewis.   See What I Mean?   New York: Ran-
       dom House, 1943.
       Pre-Pearl Harbor American fascist organization
       revealed in its Jew-baiting and professional hate-
       mongering activities.

230.   Bruce, Miriam.   Linden Road.   New York: Harper,
       1951.
       Themes of Jewish self-hatred and self-acceptance
       developed through New York suburbanite Jew who
       finally rejects her anti-Semite lover.

231.   Brutus (pseud.).   Class.   Boston: Little, Brown,
       1973.
       Class battle erupts when son of long-established
       gentile family intends to marry Jewish girl.

232.   Bryks, Rachmil.   A Cat in the Ghetto: Four Novel-

ettes.   Translated by S. Morris Engel.   New York:
Bloch, 1959.
Four novelettes set in Polish ghetto and Auschwitz concentration camp portray horror of Nazi
holocaust.

233. Buber, Martin. For the Sake of Heaven. Translated
by Ludwig Lewisohn. Philadelphia: Jewish Publication Society, 1945.
Central figures are Polish Hasidic rabbis against
background of Napoleonic wars.

234. _____. Tales of the Hasidim. 2 vols. New York:
Schocken, 1947-48.
Legends told by the disciples of the Early Mas-
ters and the Later Masters.

235. Buck, Pearl S. Peony. New York: Day, 1948.
Assimilation of Chinese-Jewish community depicted in nineteenth-century through marriage en-
gineered by bondmaiden.

236. Buckman, Peter. The Rothschild Conversion. New
York: McGraw-Hill, 1979.
Protégé of Baron James de Rothschild engineers
embezzlement within the financial world of Paris in
1848.

237. Buckmaster, Henriette. Bread from Heaven. New
York: Random House, 1952.
Victims of concentration camp experience anti-
Semitism in New England town.

238. _____. And Walk in Love: A Novel Based on the
Life of the Apostle Paul. New York: Random House,
1956.
Life of Saul (St. Paul) showing early influence on
his development by Jewish teachers.

239. Burgess, Anthony. Man of Nazareth. New York:
McGraw-Hill, 1979.
A vigorous portrayal of Jesus, a young widower,
through the crucifixion, the outgrowth of a previous
portrayal on television by this author.

240. Burnet, William Riley. Little Man, Big World. New
York: Knopf, 1951.

Newspaper world described in work of Jewish
columnist to expose corruption in big city.

241. Burns, John Horne. <u>Lucifer with a Book</u>. New York:
Harper, 1949.
Jewish student in New England private school
victim of plot to deprive him of earned honors.

242. Burns, Robert. <u>The Perfect Invader</u>. New York,
and Indianapolis: Bobbs-Merrill, 1950.
Displaced persons, Nazi leaders, main characters at the time of occupation of Austria.

243. Busch, Niven. <u>The Hate Merchant</u>. New York: Simon & Schuster, 1953.
Fundamentalist preacher incites hatred of Negroes
and Jews in Detroit, culminating in race riots and
his move to South America.

244. Butler, William. <u>A God Novel</u>. New York: Scribner's, 1970.
Jew, Negro, Lebanese, and Indian combine to
gain possession of a Virgin Mary crown aboard a
Japanese ship leaving Yugoslavia.

245. Cabries, Jean. Jacob. Translated by Gerald Hop-
kins. New York: Dutton, 1958.
Life of Jacob following quarrel with Esau, his
marriage to Leah and Rachel, and his encounter
with God.

246. Cahan, Abraham. <u>The Rise of David Levinsky</u>. Revised edition. New York: Harper, 1960.
Reissue of classic novel of the career of immigrant in New York, his financial success and spiritual dilemma.

247. Calisher, Hortense. <u>The Collected Stories</u>. New
York: Arbor House, 1975.
One of the tales is about a Jewish family that
moves from the Old South to New York and the
clashes between the generations.

248. _____. <u>Eagle Eye</u>. New York: Arbor House,
1973.
The growing up to manhood and failure by upper-
class Jewish boy in New York who is sensitive to
social wrongs.

249.   _____. The New Yorkers. Boston: Little, Brown,
        1969.
            New York City Jewish judge who moves within
        non-Jewish society as well and is involved in sen-
        sational trial.

250.   _____. Textures of Life. Boston: Little, Brown,
        1963.
            Rebellion by Jewish bohemians against parents'
        middle-class values and their ultimate recognition
        of the worth of the older generation.

251.   Carleton, Verna B. Back to Berlin: An Exile Re-
        turns. Boston: Atlantic/Little, Brown, 1959.
            Identity denial by German claiming to be an Eng-
        lishman results in breakdown and subsequent return
        to Germany for readjustment.

252.   Carnegie, Sacha. The Devil and the Deep. New
        York: Appleton-Century-Crofts, 1959.
            Hungarian woman's love for Polish refugee im-
        pels her to assist him and other Jews to hide from
        the Germans.

253.   Carney, Aubrey. No Odds, No Victory. New York:
        Scribner's, 1951.
            A false charge of Communism causes dismissal
        of Jewish faculty member from New England College.

254.   Carson, Robert. The Magic Lantern. New York:
        Holt, 1952.
            Pioneer days of motion-picture industry in New
        York and Hollywood linked to father-and-son studio
        dynasty.

255.   Caspary, Vera. A Chosen Sparrow. New York:
        Putnam, 1964.
            Jew emerges from Nazi prison, becomes coffee-
        house entertainer, marries a rich Prussian whom
        she exposes as a pervert.

256.   Chandler, David. The Gangsters. New York: Mor-
        row, 1975.
            A Jewish gangster becomes a trusted associate
        and brother to the big boss in the Mafia, an Italian
        Catholic.

257. Chapman, Abraham. Jewish-American Literature: An
      Anthology. New York: Mentor, 1974.
          Chapman's anthology includes fiction, poetry, and
      autobiography and a critical introduction of each
      writer.

258. Charles, Gerda. The Destiny Waltz. New York:
      Scribner's, 1972.
          Television producers in England develop documen-
      tary on young East End Jewish poet whose short
      life produced inspiring poetry.

259. _____. Modern Jewish Stories. Englewood Cliffs,
      N.J.: Prentice-Hall, 1966.
          Jewish short-story writers from United States,
      Soviet Union, South Africa, and England develop
      themes of anti-Semitism and acculturation.

260. _____. A Slanting Light. New York: Knopf, 1963.
          An English housekeeper recounts the family life
      of an American-Jewish playwright now residing in
      London.

261. Charyn, Jerome. Blue Eyes. New York: Simon &
      Schuster, 1975.
          A blue-eyed Jewish policeman uncovers a white-
      slavery scheme in New York.

262. _____. The Education of Patrick Silver. New
      York: Arbor House, 1976.
          The completion of a trilogy in which the central
      characters are a former cop, now the custodian of
      an Irish-Jewish synagogue, and his colleague, a
      Jewish police commissioner.

263. _____. The Man Who Grew Younger. New York:
      Harper & Row 1966.
          New York is setting for stories of Jews in the
      Bronx and East Side on mythical and extraordinary
      themes; struggle against the police, a weightlifter
      author, returned veteran, and camp canoe race.

264. _____. Marilyn the Wild. New York: Arbor
      House, 1976.
          Jewish cop is bedeviled by holdups by teenagers,
      the murder of his mother, the affairs of his daugh-
      ter, and East Side Hasidic characters.

265. _____. On the Darkening Green. New York: Mc-
     Graw-Hill, 1965.
        Attendant in a home for retarded and delinquent
     Jewish boys recounts attempt of the institution's
     rabbi to overthrow the director.

266. _____. Once Upon a Droshky. New York: Mc-
     Graw-Hill, 1964.
        Golden age of Yiddish theater in New York woven
     into generational conflict between actor and his law-
     yer son.

267. Chatterton, Ruth. Homeward Borne. New York:
     Simon & Schuster, 1950.
        Anti-Semitic husband resents wife's adoption of
     Jewish refugee child.

268. Cherniak, Judith. Double Fault. New York: Putnam,
     1975.
        Husband and wife, both academics, examine their
     marriage and professional lives during a crisis per-
     iod in their mid-30s.

269. Chesnoff, Richard Z.; Klein, Edward; and Littell,
     Robert. If Israel Lost the War. New York: Cow-
     ard-McCann, 1969.
        A fictional presentation of what might have hap-
     pened if Israel had lost the 1967 war, American
     loss of face, detente of China and Russia, and emer-
     gence of Israeli underground movement.

270. Chidsey, Alan Lake. Abraham: Father of Nations.
     New York: Pageant, 1956.
        Conventional Biblical novel of career of Abraham
     as prophet and warrior.

271. Child, Philip. Day of Wrath. Boston: Humphries,
     1945.
        Jewish couple in Germany persecuted by Nazis
     in unending series of anti-Semitic incidents.

272. Chinn, Laurene. The Soothsayer. New York: Mor-
     row, 1972.
        The Apostle Paul meets Timothy, half-Greek and
     half-Jew, in Lystra, converts him, and the two trav-
     el together in their missionary goals.

273. _____. The Unanointed. New York: Crown, 1958.

Joab's loyalty to King David and his relationships
to Absolom, Bath Sheba, and Solomon.

274. Clarke, Austin C. The Meeting Point. Boston: Little, Brown, 1972.
West Indian domestic in Toronto Jewish family
center of complex black-white relationships in a
troubled world.

275. Cleary, Jon. The Safe House. New York: Morrow,
1975.
Jewish DPs attempting to get to Palestine and
Nazis fleeing to South America cross paths in Rome.

276. Cohen, Arthur A. The Carpenter Years. New York:
New American Library, 1967.
Unsuccessful tax accountant changes identity, becomes YMCA executive, marries a non-Jew, and
finally faces estranged son of his first marriage.

277. _____. In the Days of Simon Stern. New York:
Random House, 1973.
Philosophical novel searching meaning of Judaism
through a narrator who is the biographer of a real-
estate tycoon who builds a refuge for Jews in the
New World.

278. _____. A Hero in His Time. New York: Random
House, 1975.
Russian-Jewish poet and editor attends interna-
tional conference in New York and is pressured by
Soviet agents to transmit information, by American
lover, and by American Jews.

279. Cohen, Edward M. $250,000. New York: Putnam,
1967.
East Side family wracked by greed as daughter
tries to hold on to bank account against senile mother and gambling son.

280. Cohen, Irving R. The Passover Commando. New
York: Crown, 1979.
Several persons form commando unit to exact
revenge on a former Nazi now living in San Francisco.

281. Cohen, Leonard. The Favorite Game. New York:
Viking, 1963.

Canadian poet who explores meaning of his past
and his family relationships.

282.   Cohn, Emil Bernhard.   Stories and Fantasies from the
       Jewish Past.   Translated by Charles Reznikoff.
       Philadelphia: Jewish Publication Society, 1951.
           Imaginative stories on historic Jewish themes
       and personalities including Solomon, Gamaliel, Sim-
       eon ben Yohai, Akiba, and the Crusaders in Worms.

283.   Cole, Connor Hammond.   The Cross and the Star.
       New York: Vantage, 1960.
           Korean War setting viewed through service of
       three chaplains, one of whom is Jewish.

284.   Comfort, Alexander.   On This Side Nothing.   New
       York: Viking, 1949.
           Jewish poet returns to North African town now
       under German control, helps organize resistance
       in ghetto and leaves on arrival of British.

285.   Condon, Richard.   An Infinity of Mirrors.   New York:
       Random House, 1964.
           Precarious existence of Jewish woman married
       to Prussian officer in Germany and occupied France
       during World War II.

286.   Cook, Fannie Frank.   Storm Against the Wall.   New
       York: Doubleday, 1948.
           Varied aspects of anti-Semitism in America and
       Europe covered in life of a St. Louis German-Jew-
       ish family from 1904 through World War II.

287.   Cooper, Brian.   Maria.   New York: Vanguard, 1956.
           A suspense and mystery story of Englishman who
       discovers that his fiancee had been married to a
       Nazi and was herself a war criminal.

288.   Cooper, Morton.   The Queen.   Englewood Cliffs, N.J.:
       Prentice-Hall, 1974.
           Rabbi's daughter leaves home, becomes TV and
       movie star, then queen of the woman's-liberation
       movement.

289.   _____.   Resnick's Odyssey.   New York: Morrow,
       1978.
           Fifty-year-old Jewish executive in male meno-

pause escape tries farming and porno star in Hollywood before he accepts reality.

290. Coover, Robert. The Public Burning. New York:
Seaver/Viking, 1977.
The Rosenbergs are electrocuted in Times Square
in a public burning staged by an entertainment committee while Richard Nixon has sexual fantasies
about Ethel Rosenberg.

291. Coppel, Alfred. The Gate of Hell. New York: Har-
court, Brace & World, 1967.
The 1956 Sinai War background to love story of
American volunteer and wife of European émigré.

292. Corcyra, Vicastro de. The Virgin Widow. Boston:
Humphries, 1952.
A tangled story of an Austrian widow of a Nazi
party member who falls in love with an American
Jew.

293. Corley, Edwin. The Jesus Factor. New York: Stein
and Day, 1970.
The Arab-Israeli conflict is a part of an international spy thriller that includes Chinese leader and
the ABM.

294. Corman, Avery. Oh, God! New York: Simon &
Schuster, 1971.
God returns to earth as ordinary Jewish guy and
appears to writer to convince world that He still exists.

295. Cost, March. I, Rachel. New York: Vanguard,
1957.
The career of Rachel, great French actress,
child of a Jewish peddler, spans the nineteenth century from Paris to St. Petersburg and America.

296. Costain, T. B. Silver Chalice. New York: Doubleday, 1952.
Antioch, Rome, and Jerusalem locales for legends
following crucifixion of Jesus.

297. Cotton, Ella Earls. Queen of Persia, The Story of
Esther Who Saved Her People. New York: Exposition, 1960.

Role of the Biblical Esther, who saved her people from destruction in Persia.

298. Cox, Richard. <u>Sam 7</u>. New York: Reader's Digest Press, 1977.
      Palestinian terrorists blow up an Israeli plane carrying a Sam 7 missile in London in retaliation for a raid on a Palestinian camp.

299. Craig, William. <u>The Strasbourg Legacy</u>. New York: Reader's Digest Press/Crowell, 1975.
      Resurrected SS men, led by Martin Bormann, use hidden wealth to destroy West German government in attempt to create new Reich.

300. Crawford, Kathleen. <u>Straw Fire</u>. New York: Morrow, 1947.
      Liberal Virginia girl clashes with family on Negro problem and falls in love with Jewish violinist.

301. Crawford, Oliver. <u>The Execution</u>. New York: St. Martin's, 1978.
      Five survivors of a concentration camp, now weekly mah jongg players in the U.S., plot the death of the man who performed medical experiments, now living under an assumed identity.

302. Crosby, John. <u>An Affair of Strangers</u>. New York: Stein and Day, 1975.
      A French Jew who is an Israeli agent and a young Syrian Maoist terrorist become intertwined in their missions through torrid love affair.

303. Croxford, Leslie. <u>Solomon's Folly</u>. New York: Vanguard, 1978.
      Beginning in Egypt a century ago, a Jewish merchant family is depicted with generational rivalries in a setting that includes Arabs, Frenchmen, and Englishmen.

304. Dabney, Dick. <u>Old Man Jim's Book of Knowledge</u>. New York: Random House, 1973.
      A Southerner, in the period of 1917-1922, alienates his town when falling in love with a Jewish woman and battling the bigots.

305. Dan, Uri, with Radley, Edward. <u>The Eichmann Syndrome</u>. New York: Leisure Books, 1977.

Israeli agents search out former Nazi now living
under assumed identity in Rome.

306.   Dann, Jack, ed. Wandering Stars. New York: Harper
       & Row, 1974.
       Delightful anthology of Jewish science fiction and
       fantasy that includes some of I. B. Singer's stories.

307.   Davenport, Marcia. East Side, West Side. New
       York: Scribner's, 1947.
       Love story of wealthy daughter of an intermar-
       riage and an Air Force general against background
       of New York's teeming life.

308.   Davey, Charles. David. Philadelphia: Muhlenberg,
       1960.
       High Priest of Israel views multifaceted public
       and private life of King David.

309.   Davidson, David. The Steeper Cliff, A Novel. New
       York: Random House, 1947.
       American newspaperman in Bavaria learns
       strength of anti-Nazis and philosophy of surviving
       Jews.

310.   Davidson, Lionel. Making Good Again. New York:
       Harper & Row, 1968.
       Englishman, Holocaust survivor, and German
       lawyer settle claim under Indemnification Law of
       Swiss fortune of a German-Jewish banker who dis-
       appeared during the war.

311.   _____. The Menorah Men. New York: Harper &
       Row, 1966.
       Jerusalem Temple menorah center of conflict be-
       tween archaeologists and real-estate developers.

312.   _____. Smith's Gazelle. New York: Knopf, 1971.
       A Bedouin, Arab boy, and Jewish youth join forc-
       es to care for a rare herd of gazelles prior to the
       Six Day War.

313.   _____. The Sun Chemist. New York: Dutton,
       1976.
       Expatriate Russian Jew in England finds in Chaim
       Weizmann's papers a forgotten discovery for a pe-
       troleum and oil substitute.

314. Davis, Burke. Whisper My Name. New York: Rine-
     hart, 1949.
        Philadelphia Jew changes identity and lives as
     Baptist in bustling North Carolina town.

315. Davis, Christopher. Belmarch: A Legend of the
     First Crusade. New York: Viking, 1964.
        Massacre of Jews during First Crusade to the
     Holy Land seen through eyes of foot soldier.

316. _____. Ishmael. New York: Harper & Row, 1969.
        Biblical novel based on imaginative conjectures
     concerning the life of Ishmael.

317. Davis, Maggie. Rommel's Gold. Philadelphia: Lip-
     pincott, 1971.
        Israeli war-criminal hunter and German treasure
     seeker clash in hunt for Nazi treasures.

318. Davis, Saul. The Adventures of Shlomele. New York:
     Yoseloff, 1956.
        Provincial Russian town seen through boyhood es-
     capades in period prior to World War I.

319. Dayan, Yael. Dust. Cleveland and New York:
     World, 1963.
        Young Sabra girl in new settlement tells story
     of survivor of Holocaust and her love and absorp-
     tion into his past.

320. _____. Death Had Two Sons. New York: McGraw-
     Hill, 1968.
        Father-and-son conflict centered about differing
     life experiences in European Holocaust and Israeli
     upbringing.

321. _____. Envy the Frightened. New York: World,
     1961.
        Israeli father realizes through his son his
     own mistaken values of reliance upon hardiness and
     fearlessness.

322. _____. New Face in the Mirror. Cleveland:
     World, 1959.
        Individualistic Israeli girl rebels against com-
     pulsory military service and involves herself in
     youthful romances.

323. _____. Three Weeks in October. New York: Delacorte Press, 1979.
Israeli couple whose marriage relationship is ex-
plored through the strains that develop during the
Yom Kippur War.

324. Deighton, Len. Funeral in Berlin. New York: Putnam, 1965.
British agent seeks to smuggle Russian scientist
out of East Berlin with assistance of Israeli girl.

325. Delman, David. One Man's Murder. New York: Mc-
Kay, 1975.
Jewish policeman investigates murder that in-
volves aged advertising-agency executive and his
successors.

326. Delmar, Vina. Beloved. New York: Harcourt,
Brace, 1956.
Career of Judah Benjamin, the "Brains of the
Confederacy," is interspersed with his unusual mar-
riage.

327. DeMille, Nelson. By the Rivers of Babylon. New
York: Harcourt Brace Jovanovich, 1978.
Survivor of ancient exiled community in Babylon
assists in rescue of El Al Concorde group hijacked
by Arab terrorists.

328. Denker, Henry. Horowitz & Mrs. Washington. New
York: Putnam, 1979.
After suffering a stroke caused by black muggers,
Horowitz is nursed back to health by black nurse.

329. _____. I'll Be Right Home, Ma. New York:
Crowell, 1959.
Jewish fight manager assists Irish boy to cham-
pionship and helps him overcome frightful childhood
memories of his parents.

330. _____. The Kingmaker. New York: McKay, 1972.
Head of talent agency manipulates small-time
movie actor into TV star and then governor of California.

331. _____. My Son, the Lawyer. New York: Crowell,
1950.

Struggle of young New York Jew to become a
lawyer and then to survive during the Depression
of the 30s.

332. Denzer, Peter W. The Last Hero. New York: Holt,
      1957.
          Child of intermarriage rebels against puritanical
      mother and his father, a Jewish doctor.

333. DeRopp, Robert S. If I Forget Thee. New York:
      St. Martin's, 1956.
          Love story of young man, half-Roman and half-
      Jewish, for daughter of High Priest during time of
      Roman conquest of Jerusalem.

334. Deutsch, Babette. The Welcome. New York: Harper,
      1943.
          German-Jewish refugee boy finds friendship and
      happiness in a New York boys' school.

335. DeWohl, Louis. David of Jerusalem. Translated by
      Elisabeth Abbott. Philadelphia: Lippincott, 1963.
          King David's tumultuous life developed from
      shepherd-boy days to career's end.

336. _____. The Spear. New York: Lippincott, 1955.
          Recreation of career of Jesus and his life cycle
      through the resurrection.

337. Diamond, Joseph S. Door of Hope. New York:
      Greenberg, 1951.
          Peasants' revolt against oppression in Rumania
      at turn of century led by band of Jews and non-Jews.

338. Dibner, Martin. The Bachelor Seals. New York:
      Doubleday, 1948.
          Four men followed from college career through
      World War II exhibit bigotry in their various life
      settings.

339. _____. Showcase. New York: Doubleday, 1958.
          Garment-industry setting of troubleshooter hired
      to save department store from bankruptcy.

340. Dick, Philip K. The Man in the High Castle. New
      York: Putnam, 1962.
          Science-fiction setting after Japanese and German

victory in World War II in which Jew is in hiding
on West Coast.

341. Dim, Joan. Recollections of a Rotten Kid. Indian-
      apolis: Bobbs-Merrill, 1975.
          Through two summers at Rockaway Beach and one
      Manhattan winter, Jewish girl grows up experiencing
      pregnancy, father's infidelity, mother's mastectomy,
      and uncle's death.

342. Dintenfass, Mark. The Case Against Org. Boston:
      Little, Brown, 1970.
          Obese New Yorker creates cult-like newsletter
      based upon worship of gluttony while attempting to
      free himself from his mother's influence.

343. _____. Make Yourself an Earthquake. Boston:
      Little, Brown, 1969.
          Retired schoolteacher escapes from nursing home
      and engages in adventures, some of which are
      couched in African mythic reveries.

344. _____. Montgomery Street. New York: Harper
      & Row, 1978.
          A filmmaker recreates his old neighborhood in
      Brooklyn and his struggle to free himself of his
      family while an old shopkeeper tries to cope with
      the world.

345. Dixon, Roger. Going to Jerusalem. New York:
      Coward, McCann & Geoghegan, 1977.
          British filmmaker and assistant find themselves
      in midst of Nazi war-criminal trial and Israeli
      Arab's terrorist mission.

346. Doctorow, E. L. The Book of Daniel. New York:
      Random House, 1971.
          Bitter political novel, based on the Rosenberg
      case, of son of executed Jewish spies seeking the
      truth about his parents.

347. _____. Ragtime. New York: Random House,
      1974.
          A fictional recreation of early-twentieth-century
      family in New York suburb with real people like
      Kord, Emma Goldman, Freud, Houdini, and a great
      cast.

348. Doliner, Roy. For Love or Money. New York:
      Simon & Schuster, 1974.
          Dead delicatessen owner returns to earth to get
      revenge and to get his loot and take it back to para-
      dise.

349. Dortort, David. Burial of the Fruit, a Novel. New
      York: Crown, 1947.
          Bronxville boy becomes top gunman of a Brook-
      lyn gang and is finally killed by associates.

350. _____. The Post of Honor. New York: Whittle-
      sey, 1949.
          Frustrations spawned by the Depression cause
      ideological outlets to be sought by Brownsville
      youths.

351. Douglas, Lloyd C. The Big Fisherman. Boston:
      Houghton Mifflin, 1949.
          Christological novel with emphasis on career of
      Peter.

352. _____. The Robe. Boston: Houghton Mifflin,
      1942.
          Roman senator's son in charge of Crucifixion
      accepts death rather than recant his Christian faith.

353. Drapkin, Frita Roth. Papa's Golden Land. New York:
      Comet, 1960.
          East European immigrant family finds fulfillment
      in America as seen through daughter's appreciative
      eyes.

354. Drexler, Rosalyn. I Am the Beautiful Stranger. New
      York: Grossman, 1965.
          Through diary covering early adolescence in
      1930s, Bronx girl reveals her illusions, self-knowl-
      edge, and exploitation by men.

355. Duerrenmatt, F. The Quarry. New York: Graphic,
      1962.
          Retired Swiss police officer saved by survivor
      of concentration camp during investigation of sus-
      pected Nazi doctor.

356. Duke, Madelaine. The Bormann Receipt. New York:
      Stein and Day, 1978.

Daughter of Jewish family of Vienna, now a
British citizen, seeks to recover art treasures
stolen by the Nazis.

357. Dunscomb, C. The Bond and the Free. Boston:
      Houghton Mifflin, 1955.
          Young Roman noblewoman visits uncle, Pontius
      Pilate, during trial of Jesus and reveals impact of
      new religion on provincial Jews.

358. Durrell, L. Justine. New York: Dutton, 1957.
          Four-sided love story set in Alexandria, Egypt,
      with Jew married to Coptic native.

359. _____. Mountolive. New York: Dutton, 1959.
          Jew and Coptic Egyptian husband assist in smug-
      gling arms to Palestine to save Jews and Arab mi-
      norities from Moslem domination.

360. Duvedon, A. Hatzkel the Water-carrier. New York:
      Pageant, 1963.
          Polish-Jewish village setting in pre-World War II
      days illustrates lives of simple people.

361. Dwoskin, Charles. Shadow over the Land. New
      York: Beechhurst, 1946.
          Right-wing patriotic group from Detroit stirs up
      anti-Semitism in Connecticut town.

362. Eberle, Gertrude. Charioteer. Grand Rapids: Eerd-
      mans, 1946.
          Joseph's career in Egypt as representative of
      Pharaoh is illumined with conversion to Jewish god
      by a bond-slave who wanted to be a charioteer.

363. Edelman, Maurice. All on a Summer's Night. New
      York: Random House, 1970.
          Jewish businessman seeks to take over one of
      oldest English industries and encounters anti-Sem-
      itism, conservative thinking, while wife seduces
      son's classmate.

364. _____. Disraeli in Love. New York: Stein and
      Day, 1972.
          Inner conflicts of the young Disraeli seeking his
      future through political campaigns and love affairs.

365. _____. Disraeli Rising. New York: Stein and
     Day, 1975.
          In this sequel to Disraeli in Love, the novelist-
     politician becomes the Chancellor of the Exchequer
     proceeding through love affair and bad debts.

366. Edelman, Rosemary. Fireworks. New York: Arbor
     House, 1979.
          Magazine writer and her TV journalist lover op-
     pose federal-government-supported conspiracy to
     burn down houses in the South Bronx.

367. Edwards, Samuel (pseud. Noel B. Gerson). The
     Exploiters. New York: Praeger, 1974.
          American oil-company executive seeks to win
     over Arab ruler with use of sexy females while
     French compete against him.

368. Elkin, Stanley. A Bad Man. New York: Random
     House, 1967.
          Department-store owner jailed for providing abor-
     tions, drugs, and illicit services realizes prison
     limits freedom.

369. _____. Criers and Kibitzers, Kibitzers and Criers.
     New York: Random House, 1966.
          Allegory and fantasy are present in short-story
     collection with themes of bitterness, sadism, and
     tragedy.

370. _____. Searches and Seizures. New York: Ran-
     dom House, 1973.
          A collection of three novellas of alienated per-
     sons whose searches end in horror and despair.

371. Elliot, John. Blood on the Snow. New York: St.
     Martin's, 1977.
          The Czarist massacre of Jews is part of the
     events leading to the Bolshevik Revolution; Keren-
     sky and Trotsky are depicted.

372. Elman, Richard M. A Coat for the Tsar. Austin:
     University of Texas Press, 1958.
          A novella of tension of deserter from Tsarist
     army torn between confessing his "sin" or emigrat-
     ing to America.

373. _____. Crossing Over and Other Tales. New
York: Scribner's, 1973.
These short stories include attachment of a Jewish matron for her black maid, a teenager in ther-
apy, and sex orgies.

374. _____. Freddie & Shirl & the Kids. New York:
Scribner's, 1972.
An autobiographical account of the growing into
manhood of son of middle-class Jewish parents, his
college life in Syracuse, and a doomed marriage.

375. _____. Lilo's Diary. New York: Scribner's,
1968.
Record of Hungarian girl's betrayal in 1944 by
fiancee and her family to escape Nazi imprisonment
and death.

376. _____. The Reckoning. New York: Scribner's,
1969.
Hungarian businessman and family destined for
crematoria reveals his weakness, venality, and
crudeness.

377. _____. The 28th Day of Elul. New York: Scribner's, 1967.
Hungarian refugee in Israel must prove he is a
professing Jew to receive a legacy and tells of
greed and betrayal in Hungary and escape from
Nazis.

378. Engel, Monroe. Voyager Belsky. New York: Atheneum, 1963.
Part-time stockbroker searches for meaning
through travel, new marriage, trade as carpenter,
and returns to New York urban life.

379. Epstein, Leslie. King of the Jews. New York:
Coward, McCann & Geoghegan, 1979.
Fictionalized account of Jewish ruler of Polish
town made head of the Judenrat by the Nazis.

380. _____. The Steinway Quintet: Plus Four. New
York: Little, Brown, 1976.
Among the five stories is one narrated by an
aging Jewish musician of the night when Puerto
Ricans terrorize an East Side restaurant.

381. Epstein, Seymour. <u>Caught in That Music.</u> New York:
      Viking, 1967.
          Awakening of young man to love and friendship,
      exposure to loosening of family ties and suicide of
      friend prior to embarking in World War II trans-
      port ship.

382. _____. <u>The Dream Museum.</u> New York: Double-
      day, 1971.
          Cuckolded husband begins life anew after twenty-
      three years of marriage to discover a new maturity
      in himself.

383. _____. <u>Leah.</u> Boston: Little, Brown, 1964.
          New York single woman, employee of importer,
      intelligent and witty, finds people assuaging their
      loneliness at her expense.

384. _____. <u>Looking for Fred Schmidt.</u> New York:
      Doubleday, 1973.
          Middle-aged successful Jewish businessman seeks
      meaning in life, fearful of growing older, while
      searching for his first partner, whom he had wronged.

385. _____. <u>A Penny for Charity.</u> Boston: Little,
      Brown, 1965.
          Familiar scenes and persons in New York Jewish
      environment including Broadway theater director,
      parent-child concerns, small-store owner, and gen-
      eral aura of estrangement of human beings.

386. _____. <u>Pillar of Salt.</u> New York: Scribner's,
      1959.
          Marriage of Jewish girl of German refugee back-
      ground threatened because of husband's East Euro-
      pean parentage.

387. Erdman, Paul E. <u>The Crash of '79.</u> New York:
      Simon & Schuster, 1976.
          The Shah of Iran's strategy to create a new Per-
      sian empire involves financial ruin of West, capture
      of oilfields, but is foiled by Jewish nuclear scien-
      tist and Israel is saved.

388. Ettinger, Elzbieta. <u>Kindergarten.</u> Boston: Houghton
      Mifflin, 1970.
          Teenage survivor of Nazi terror in Warsaw be-

comes inhuman madwoman because of horrifying experiences.

389. Faber, Nancy W. Strange Way Home. Chicago: Regnery, 1963.
     Young Jewish boy, kidnapped by French-Canadian tutor, is raised in Canada, enters priesthood and ultimately is reconciled to parents.

390. Falk, Harvey. Days of Judgment. New York: Shengold, 1972.
     The generational gap is pictured in the conflict between a rabbi, his wife, and their children.

391. Falkirk, Richard. The Twisted Wire. New York: Doubleday, 1971.
     British geologist overhears telephone conversation between U.S. President and American ambassador and is involved with spies while in Israel.

392. Falstein, Louis. Face of a Hero. New York: Harcourt, Brace, 1950.
     Jewish tail-gunner of bomber crew survives fifty missions out of Italy and tells story of his comrades.

393. _____. Laughter on a Weekday. New York: Oblensky, 1965.
     Ukrainian family, rooted in Russia for generations, leaves at time of the Revolution, moves to Paris, and then to Chicago and experiences assimilation through son, who becomes baseball and poolhall addict.

394. _____. Sole Survivor. New York: Dell, 1954.
     Survivor of concentration camp discovers Nazi prison guard in America who had murdered his brother and kills him.

395. Farren, Julian. The Train from Pittsburgh. New York: Knopf, 1948.
     Alcoholic advertising man beset by decision between wife and mistress and defiance of anti-Semitic employer on behalf of a Jewish friend.

396. Fast, Howard. Agrippa's Daughter. New York: Doubleday, 1964.
     Daughter of King Herod the Great caught in fac-

tionalism of Sicarii and zealots in Jerusalem and
witnesses Roman destruction of Jerusalem.

397. _____. The Children. New York: Duell, Sloan
and Pearce, 1947.
New York slum children come up to maturity
with warped souls because of society's neglect.

398. _____. Departure and Other Stories. Boston:
Little, Brown, 1949.
Short stories, including one about a Jew who
dies in Spanish Civil War for Loyalist cause and a
vignette of anti-Semitism in Colonial America.

399. _____. The Establishment. Boston: Houghton
Mifflin, 1979.
The third in the Lavette family series, this one
includes the McCarthy period and smuggling of
planes for the 1948 Israeli War of Independence.

400. _____. The Immigrants. Boston: Houghton Mifflin, 1977.
A Jewish partner is involved with French-Italian
immigrant who moves up the social and financial
ladder in San Francisco following the earthquake.

401. _____. Moses, Prince of Egypt. New York:
Crown, 1958.
The early years of Moses in Pharaoh's court are
recreated and his decision to renounce royal state
to join the Hebrews.

402. _____. My Glorious Brothers. Boston: Little,
Brown, 1948.
Last surviving Hasmonean brother retells the
epic of the Maccabean revolt and victory against
the Syrians.

403. _____. The Proud and the Free. Boston: Little,
Brown, 1950.
Pennsylvania regiment revolts in 1781, and narrator describes anti-Semitism against Jewish soldiers.

404. _____. Second Generation. Boston: Houghton
Mifflin, 1978.
The years covering World War II, including the

Holocaust and Nazis, are portrayed in the sequel to The Immigrants.

405. _____. Spartacus. New York: Author, 1951.
David, a Jewish zealot, inspires Spartacus to lead the gladiators' revolt against the Romans.

406. _____. Torquemada. New York: Doubleday, 1966.
The best friend of Torquemada, the Spanish Inquisitor, is accused of being a Jew.

407. Faure, Raoul Cohen. Lady Godiva and Master Tom: With Drawings by Aurelius G. Battaglia. New York: Harper, 1948.
Lady Godiva's ride presented in psychological setting of hate of husband while being counseled by his Jewish treasurer.

408. Faust, Irvin. Foreign Devils. New York: Arbor House, 1973.
Jewish correspondent for New York newspaper covers the Boxer Rebellion in China as a comic-tragic personality.

409. _____. Roar Lion Roar and Other Stories. New York: Random House, 1965.
Pathetic individuals in New York include Nazi survivor who becomes self-hating Jew.

410. _____. A Star in the Family. New York: Doubleday, 1975.
A legendary comic star of stage, screen, and radio tells his biographer of his growing up in Brooklyn, war service, and hectic career.

411. _____. The Steagle. New York: Random, 1966.
English professor, during Cuban missile crisis in 1962, retraces past through cross-country journey.

412. Federman, Raymond. Take It or Leave It. New York: Braziller, 1976.
French Jew comes to U.S. after World War II and travels, changes jobs, experiences loves, all in a search to find the truth about himself.

413. Feierberg, Mordecai Zeeb. Whither. Translated

by Ira Eisenstein. New York: Abelard-Schuman, 1959.
   Classic conflict in youth between tradition and nationalism in Russian setting of close of nineteenth century seems to be resolved in early Zionist movement.

414. Fein, Harry H. Farewell to Samaria: A Story of the Last Years of the Kingdom of Israel. Boston: Verndale, 1955.
   Fall of Samaria and Kingdom of Israel backdrop for love story.

415. Feinstein, Alan S. Triumph! Boston: Citadel, 1960.
   Outstanding student in college class beset by ambitious drive for success and recognition.

416. Fergusson, Harvey. The Conquest of Don Pedro. New York: Morrow, 1954.
   New York Sephardic Jew seeks health in New Mexico town after Civil War, marries younger woman, and leaves after she falls in love with Texas.

417. Feuchtwanger, Lion. Jephta and His Daughter. Translated by Eithne Wilkins and Ernst Kaiser. New York: Putnam, 1958.
   Jeptha sacrifices daughter through vow to prove his faith in Yahweh.

418. _____. Josephus and the Emperor. Translated by Caroline Oram. New York: Viking, 1942.
   Last volume of Josephus trilogy, in which he loses favor of Roman emperor, Domitian, and is killed by Roman troops in Judea while trying to reach rebels.

419. _____. Paris Gazette. Translated by Willa and Edwin Muir. New York: Viking, 1940.
   Indictment of Hitlerism conveyed in story of Paris of 1935 and German-language newspaper.

420. _____. Raquel. Translated by Ernst Kaiser and Eithne Wilkins. New York: Messner, 1955.
   Love story of twelfth-century Castillian king and daughter of his finance minister, a Jew of Seville.

421. _____. Short Stories from Far and Near. New York: Viking, 1945.

Most stories deal with Nazi era and the effect
of Facism on Europe.

422.   Fiedler, Leslie. Back to China. New York: Stein
       and Day, 1965.
            Death of American Indian friend causes middle-
       aged Jewish professor to confront problems of Jap-
       anese mistress, gentile wife, and war guilt.

423.   _____. The Last Jew in America. New York:
       Stein and Day, 1966.
            Trilogy of comic stories include alienated Jews
       and minority types who happen to be Protestants
       and Negroes.

424.   _____. The Messenger Will Come No More. New
       York: Stein and Day, 1975.
            Science-fiction novel of twenty-fifth-century ar-
       chaeologist who discovers Jerusalem scrolls that
       reveal role of space messengers in creating Judeo-
       Christian myths.

425.   _____. Nude Croquet. New York: Stein and Day,
       1969.
            Short stories include academic setting, New York
       storekeepers, middle-class country club set, and
       Passover scene in Russia.

426.   _____. The Second Stone. New York: Stein and
       Day, 1963.
            First International Conference in Love in Rome
       provokes triangular relationship between director,
       his pregnant wife, and boyhood friend, his alter
       ego.

427.   Field, Ben. Jacob's Son. New York: Crown, 1971.
            Son of a teacher and poet seeks his own identity
       finally as farmer as symbol of his independence.

428.   _____. The Outside Leaf. New York: Reynal
       and Hitchcock, 1943.
            Orthodox Jewish tobacco-growing family in Con-
       necticut becomes reconciled to son's marriage to
       non-Jew.

429.   _____. Piper Tompkins. Garden City: Doubleday,
       Doran, 1946.

Farmboy works in defense factory and develops
into strong unionist.

430. Field, Francis T. McDonough: A Novel. New York:
      Duell, Sloan and Pearce, 1951.
          New Jersey politics revealed through Irish party
      leader and existence of a Jewish voting bloc.

431. Field, Hermann, and Mierzenski, Stanislav. Angry
      Harvest. New York: Crowell, 1958.
          Polish girl, fleeing from Germans, finds tempor-
      ary refuge on farm of peasant who turns her out to
      save himself.

432. Fielding, Gabriel. The Birthday King. New York:
      Morrow, 1963.
          Jewish-Catholic steel magnate family is oblivious
      to Nazi morality while one son is imprisoned for
      political crimes, survives, and returns to accept
      German guilt.

433. _____. In the Time of Greenbloom. New York:
      Morrow, 1957.
          Adolescent English boy recognizes murderer of
      friend and is assisted by Oxford student to achieve
      resolution of inner questioning and doubts.

434. Fifield, William. The Sign of Taurus. New York:
      Holt, Rinehart and Winston, 1960.
          Polish-Jewish refugee countess finds haven in
      Mexico and earns a living with Italian ex-Fascist
      by telling fortunes and discovers she possesses
      extrasensory powers.

435. Finas, Lucette. The Faithful Shepherd. Translated
      by Ralph Manheim. New York: Pantheon, 1963.
          Parisian civil servant, obsessed by guilt for
      Nazi persecution of Jews, imposes Jews on anti-
      Semitic wife, who takes revenge through extramar-
      ital affair.

436. Finegan, Jack. Wanderer upon Earth. New York:
      Harper, 1956.
          Fugitive Jew at time of Ezekiel and fall of Jer-
      usalem journeys eastward in search for truth in
      Orient and India and returns when Babylon falls.

437.   Fineman, Irving. Jacob: An Autobiographical Novel.
       New York: Random House, 1941.
            First-person tale by Jacob to his son Joseph
       covering early years of lives of Isaac and Esau,
       Jacob's return to Canaan, and Rachel's and Isaac's
       deaths.

438.   _____. Ruth. New York: Harper, 1949.
            Parable of tolerance through story of Ruth the
       Moabite and her marriage to Boaz.

439.   Finnegan, Robert. Many a Monster. New York:
       Simon & Schuster, 1948.
            San Francisco reporter encounters anti-Semitic
       organization while searching for suspect in murder
       of three women.

440.   Fischer, Marjorie. Mrs. Sherman's Summer. Phil-
       adelphia: Lippincott, 1960.
            Matriarch of German-Jewish clan has entire fam-
       ily together for summer in Long Island and is chal-
       lenged by oldest son, who controls family money.

441.   Fisher, Vardis. The Island of the Innocent. New
       York: Abelard, 1952.
            Greek physician involved with sister of Jewish
       friend in Maccabean times.

442.   _____. The Valley of Vision. New York: Abelard,
       1951.
            Solomon the King presented as realistic and so-
       phisticated ruler of impressive magnitude.

443.   Fitzgerald, F. Scott. The Last Tycoon. New York:
       Scribner's, 1941.
            Unfinished novel of impact of motion-picture in-
       dustry, with Jewish personnel, on whole fabric of
       American life.

444.   Forsyth, Frederick. The Odessa File. New York:
       Viking, 1972.
            Journalist tracks down former Nazi SS officers
       now working on rockets for Egypt to bomb Tel Aviv
       with deadly bacilli and radioactive cobalt.

445.   Frank, Bruno. One Fair Daughter. Translated by
       Claire Trask. New York: Viking, 1943.

Effect of anti-Semitism on Viennese army officer, his wife of Polish-Jewish background, and their daughter.

446.   Frank, Waldo David. Island in the Atlantic. New York: Duell, Sloan and Pearce, 1946.
Three-generation sweep of interrelationships between Jewish and non-Jewish New York families, with themes of civic reform, social life, and early Zionism.

447.   Frankel, Sandor, and Mews, Webster (pseud.). The Aleph Solution. New York: Stein and Day, 1979.
Israeli counter-terrorist pitted against Arabs who hold entire UN General Assembly hostage as blow against Israel.

448.   Frankel, Zygmunt. Short War, Short Lives. New York: Abelard-Schuman, 1971.
The Six Day War is seen through the eyes of the production manager of an ammunition factory who views war as waste of human lives.

449.   Franklin, F. K. The Cleft in the Rock. New York: Crowell, 1955.
A neurotic intellectual seeks peace in solitude of Aleutian Islands and is destroyed by sadistic construction foreman.

450.   Fredman, John. The Wolf of Masada. New York: Morrow, 1979.
A fictionalized account of the life of Simon ben Eleazar, the hero of Masada, includes a friendship with Vespasian and service in the Roman invasion of Britain.

451.   Freedman, Benedict and Nancy. The Spark and the Exodus. New York: Crown, 1954.
Early-twentieth-century pilgrimage of rural Polish Jews seeking freedom in Palestine.

452.   Freedman, Nancy. The Immortals. New York: St. Martin's, 1976.
Creator of oil dynasty acquires a Jewish mistress who is a fervent Zionist, is involved with Ibn Saud, FDR, and King David Hotel bombing and is opposed by grandchildren who seek other energy solutions.

453. Freedman, Ralph. <u>Divided</u>. New York: Dutton,
     1948.
     Account of denazification program by Americans
     in Austrian village prior to Russian takeover.

454. Freeman, Cynthia. <u>Days of Winter</u>. New York: Ar-
     bor House, 1978.
     Of five lawyer sons in London firm, Rubin
     marries a Rumanian, fathers a daughter, and
     leaves his unfaithful wife to save her from the
     Gestapo.

455. _____. <u>Portraits</u>. New York: Arbor House,
     1979.
     Daughter of immigrant married to a Jewish Ameri-
     can Princess in San Francisco writes a best-seller
     on Jewish immigrant family.

456. _____. <u>A World Full of Strangers</u>. New York:
     Arbor House, 1975.
     Successful real-estate man in California is Jew
     from East Side of New York who changed his name
     and abandoned his background and whose son seeks
     his Jewish heritage.

457. Freemantle, Brian. <u>The Man Who Wanted Tomorrow</u>.
     New York: Stein and Day, 1976.
     Israelis, Russians, and Nazis search for list of
     disguised Nazis hidden in Lake Toplitz.

458. Friedman, Ben. <u>The Anguish of Father Rafti</u>. New
     York: Two Continents, 1978.
     Catholic priest charged with murder of son of
     Holocaust survivor in small Texas town.

459. Friedman, Bruce Jay. <u>The Dick</u>. New York: Knopf,
     1970.
     Jewish "detective" changes identity and is in-
     volved with underworld characters in comic rela-
     tionships.

460. _____. <u>A Mother's Kisses</u>. New York: Simon
     & Schuster, 1964.
     Ambivalent relationship between possessive Jew-
     ish mother and college-age son.

461. _____. <u>Stern</u>. New York: Simon & Schuster, 1962.

Emotional upheaval in life of Jew who buys isolated home in suburbs and fears anti-Semitism.

462.   Friedman, Sanford. Totempole. New York: Dutton, 1965.
Life of New York Jewish boy traced from summer camps, to college and to Korea and his homosexual relationships.

463.   Friedrich, Otto. The Poor in Spirit. Boston: Little, Brown, 1952.
American-Jewish press officer's relationship with German girl and their attendant conflicts and problems.

464.   Frischauer, Paul. So Great a Queen: The Story of Esther, Queen of Persia. New York: Scribner's, 1950.
Story of Esther embellished with sex customs of natives and conspiracy of neighboring nations against Ahasuerus.

465.   Fruchter, Norman. Coat upon a Stick. New York: Simon & Schuster, 1963.
Lonely old men in East Side find solace in rundown synagogue but realize that their middle-class children can become compassionate.

466.   Fuks, Ladislav. Mr. Theodore Mundstock. Translated by Iris Urwin. New York: Orion, 1968.
Czech Jew, during German occupation of Prague in 1942, prepares for inevitable concentration-camp internment.

467.   Gabriel, Gilbert Wolf. Love from London. New York: Macmillan, 1946.
Three American soldiers, one of whom is an anti-Semitic Bostonian, fall in love with part-Jewish refugee while billeted in London.

468.   Gaer, Joseph. Heart upon the Rock. New York: Dodd, Mead, 1950.
Conflict between generations set in poverty-stricken Jewish community in Bessarabia.

469.   Gainham, Sarah. Night Falls on the City. New York: Holt, Rinehart and Winston, 1967.

Non-Jewish Viennese actress attempts to shield
Jewish husband prior to Nazi control of Austria.

470.   _____. Private Worlds. New York: Holt, Rinehart and Winston, 1971.
The third in the Julia Homburg saga, centering
on the return to Vienna of a former SS general and
the threat to her husband.

471. Gallico, Paul. The Foolish Immortals. Garden City:
Doubleday, 1953.
Hoax perpetrated on group seeking easy money,
then secret of longevity in Palestine.

472. Gann, Ernest K. The Antagonists. New York: Simon & Schuster, 1970.
Masada is the scene of the final revolt of the
Jews against the Romans, with focus upon Eleazar
ben Yair and General Flavius Silva.

473. Garbo, Norman. The Artist. New York: Norton,
1978.
Jewish artist fights against anti-Semitism in
Czarist Russia, in the U.S., and in Germany while
pursuing three loves.

474.   _____. Cabal. New York: Norton, 1978.
The pre-emptive strike of Israel in the Six Day
War is assisted by secret group of wealthy and
prominent Jews who defy U.S. President.

475. Garnett, David. Two by Two: A Story of Survival.
New York: Atheneum, 1963.
Reinterpretation of Biblical account of Noah and
the flood through eyes of twin girls on the Ark.

476. Gary, Romain. The Dance of Genghis Cohn. New
York: World, 1963.
Jewish night-club comic in Berlin is executed
and becomes a dybbuk in the subconscious of his
murderer.

477.   _____. The Guilty Head. New York: World,
1969.
Adventurer in form of dybbuk imitates Gauguin in
Tahiti to bilk tourists.

478. Gates, Susa Young, and Widtsoe, Leah Endora Dun-

can. The Prince of Ur. Salt Lake City: Book-
craft, 1946.
Early life of the patriarch Abraham, set in the
city of Ur of the Chaldees.

479.   Gavron, Daniel. The End of Days. Philadelphia:
Jewish Publication Society, 1970.
Masada is the scene of the final siege of the
Romans against the Zealot rebellion.

480.   Geilich, Rachel Levin. Yudel: A Novel. Philadelphia: Dorrance, 1955.
Russian-Jewish immigrant and his adjustment to
life in the United States.

481.   Geissler, Christian. The Sins of the Fathers. Translated by James Kirkup. New York: Random House,
1962.
German physicist and gardener join forces to
find surviving member of Jewish family extermin-
ated by Nazis to atone for guilt.

482.   Gellhorn, Martha. The Wine of Astonishment. New
York: Scribner's, 1948.
A Jewish jeep-driver for a Southern officer in
Germany learns meaning of his struggle for self-
recognition after viewing Dachau.

483.   Gerber, Albert. The Lawyer. New York: World,
1972.
The world of a successful Jewish lawyer is ex-
plored while stripping bare the legal profession.

484.   Gerber, Israel Joshua. Man on a Pendulum: A Case
History of an Invert. New York: American, 1956.
Fictional biography of homosexual who achieves
normal adjustment through psychological and religious counseling.

485.   Gerber, Merrill Joan. An Antique Man. Boston:
Houghton Mifflin, 1967.
Eldest daughter tells family story of interrelationships between parents and children, centered on
death of father, a former junkman and antique dealer.

486.   _____. Stop Here, My Friend. Boston: Houghton
Mifflin, 1965.

Among the maiden ladies in these short stories
are a witch-like piano teacher and a cross-eyed
hairdresser.

487. Gerchunoff, Alberto. The Jewish Gauchos of the Pampas. Translated by Prudencio de Pereda. New
York: Abelard-Schuman, 1955.
Sketches of Jews who settle in the Baron de
Hirsch colonies in Argentina in the early 1900s.

488. Gerenstain, Grigori. The Fall and Other Stories.
Translated by Antonina W. Bouis. New York:
Harper & Row, 1976.
Thirteen stories of Jewish life in Soviet Union
written by émigré to Israel.

489. Gerlitz, Menachem. Heavenly City. New York:
Feldheim, 1978.
This collection of stories from a wide variety of
Jewish sources all deal with the city of Jerusalem.

490. Gerson, Noel B. The Hittite. New York: Doubleday, 1961.
Hittite army commander opposes Hebrew invaders under the command of Joshua.

491. Gessner, Robert. Here Is My Home. New York:
Alliance, 1941.
Jewish immigrant prospers in Midwest lumber
city, marries a non-Jew, and is seized by Ku Klux
Klan.

492. _____. Treason. New York: Scribner's, 1944.
American Revolutionary background to person of
Benedict Arnold; Haym Solomon is portrayed, too.

493. Gilbert, Julie Goldsmith. Umbrella Steps. New
York: Random House, 1972.
Two private-school teenagers in Manhattan find
themselves involved with each other's father and
the eventual marriage of one pair.

494. Gillon, Adam. Cup of Fury. New York: Astra,
1962.
Palestine just before the creation of the State
of Israel is scene of illegal Jewish army and intrigues involving British and Arabs.

495.   Gillon, Diana and Meir. Vanquish the Angel. New
       York: Day, 1956.
            Native-born Jerusalemite marries English non-
       Jew; plot moves from time of British mandate
       through establishment of State of Israel.

496.   Gilner, Elias. Prince of Israel: A Novel on Bar-
       Kokba's Uprising Against Rome. New York: Ex-
       position, 1952.
            Jerusalem, Antioch, and Rome are key settings
       for last war of Judea for independence against Rom-
       ans led by Bar Kochba.

497.   Ginsburg. Natalia. A Light for Fools. Translated
       by Angus Davidson. New York: Dutton, 1957.
            Effects of war on two families in small town in
       northern Italy, where German Jew and his Italian
       protector are executed.

498.   Gitlin, Murray. The Embarkation. New York:
       Crown, 1950.
            American army deserter in Rome refuses to be-
       tray Jewish refugees sailing for Palestine in return
       for immunity from court-martial.

499.   Glanville, Brian. The Bankrupts. New York: Double-
       day, 1958.
            English girl revolts against parents' middle-class
       values, marries Ph.D. student, moves to Israel,
       suffers death of husband, and remains with unborn
       child.

500.   _____. Diamond. New York: Farrar, 1962.
            Middle-class English Jewish life sketched through
       Irish Jew married to Cockney wife and their battles
       with their children.

501.   _____. Money Is Love. New York: Doubleday,
       1972.
            An English rabbi's son and a New York financier
       create a megafund to transfer financial power to
       the young.

502.   _____. A Second Home. New York: Delacorte,
       1966.
            Impetuous English-Jewish actress ensnared in
       love affair with playwright and involved with London
       TV literary set.

503.   Glatstein, Jacob. Homecoming at Twilight. Trans-
       lated by Norbert Guterman. New York: Yoseloff,
       1962.
            Polish Jew returns for mother's funeral on eve
       of Nazi Holocaust and discovers courage of Jews
       as they face death.

504.   _____. Homeward Bound. Translated by Abraham
       Goldstein. New York: Yoseloff, 1969.
            Yiddish poet recreates return to Lublin from
       America to visit his mother and in fiction form
       summarizes Jewish history.

505.   Goes, Albrecht. Burnt Offering. Translated by
       Michael Hamburger. New York: Pantheon, 1956.
            German butcher's wife executed because of con-
       cern for Jews hounded by the Nazi SS men.

506.   Gold, Herbert. Fathers. New York: Random House,
       1967.
            Themes of the American dream and dislocation
       between generations developed in autobiographical
       novel of immigrant and his family in America.

507.   _____. Love and Like. New York: Dial, 1960.
            Short stories dealing with family and childhood,
       failing marriages, and assimilation.

508.   _____. The Prospect Before Us. Cleveland:
       World, 1954.
            Cleveland hotel owner becomes involved in racial
       conflict when he permits Negro to register as guest.

509.   _____. Therefore Be Bold. New York: Dial,
       1960.
            Love of adolescents in Midwest upset by anti-
       Semitic father of hero's girlfriend.

510.   Goldemberg, Isaac. The Fragmented Life of Don
       Jacobo Turner. Translated by Robert S. Picciotto.
       New York: Persea, 1977.
            Immigrant from Czarist Russia tries to survive
       in small community in Peru in the 1930s.

511.   Golding, Louis. In the Steps of Moses. Philadelphia:
       Jewish Publication Society, 1943.
            Condensation of two earlier books following trail
       of Moses and Israelites to Promised Land.

512.   _____ . The Glory of Elsie Silver. New York:
        Dial, 1946.
            Former English cabaret singer, married to Nazi
        general, reaffirms Jewishness by participation in
        Warsaw ghetto battle.

513.   Goldreich, Gloria. Leah's Journey. New York:
        Harcourt Brace Jovanovich, 1978.
            Panoramic sweep of Russian-Jewish family's
        saga, immigrants to East Side in the 20s through
        Depression, Holocaust, World War II, and Israel's
        kibbutzim.

514.   Goldring-Goding, Henry. Out of Hell. Boston: Chap-
        man & Grimes, 1955.
            Escape from German concentration camp of ex-
        officer in Polish army and his wife.

515.   Goldstein, Arthur D. Nobody's Sorry He Got Killed.
        New York: Random House, 1976.
            New Yorker leads senior citizens of California
        center in investigation of murder of lover of one
        of their granddaughters.

516.   _____ . A Person Shouldn't Die Like That. New
        York: Random House, 1972.
            Retired clothing cutter is plunged into a new
        world when he investigates death of friend whom he
        believes was murdered.

517.   Goldstein, Ruth Tessler. The Heart Is Half a Prophet.
        New York: Macmillan, 1976.
            A pious Orthodox Jew struggles to support his
        family during the Depression and creates havoc in
        the lives of his wife and children because of his
        fanaticism.

518.   Goldthorpe, John. The Same Scourge. New York:
        Putnam, 1956.
            The Last Supper and the Crucifixion are the high-
        lights of the drama of Jesus and his disciples.

519.   Goodman, Paul. The Facts of Life. New York: Van-
        guard, 1945.
            Pieces include play based on the prophet Jonah
        and group of refugees joined in a university in ex-
        ile.

520. _____ . The Break-up of Our Camp.   Norfolk,
     Conn.: New Directions, 1949.
         Avant-garde short stories centered mainly around
     Jews who seek meaning in the void of the universe.

521. Goran, Lester. The Demon in the Sun Parlor.   New
     York: New American Library, 1968.
         Former army captain who is a failure as a sales-
     man and as a fireman is determined to provide for
     his family in Miami.

522. _____ . The Keeper of Secrets.   New York: Mc-
     Call, 1971.
         Jewish-Irish novelist journeys across America to
     collect parts of his novel from his many ex-wives.

523. _____ . The Stranger in the Snow.   New York:
     New American Library, 1966.
         Middle-aged Jewish failure haunted by ghost of
     Methodist killed in his stead during World War II
     patrol.

524. Gorbatov, Boris. Taras' Family.   Translated by
     Elizabeth Donnelly.   New York: Cattell, 1946.
         During German occupation of the Ukraine, Rus-
     sian seeks to offer refuge to aged Jewish doctor.

525. Gordimer, Nadine. The Lying Days: A Novel.   New
     York: Simon & Schuster, 1953.
         Middle-class Protestant girl reminisces about
     adolescence and college years in Johannesburg and
     friendship with Jewish boy.

526. Gordon, Noah. The Jerusalem Diamond.   New York:
     Random House, 1979.
         A diamond from the ancient Jerusalem Temple
     is sought by diamond merchant who is commissioned
     by three religious groups to return it.

527. _____ . The Rabbi.   New York: McGraw-Hill,
     1965.
         Career of rabbi married to convert covers is-
     sues like civil rights and normal congregational
     problems.

528. Gorm, Lester H. The Anglo-Saxons.   New York:
     Sagamore, 1958.

World War II veteran, reacting to anti-Semitism, joins with Canadians, British, and Americans in volunteer brigade in Israel in 1948 war.

529. Gottlieb, Hinko. The Key to the Great Gate. Translated by Fred Bolman and Ruth Morris. New York: Simon & Schuster, 1947.
      Three Jews in German prison all sustained by magical powers of one of them who convinces them that salvation is in their own lives.

530. Goudge, Elizabeth. Castle on the Hill. New York: Coward-McCann, 1942.
      Brief relationship, in castle following Dunkirk, of assorted characters, including Jewish violinist.

531. Gould, Heywood. One Dead Debutante. St. Martin's, 1975.
      A Jewish investigative reporter runs into case involving Mafia, dope dealers, and is almost killed by incompetent gangsters.

532. Gould, Lois. Necessary Objects. New York: Random House, 1972.
      New York heiresses to department-store fortune pictured pitilessly with lovers, harassed children, and sterile existences.

533. Gouri, Haim. The Chocolate Deal. New York: Holt, Rinehart and Winston, 1968.
      Two survivors of the Holocaust seek families and black-market deals in Germany.

534. Gourse, R. Leslie. With Gall and Honey. New York: Doubleday, 1961.
      American girl in Israel attracted to Argentinian fighter-intellectual and older businessman in Jerusalem.

535. Grade, Chaim. The Agunah. Translated by Curt Leviant. New York: Twayne/Bobbs-Merrill, 1974.
      The plight of a woman whose husband is not declared officially dead is developed in a Vilna setting between the two World Wars.

536. _____. The Well. Philadelphia: Jewish Publication Society, 1967.

Panoramic view of Vilna Jews, their religiosity
and radicalism, prior to World War I.

537. _____. The Yeshiva. Translated by Curt Leviant.
Indianapolis: Bobbs-Merrill, 1977.
Pious son of a Hebrew teacher once active in
the Haskalah is beset by doubts as student in a
"musar" Yeshiva.

538. _____. The Yeshiva Vol. 2: Masters and Disciples. Indianapolis: Bobbs-Merrill, 1977.
The Yeshiva student, now in his late teens, begins to doubt God's existence as he becomes aware
that the founder of the Yeshiva suffers great doubts
too.

539. Graham, Gwenthalyne. Earth and High Heaven. New
York: Lippincott, 1944.
Plea for tolerance and understanding in Canadian
setting of intermarriage when problems increase
after the ceremony.

540. Granit, Arthur. The Time of the Peaches. New
York: Abelard-Schuman, 1959.
Adolescent views with pessimism the clash be-
tween Brownsville Jewish culture and pressures of
American life.

541. Grass, G. Dog Years. New York: Harcourt, 1956.
Jewish maker of scarecrows is narrator of
apocalyptic period in Germany from 1920s through
the end of World War II.

542. Graves, Robert. King Jesus. New York: Creative
Age, 1946.
Radical departure from usual biographical approach to life of Jesus with use of Jewish and
pagan folklore.

543. Green, Gerald. Cactus Pie: Ten Stories. Boston:
Houghton Mifflin, 1979.
Among the stories is one of an elderly Jewish
businessman who changes a Hare Krishna retreat
into a capitalist money-maker.

544. _____. Faking It: Or, The Wrong Hungarian.
New York: Trident, 1971.

Frustrated writer acts as secret agent in international Paris conference and becomes enmeshed with CIA, Russian spies, and Israeli agents.

545. _____. The Healers. New York: Putnam, 1979.
Massive saga of doctors who crusade for better hospital care includes Italian, Jewish, and WASP personalities.

546. _____. Holocaust. New York: Bantam, 1978.
The novel served as the basis of the teleplay, or vice versa, of NBC-TV's "Holocaust" spectacular.

547. _____. The Last Angry Man. New York: Scribner's, 1957.
Elderly Brooklyn doctor becomes subject for new TV show.

548. _____. The Legion of Noble Christians. New York: Trident, 1965.
Jewish group seeks to identify and honor Christians who saved Jewish lives during Hitler period.

549. _____. The Lotus Eaters. New York: Scribner's, 1959.
Anthropologist assails white-superiority attitude in Southern setting very much like Miami Beach.

550. _____. To Brooklyn with Love. New York: Trident, 1967.
Adolescent in Bronxville in 1934 reflects struggle of growing up with street gangs and effects of Depression on family life.

551. _____. Tourist. New York: Doubleday, 1973.
American tourists on trip to London, Leningrad, Vienna, Jerusalem, etc., become involved in plot to free a Russian-Jewish scientist.

552. Greenberg, Joanne. The King's Persons. New York: Holt, 1963.
Jewish moneylenders in England in the twelfth century are protected by the King until blood-libel massacre in York.

553. _____. Summering. New York: Holt, Rinehart and Winston, 1966.

Short stories illuminate themes of the outsider
and stranger in characters of Jewish girl's return
to New York ghetto and life among the Navahos.

554.   Greenburg, Dan. Kiss My Firm but Pliant Lips. New
        York: Grossman, 1965.
            Art-school graduate holds down two jobs in office
        building and also is involved with two mistresses.

555.   Greene, Harris. Cancelled Accounts. New York:
        Doubleday, 1973.
            SS survivors seek to collect money stolen from
        Jews killed in concentration camps and are caught
        between Arab and Israeli agents in South America.

556.   Greenfield, Josh. O for a Master of Magic. New
        York: New American Library, 1968.
            Ex-New York academic married to Japanese wife
        and the conflicts arising from differences in culture.

557.   Grendahl, J. Spencer. The Mad Dog Press Archives.
        New York: Putnam, 1970.
            Former Peace Corps member establishes revolu-
        tionary magazine in Tangier; the young Jewish in-
        terpreter is later killed in Arab section of the me-
        dina.

558.   Gresham, William Lindsay. Limbo Tower. New
        York: Rinehart, 1949.
            Young Jewish radical and elderly Jew of faith in-
        teract in tuberculosis ward of a city hospital.

559.   Grey, Harry. The Hoods. New York: Crown, 1952.
            East Side juvenile delinquent rises to become
        leader of crime syndicate.

560.   Grisman, Arnold E. Early to Rise. New York: Har-
        per, 1958.
            Ambitious veteran establishes dye business and
        marries Fifth Avenue girl who differs from his
        Bronx background.

561.   Gross, Joel. The Young Man Who Wrote Soap Op-
        eras. New York: Scribner's, 1975.
            A Yeshiva student from Long Island writes soap
        operas but withdraws from brutal world through at-
        traction to former schoolmate.

562. Grossbach, Robert. The Frisco Kid. New York:
Warner, 1979.
Based on a screenplay, this novel tells of the
Polish Rabbi from Cracow who teams up with bank
robbers to cross U.S. in order to establish a syna-
gogue in San Francisco during the Gold Rush.

563. _____. Someone Great! New York: Harper and
Row, 1971.
A thirty-year-old failure from the South Bronx
seeks company and admiration in cheap dance halls.

564. Grosser, Morton. The Hobby Shop. Boston: Houghton Mifflin, 1967.
Middle-aged widowed professor finds solace
through a hobby shop and second marriage to a
young non-Jew.

565. Grossman, Ladislav. The Shop on Main Street. New
York: Doubleday, 1970.
Old Jewish woman befriended and aided by Slovak
during Czech crisis of 1942, when Nazis invade her
town.

566. Haas, Ben. The House of Christina. New York:
Simon & Schuster, 1977.
Vienna in pre-World War II days is setting for
the relationships between a beauty and a Nazi, Jew,
and an American writer all attracted by her.

567. Habe, Hans. Christopher and His Father. Translated
by Michael Bullock. New York: Coward-McCann,
1968.
Son of German Nazi fails to find expiation by
working on a kibbutz and flees behind the Iron Cur-
tain.

568. _____. Off Limits: A Novel. Translated by
Ewald Osers. New York: Fell, 1957.
American Jewish officer loves German fräulein
during early years of occupation of Germany.

569. _____. The Mission. New York: Coward-McCann,
1966.
Nations doom Jews to Nazi death due to inability
to resolve refugee problem at Swiss conference.

570. _____. Walk in Darkness. New York: Putnam, 1948.

Jewish woman helps child of Negro soldier and his German wife after he is involved with black marketeers and kills a soldier.

571. Haddad, C. A. Bloody September. New York: Harper & Row, 1976.
Iraqi Jew, an Israeli secret agent, investigates the disappearance of a Jewish missile scientist and uncovers Arab plot to destroy Israel.

572. _____. The Moroccan. New York: Harper & Row, 1975.
A Moroccan Jew married to a blonde Israeli is recruited into Israeli secret service to infiltrate Palestinian Arab organization.

573. _____. Operation Apricot. New York: Harper & Row, 1978.
Israeli businessman, former intelligence agent, pressed into service to uncover conspiracy of fanatic Israelis and Arabs to bring down Israeli government.

574. Haine, Victor. Gabe's Challenge: A Novel of Love's Victory Over Religious Conflict. New York: Exposition, 1953.
Rabbi falls in love with minister's daughter, leaves his congregation and creates new humanistic religion.

575. Halberstam, Michael. The Wanting of Levine. Philadelphia: Lippincott, 1978.
Jewish presidential candidate in 1988 is beset by anti-Semitism, earlier sexual antics, and radical son in his campaign.

576. Haldeman, Charles. The Snowman. New York: Simon & Schuster, 1965.
Small upstate New York town is scene of anti-Semitism directed against new Jewish doctor.

577. Hallahan, William H. Catch Me, Kill Me. Indianapolis: Bobbs-Merrill, 1977.
American Immigration Service and CIA are involved with pursuing an exiled Russian-Jewish poet kidnapped by Russian agents in Grand Central Station.

578. Halper, Albert. The Fourth Horseman of Miami
      Beach. New York: Norton, 1966.
           Vacationer in Miami Beach befriends retired man
      while searching for cousin who stole money from
      his firm.

579. _____. The Golden Watch. New York: Holt,
      1953.
           Vignettes of boy growing up in Chicago before
      World War I in and around father's delicatessen
      store.

580. _____. The Little People. New York: Harper,
      1942.
           Clerk's-eye view of workers in exclusive clothing
      store in Chicago.

581. _____. Only an Inch from Glory. New York:
      Harper, 1943.
           Art student, accountant, press agent, and his
      wife are principal characters in New York setting
      of people trying to achieve ambitions.

582. Halsey, Margaret. Some of My Best Friends Are
      Soldiers. Simon & Schuster, 1944.
           Letters written by young woman to army brother
      in which she describes race prejudice and anti-Sem-
      itism at servicemen's canteen.

583. Hameiri, Avigdor. The Great Madness. New York:
      Vantage, 1952.
           The plight and antics of a Hungarian Jew drafted
      into German army in World War I.

584. Hamilton, Wallace. David at Olivet. New York: St.
      Martin's, 1979.
           The lives of David, Saul, and Jonathan are linked
      together in this retelling of David's life through
      flashbacks.

585. Handel, Yudit. The Street of Steps. Translated by
      Rachel Katz and David Segal. New York: Yoseloff,
      1963.
           Modern Israel's social problems, slums, prosti-
      tutes, thievery, seen in squalid section of Haifa.

586. Hardy, William George. All the Trumpets Sounded:

<u>A Novel Based on the Life of Moses</u>.   New York:
Coward-McCann, 1942.
   Imaginative retelling of story of Moses with great
emphasis on his years as a Prince of Egypt.

587.   Hareven, Shulamith.   <u>City of Many Days</u>.   Translated
       by Hillel Halkin.   New York: Doubleday, 1977.
          The city of Jerusalem and a Sephardic Jewish
       family are the heroes in this novel of the period of
       1917-1948 in Palestine.

588.   Harmon, Sandra.   <u>A Girl Like Me</u>.   New York: Dut-
       ton, 1975.
          Brooklyn Jewish girl makes good in the entertain-
       ment world as talented scriptwriter while realizing
       that sex isn't the key to success.

589.   Harriman, John.   <u>The Magnate</u>.   New York: Random
       House, 1946.
          Humanistic Jewish banker involved with financial
       wizard who creates public utilities empire.

590.   Harris, Leonard.   <u>The Masada Plan</u>.   New York:
       Crown, 1976.
          Suspense fiction based on Israel's Masada Plan
       to stave off Arab attack and intrigue involving journ-
       alist, an Israeli ambassador, and the American
       Secretary of State.

591.   Harris, Mark.   <u>The Goy</u>.   New York: Dial, 1970.
          Non-Jewish historian drawn to Jews through mar-
       riage and associations seeks to manipulate their
       lives through his loving deeds.

592.   _____.   <u>Something About a Soldier</u>.   New York:
       Macmillan, 1957.
          Small-town Jewish son of a pawnbroker has short
       career in Georgia camp.

593.   Harris, Rosemary.   <u>Nor Evil Dreams</u>.   New York:
       Simon & Schuster, 1973.
          English schoolteacher falls in love with Jewish
       colleague and both are subject to anti-Semitic inci-
       dents.

594.   Harris, Thomas.   <u>Black Sunday</u>.   New York: Put-
       nam, 1975.

Arab terrorists seek to blow up Super Bowl using a former American POW piloting a television
blimp.

595. Harrison, Marcus. The Memoirs of Jesus Christ.
New York: Ballantine, 1975.
    Jesus retells his life story now that he is in a
monastery on the Damascus Road, in retirement
and having escaped from the Crucifixion.

596. Hartley, J. M. The Way. New York: Crowell, 1944.
    Roman centurion sent on mission to discover
those who announced Jesus' birth brings death upon
his Jewish mistress.

597. Hartog, Jan de. The Inspector. New York: Atheneum, 1960.
    Middle-aged Dutch policeman tries to get Jewish
girl, victim of concentration-camp medical experiments, to Israel.

598. Harwood, Ronald. The Guilt Merchants. New York:
Holt, Rinehart and Winston, 1969.
    South American town scene of search for Nazi
war criminal by Israeli agent.

599. Haydn, Hiram Collins. The Time Is Noon. New
York: Crown, 1948.
    Only one Jewish intellectual of a group of six
young people at New England college in the 1920s
understands the real world outside.

600. Hayward, Louis M. Grandpa and the Girls. New
York: Random House, 1960.
    Elderly Jewish Talmudic scholar visits daughter
in Tulsa who is a successful "madam" and befriends
her girls.

601. Hazaz, Haim. Gates of Bronze. Translated by Ger-
shon Levi. Philadelphia: Jewish Publication Society, 1975.
    An Eastern European Jewish shtetl is destroyed
in the Bolshevik Revolution.

602. _____. Mori Sa'id. Translated by Ben Halpern.
New York: Abelard-Schuman, 1956.
    Portrayal of lives of three generations of Yemen-
ite Jews in Israel during World War II.

603. Heard, Gerald. The Gospel According to Gamaliel.
      New York: Harper, 1945.
         Jesus seen in journal of Gamaliel, grandson of
      Hillel and teacher of Paul, which tries to bridge
      chasm between Pharasaic teachings and Christianity.

604. Hearne, John. Land of the Living. New York: Har-
      per & Row, 1962.
         Jewish-refugee scientist drawn back into main-
      stream of life by sympathetic natives of West Indian
      island.

605. Heatter, Basil. The Dim View, a Novel. New York:
      Farrar, Straus, 1946.
         German-Jewish psychiatrist seeks to help Amer-
      ican naval lieutenant in command of PT boat.

606. Heller, Joseph. Good as Gold. New York: Simon
      & Schuster, 1979.
         Middle-aged professor sells idea for book on the
      Jewish experience in America while yearning for
      glamorous job in Washington.

607. Helprin, Mark. A Dove of the East. New York:
      Knopf, 1975.
         Among the twenty stories is that of the Jewish
      cowboy on the Golan Heights who had fled to Israel
      from Paris during the Holocaust period.

608. _____. Refiner's Fire, The Life and Adventures
      of Marshall Pearl, A Foundling. New York: Knopf,
      1977.
         The hero is born on an illegal ship bound for
      Palestine in 1947 and searches for his father as he
      grows up and undergoes adventures.

609. Hempstone, Smith. In the Midst of Lions. New York:
      Harper & Row, 1968.
         Veteran war photographer falls in love with daugh-
      ter of old friend during the 1967 Arab-Israeli war.

610. Henderson, Lois T. Hagar: A Novel. Chappaqua:
      Christian Herald, 1978.
         The conflicts and tensions among Sarah, Hagar,
      and Abraham are explored in this fictionalized Bib-
      lical account.

611. Henissart, Paul. Narrow Exit. New York: Simon
         & Schuster, 1974.
            Israeli and Arab agents cross in Jewish scheme,
         to kidnap a Palestinian guerrilla leader, highlighted
         by Arab disunity and Israeli inefficiency.

612. Henriques, Robert. The Commander. New York:
         Viking, 1968.
            Jewish officer suffers discrimination in comman-
         do unit of British armed forces.

613. _____. Too Little Love. New York: Viking,
         1968.
            Chronicles of landed English gentry and Jewish
         neighbors in countryside setting for two decades
         prior to World War II.

614. Henry, B. A. The Gutenheim Way. New York:
         Yoseloff, 1957.
            Upper-middle-class New York German Jews face
         adjustment when daughter marries boy below her
         station in life from immigrant family.

615. Herrick, William. Hermanos! New York: Simon &
         Schuster, 1969.
            Jewish fighter in Spanish Civil War from unionist
         and Communist background suffers defeat in battle.

616. _____. The Itinerant. New York: McGraw-Hill,
         1967.
            Escapades of East Side boy growing up in Depres-
         sion, involvement with sharecroppers and Spanish
         Civil War, and final adjustment in marriage and
         civil-rights movement.

617. Hesky, Olga. The Different Night. New York: Ran-
         dom House, 1971.
            Israeli agent searches for Jewish boy kidnapped
         on the eve of Passover.

618. _____. The Sequin Syndicate. New York: Dodd,
         Mead, 1969.
            American girl with CIA connections and Israeli
         undercover agent join forces to solve murder of
         Tel Aviv antiquities dealer.

619. Hersey, John. The Wall. New York: Knopf, 1950.

Detailed account of Nazi occupation of Poland,
the physical walling-in of the Jews, and the revolt
in the Warsaw ghetto.

620.   Herzl, Theodor.   Old-New Land.   Translated by Lotta
Levensohn.   New York: Bloch, 1960.
New edition of Herzl's visionary novel, which
described a cooperative Jewish society established
in Palestine, Jerusalem restored, harnessing of the
Jordan River, all of this with a Viennese flavor.

621.   Heym, Stefan.   The King David Report.   New York:
Putnam, 1973.
A modern political parable based on a recreation
of the life of King David as commissioned by his
son Solomon.

622.   Heuman, William.   Strictly from Brooklyn.   New
York: Morrow, 1956.
Narrative of Dodgers' fan and his problems, al-
so daughter's intermittent romances.

623.   Higgins, Aldan.   Balcony of Europe.   New York: Delacorte, 1973.
Irish painter in Spanish artists' colony is fascin-
ated by friend's wife and her American-Jewish background.

624.   Hilsenrath, Edgar.   The Nazi and the Barber.   New
York: Doubleday, 1971.
Former SS machine-gunner assumes identity of
former friend and victim, a Jewish barber, and
escapes to Palestine to fight in Jewish underground.

625.   _____ .   Night.   New York: Doubleday, 1966.
Documentary account of harshness of life in
Ukrainian ghetto in 1942.

626.   Himmel, Richard.   The Twenty-Third Web.   New
York: Random House, 1977.
Terrorists seek to withdraw Jewish financial aid
to Israel to cause its collapse.

627.   Hobart, Alice Tisdale.   The Serpent-Wreathed Staff.
Indianapolis: Bobbs-Merrill, 1951.
Intermarriage adjustment of Jew in family of doctors who are opponents on question of compulsory
medical insurance.

628. Hobson, Laura Z. First Papers. New York: Random House, 1965.
      Jewish newspaper editor and Unitarian lawyer friend allies in liberal political movements prior to World War I.

629. _____. Gentleman's Agreement, a Novel. New York: Simon & Schuster, 1947.
      Non-Jewish writer pretends to be Jewish to develop magazine article exposing discrimination and the Christian Front.

630. _____. Over and Above. New York: Doubleday, 1979.
      Three generations of women interact during the period from the UN resolution on Zionism to the Entebbe raid and reflect problems of Jewish identity.

631. _____. The Trespassers. New York: Simon & Schuster, 1943.
      Ruthless radio tycoon's fear of marriage to successful businesswoman played out behind theme of plight of refugees who are denied entrance into the United States.

632. Hochman, Sandra. Endangered Species. New York: Putnam, 1977.
      Middle-aged woman seeks to establish a woman's life-insurance company and is involved with literary world of Mailer, Jerry Rubin, and a cabbalist jockey.

633. Hoffenberg, Jack. 17 Ben Gurion. New York: Putnam, 1977.
      Intrigue and espionage mark attempt of Israelis to prevent Palestinian terrorists from destroying oilfields in the Sinai.

634. Hoffman, Michael. The Buddy System. New York: Holt, Rinehart and Winston, 1971.
      A novel of growing up Jewish spiced with sister-brother incest and nervous breakdown.

635. Hoffman, Stanley. Solomon's Temple. New York: Viking, 1974.
      A seriocomic transformation of a twenty-five-year-old graduate student from a compulsive overweight eater to a Lothario.

636. Hoffman, William. Mendel. New York: Yoseloff,
      1969.
          Eighty-year-old man crosses paths with neighbors
      and acquaintances in St. Paul Jewish neighborhood.

637. Hoffmann, Poul. The Eternal Fire. Philadelphia:
      Muhlenberg, 1962.
          Middle novel of a trilogy in which Moses returns
      to Egypt after his stay with Jethro and leads Hebrews
      into desert.

638. Holles, Robert. Spawn. New York: Doubleday,
      1978.
          Israeli intelligence, under cover of an interna-
      tional art company, tracks down German owner of
      a canister containing frozen semen of Adolf Hitler.

639. Holt, Felix. Dan'l. Boone Kissed Me. New York:
      Dutton, 1954.
          First Jew to settle in Kentucky town as merchant
      is mistaken for Daniel Boone by elderly woman.

640. Horovitz, Israel. Cappella. New York: Harper &
      Row, 1973.
          Elderly, half-crazed Jew is a hospital patient
      along with a middle-aged writer, both sharing agony
      and death wishes.

641. Horowitz, Gene. Home Is Where You Start From.
      New York: Norton, 1966.
          Recreation of East Side, New Jersey, and Brook-
      lyn seen in marriage of incompatible children of
      immigrants.

642. Horwitz, Julius. The City. Cleveland and New York:
      World, 1953.
          Alienated and lonely Jewish urbanites in New
      York City seek friendship and understanding.

643. Household, Geoffrey. Arabesque. Boston: Little,
      Brown, 1948.
          Set at the time of the British mandate in Pales-
      tine and focuses on the tensions between the British
      and the Jewish agency and between the Zionists and
      the extremist Irgun movement.

644. Howard, Elizabeth M. Before the Sun Goes Down.
      Garden City: Doubleday, Doran, 1946.

Small-town life in 1880 in Pennsylvania with plea
for tolerance toward minorities, including Jews.

645. Howe, Irving, ed. Jewish-American Stories. New
      York: Mentor/New American Library, 1977.
           Howe's introduction to this anthology emphasizes
      the role of the family in Jewish life.

646. _____, and Greenberg, Eliezer, eds. Ashes Out
      of Hope: Fiction by Soviet-Yiddish Writers. New
      York: Schocken, 1977.
           Bergelson, Kahanovitch, and Kulbak are the
      authors of short fiction depicting pre-World War II
      Russia and the disintegration of Jewish life.

647. _____. A Treasury of Yiddish Stories. New York:
      Viking, 1954.
           Jewish life in villages of Eastern Europe re-
      vealed through many diverse personalities with sev-
      eral stories describing plight of immigrants in New
      York.

648. _____. Yiddish Stories: Old and New. New York:
      Holiday House, 1974.
           Peretz, Sholom Aleichem, and Singer are among
      the authors in this collection of fourteen stories.

649. Howe, Irving, and Wisse, Ruth, eds. The Best of
      Sholom Aleichem. New York: New Republic, 1979.
           Twenty-five of Sholom Aleichem's stories recap-
      ture the flavor of the East European Jewish life-
      style.

650. Howland, Bette. Blue in Chicago. New York: Har-
      per & Row, 1978.
           The narrator grows up lonely in Chicago within
      a Jewish family that experiences weddings, death,
      old age, racial tensions.

651. Hoyer, Robert. Jabbok. Philadelphia: Muhlenberg,
      1958.
           Jacob's conflict with his brother Esau and his
      encounter with God in his dream.

652. Hubler, Richard G. Love and Wisdom. New York:
      Crown, 1968.
           King Solomon, his abilities as administrator and

his personal problems, seen through the person of
the prophet Nathan.

653. _____. The Soldier and the Sage. New York:
Crown, 1966.
The second-century rebellion against the Romans
creates a strange fellowship between Rabbi Akiba
and Bar Kochba.

654. Hudson, Helen. Meyer Meyer. New York: Dutton,
1967.
Two middle-aged history professors living in
past have friendship broken when one marries.

655. Hughes, Kathleen. Not Quite a Dream. New York:
Doubleday, 1948.
Gentile girl and older Jew marry in Midwestern
setting accompanied by anti-Semitic concerns of
family.

656. Hughes, Rupert. The Giant Awakes. Los Angeles:
Borden, 1950.
Romanticized version of life of Samuel Gompers
and impact on American labor movement.

657. Hunt, Howard. The Berlin Ending. New York: Putnam, 1973.
A rich American Jew and a French nobleman
conspire to subvert a German foreign minister in
spy thriller of American and European espionage.

658. Hurst, Fannie. Family. New York: Doubleday, 1960.
Lives of three brothers in St. Louis are affected
when a woman comes to live with the oldest brother,
a wealthy widower.

659. Hurwitz, Ken. The Line of David. New York: Norton, 1973.
A Harvard hippie pacifist falls in love with pro
Israel law student and winds up in Israel and
kills an Arab in guerrilla action.

660. Hutchinson, Ray Coryton. The Fire and the Wood.
New York: Farrar & Rinehart, 1940.
German-Jewish scientist working on cure for
tuberculosis flees with patient to tragic end in
England.

661. Hutter, Catherine. The Outnumbered. New York:
Dodd, 1944.
Jewish orphan, reared as Catholic in Austria
prior to 1938, attains maturity at period of the
Anschluss.

662. _____. On Some Fair Morning. New York: Dodd,
1946.
Tragic outcome for American Jew married to a
half-Jewish German aristocrat after Nazis achieve
power.

663. Ibn Zahav, Ari. David and Bathsheba. Translated
by I. M. Lask. New York: Crown, 1951.
King David as he lies dying, recounts life, and
his love for Bathsheba.

664. _____. Jessica, My Daughter. Translated by
Julian Meltzer. New York: Crown, 1948.
Retelling of Shylock story with action mainly in
Venetian ghetto of sixteenth century.

665. Ikor, Roger. The Sons of Avrom. Translated by
Leonard M. Friedman and Maxwell Singer. New
York: Putnam, 1958.
Family of Russian Jews find freedom in France
from Czarist tyranny; members turn to assimilation, to Palestine, to fighting in the French resistance movement.

666. Ilton, Paul, and MacLennan, Roberts. Moses and the
Ten Commandments. New York: Dell, 1956.
The classic story of the rise of Moses to lead-
ership and his role as lawgiver.

667. Ingles, James W. Woman of Samaria. Longmans,
1949.
The Biblical story of Jesus and the woman of
Samaria with much background of the people, sects,
and customs.

668. Ingram, Tolbert R. Maid of Israel. Nashville:
Broadman, 1955.
Heroine is maid of wife of Syrian leader Naaman
during days of Jehoram, son of Jezebel.

669. Isherwood, Christopher. Prater Violet: A Novel.
New York: Random House, 1945.

Austrian-Jewish movie director produces film
for British firm subsequent to early encounter with
Nazis.

670.	Israel, Charles E.	Rizpah.	New York: Simon &
Schuster, 1961.
The lives of Saul, Samuel, David, and Rizpah
are intertwined at the time of Saul's ascendency to
leadership.

671.	Jablons, Beverly.	Dance Time.	New York: Morrow,
1979.
Fun-loving Jewish family introduces middle-aged
Cleveland woman to ballroom dancing, bagels, and
sex.

672.	Jabotinsky, Vladimir.	Prelude to Delilah.	New York:
Ackerman, 1945.
Samson and the Philistines and his downfall at
the hands of Delilah.

673.	Jackson, Shirley.	The Road Through the Wall.	New
York: Farrar, 1948.
Small California town scene of death of two teenagers, part of middle-class community including
one Jewish family.

674.	Jacobs, Harvey.	The Egg of the Glak and Other
Stories.	New York: Harper & Row, 1969.
Middle-class New York Jews, including musician,
antiques dealer, and sales promoter.

675.	_____.	Summer on a Mountain of Spices.	New
York: Harper & Row, 1975.
Nostalgic view of a ten-day period in 1945 set
in the borscht circuit of the Catskill Mountains, a
vacation haven for New York City Jews.

676.	Jacobs, Israel.	Ten for Kaddish.	New York: Nor-
ton, 1972.
Rabbi's courage in opposing American Nazi speak-
er reveals bigotry in upper-middle-class community
and sparks conflict with his congregational leadership.

677.	Jacobson, Dan.	The Beginners.	New York: Mac-
millan, 1966.
Jewish girl from Lithuania comes to live with

uncles in South Africa, marries a Zionist, and
rears a troubled family.

678. _____. The Price of Diamonds. New York:
Knopf, 1958.
Pair of Jewish diamond merchants in South African mining town involved in illicit trading operation.

679. _____. The Rape of Tamar. New York: Mac-
millan, 1970.
Nephew of King David stages the tragic rape of
Tamar by her brother Amnon.

680. _____. Through the Wilderness and Other Stories.
New York: Macmillan, 1968.
Mostly South African setting for short stories
dealing with adolescence, search for meanings
among Jewish students, street hawkers, and middle-
class merchants.

681. _____. The Wonder-Worker. Boston: Atlantic/
Little Brown, 1974.
London youth lives in the midst of portents,
signs, dreams and semi-madness.

682. _____. The Zulu and the Zeide. Boston: Little,
Brown, 1974.
Short stories with South African background and
relationships of Jews to blacks and Afrikaners.

683. Jacobson, Sheldon A. Fleet Surgeon to Pharaoh.
Portland: Oregon State University Press, 1971.
Sixth-century B.C. voyage of Egyptian fleet includes Jewish physician who seeks to learn of Egyptian art of medicine.

684. Jacot, Michael. The Last Butterfly. Indianapolis:
Bobbs-Merrill, 1974.
Half-Jewish clown seeks to entertain Jewish
children at Terezin until their train trip to Auschwitz.

685. Jaffe, Rona. Family Secrets. New York: Simon &
Schuster, 1974.
Immigrant Russian Jew realizes dream of success
in America but creates nightmare for grandchildren.

686. Jameson, Storm. The Black Laurel. New York:
     Macmillan, 1948.
         Jewish-refugee art expert victim of plot by Ger-
     man aristocrat to loot art treasures in British Zone
     of Berlin.

687. _____. Europe to Let: The Memoirs of an Ob-
     scure Man. New York: Macmillan, 1940.
         Vienna, Prague, Budapest, and Rhineland viewed
     by English journalist from 1923 to rise of Nazis.

688. _____. The Green Man. New York: Harper,
     1952.
         Ambitious Englishman's drive for money and
     power colored by hatred of Jews.

689. Janney, Russel. The Miracle of the Bells. New
     York: Prentice-Hall, 1946.
         Jewish movie producer involved in story of Polish-
     American girl from Pennsylvania who dies just be-
     fore reaching stardom.

690. Jarrell, Randall. Pictures from an Institution: A
     Comedy. New York: Knopf, 1954.
         Scholar-in-residence writes savage novel on life
     in a progressive college for women.

691. Jessey, Cornelia. Consuela Bright. New York:
     Sheed & Ward, 1962.
         Jewish immigrants seek new life in America
     leaving behind anti-Semitic persecution.

692. _____. The Growing Roots. New York: Crown,
     1947.
         Immigrant family settles in Colorado and under-
     goes assimilation, as seen in later life of daughter.

693. Johnson, Uwe. Speculations About Jakob. Translated
     by Ursule Molinaro. New York: Grove, 1963.
         East German meets her death after return from
     West Berlin and refusal to collaborate with Soviet
     agent during Hungarian revolt.

694. Johnston, Avin Harry. The Golden Temple. Grand
     Rapids: Zondervan, 1963.
         Jerusalem scene of Solomon's crowning achieve-
     ment, the building of the Temple.

695. Jones, James. From Here to Eternity. New York:
      Scribner's, 1951.
           Jewish soldiers included in story of army life in
      Hawaii in the months before Pearl Harbor.

696. Jong, Erica. Fear of Flying. New York: Holt, Rine-
      hart and Winston, 1973.
           A liberated woman rushes from husband to lover
      and back again in a novel with psychiatric special-
      ists as the heroes.

697. _____. How to Save Your Own Life. New York:
      Holt, 1977.
           A sequel to Fear of Flying finds Isadora in af-
      fairs again, losing sense of guilt and finding special
      love with young screenwriter.

698. Judah, Aaron. Clown of Bombay. New York: Dial,
      1968.
           Indian-Jewish boy in prep school in Bombay is in-
      volved in comic adventures with Muslims, Indians,
      and Jews.

699. _____. Clown on Fire. New York: Dial, 1967.
           Seventeen-year-old son of Bombay lawyer of
      Iraqi-Jewish descent and Polish mother and his
      adventures at prep school.

700. Julitte, Pierre. Block 26: Sabotage at Buchenwald.
      Translated by Francis Price. New York: Double-
      day, 1971.
           French prisoners at Buchenwald attempt to sab-
      otage or destroy mysterious factory in which they
      work.

701. Kaczer, Illes. The Siege. Translated by Lawrence
      Wolfe. New York: Dial, 1953.
           Jewish life in small Hungarian village in nine-
      teenth century with highlights of holidays and folk-
      lore.

702. Kadish, Mortimer R. Point of Honor. New York:
      Random House, 1951.
           German-Jewish corporal in U.S. artillery brigade
      in Italy experiences neo-Fascists and martinets.

703. Kahn, Roger. But Not to Keep. New York: Harper,
      1979.

> Jewish writer, in midlife crisis, involved in divorce and remarriage and attempts to maintain relationship with teenaged son.

704. Kalb, Marvin, and Koppel, Ted. In the National Interest. New York: Simon & Schuster, 1977.
   A network correspondent learns of transcript of meeting between Secretary of State (Kissinger?) and Arab terrorist who kidnapped his wife.

705. Kamins, Jeanette. Everything but a Husband. New York: St. Martin's, 1962.
   Five lonely women seek husbands at plush Catskill Hotel resort one weekend.

706. Kaniuk, Yoram. The Acrophile. Translated by Zeva Shapiro. New York: Atheneum, 1961.
   Israel archaeologist in New York becomes Empire State Building guide because of emotional scars from Arab-Israeli War, in which he killed a child.

707. _____. Adam Resurrected. New York: Atheneum, 1971.
   A mental-rehabilitation center in an Israeli desert houses an ex-clown from Auschwitz who seeks sanity.

708. _____. Himno, King of Jerusalem. Translated by Yosef Shachter. New York: Atheneum, 1969.
   Israeli nurse in Jerusalem in 1948 attempts to assist young soldier horribly maimed and seriously injured.

709. _____. Rockinghorse. Translated by Richard Flantz. New York: Harper & Row, 1977.
   A native Israeli painter abandons family in New York to return to Tel Aviv to seek new inspiration for his work.

710. _____. The Story of Aunt Shlomzion the Great. Translated by Zeva Shapiro. New York: Harper & Row, 1978.
   Aged matriarch of leading Tel Aviv family still affects the lives of family members from her nursing-home bed.

711. Kantor, MacKinlay. Andersonville. New York: World, 1955.

Life in and around Civil War camp in Georgia, which includes a cultured, traveled Jewish prisoner.

712. Kaplan, Bernard. Obituaries. New York: Grossman/ Viking, 1976.
Among the six stories is that of an elderly Jew who kills his son to head off an imagined pogrom in Rhode Island.

713. _____. Prisoners of This World: Stories. New York: Grossman, 1970.
Macabre short stories featuring violence and sadism; includes flight of family from the Bronx.

714. Kaplan, Howard. The Chopin Express. New York: Dutton, 1978.
American student smuggles books into Soviet Union while Mossad, KGB, and CIA are involved in Jews escaping from USSR.

715. _____. The Damascus Cover. New York: Dutton, 1977.
Aging Israeli agent recalled to service to help bring out Jewish children from Damascus.

716. Kaplan, Johanna. Other People's Lives. New York: Knopf, 1975.
Several short stories that deal with New York Jewish girls, one of whom is a former psychiatric patient boarding in a ballet dancer's apartment.

717. Kardos, Gyorgy G. Abraham's Good Week. Translated by Ralph Manheim. New York: Doubleday, 1975.
One week in the life of an aging Palestinian farmer is covered during 1947, when he shelters a Jewish terrorist.

718. Karmel, Ilona. An Estate of Memory. Boston: Houghton Mifflin, 1969.
Four women in German camp in Poland seek to smuggle newborn baby out of the camp.

719. _____. Stephania. Boston: Houghton Mifflin, 1953.
Polish-Jewish actress, survivor of Nazi brutality, gives hope to two roommates in Swedish hospital.

720. Karmel-Wolfe, Henia. The Baders of Jacob Street.
     Philadelphia: Lippincott, 1970.
        Daughter of Jewish family in Cracow, center of
     drama of Nazi takeover of Poland.

721. Karney, Jack. Cop. New York: Holt, 1951.
        Jewish policeman's career in New York wrecked
     by graft, corruption, and anti-Semitism.

722. _____. The Ragged Edge. New York: Morrow,
     1946.
        Family in East Side New York includes prize-
     fighter and gangster, and daughter who finds hap-
     piness in second marriage.

723. _____. Work of Darkness: A Novel. New York:
     Putnam, 1956.
        Teenaged Jewish boy killed by rival hoodlum mob
     on Lower East Side.

724. Karp, David. Enter Sleeping. New York: Harcourt,
     1960.
        Aspiring song-writer becomes involved with girl-
     friend's father's secret organization, which is re-
     ported to FBI by his mother.

725. Karsavina, Jean. White Eagle, Dark Skies. New
     York: Scribner's, 1974.
        Seventeen years in the life of a Warsaw Jew,
     his family and friends, prior to the time of the
     Russian Revolution.

726. Kasdan, Sara. So It Was Just a Simple Wedding.
     New York: Vanguard, 1961.
        Mother of the bride views all the preparations
     leading to the climax of her daughter's wedding.

727. Kastle, Herbert D. Koptic Court. New York: Simon
     & Schuster, 1958.
        Conflicts and accommodations between Jews and
     blacks in Brooklyn apartment house.

728. Katkov, Norman. Eagle at My Eyes. Garden City:
     Doubleday, 1948.
        Anti-gentile feeling of Jewish family stressed in
     intermarriage of son.

729. _____. A Little Sleep, a Little Slumber. New
     York: Doubleday, 1949.
          Jewish-immigrant peddler enabled to raise four
     sons to college level and fulfill his dream of Amer-
     ica.

730. Katz, Herbert M. Love and Marriage. New York:
     Arbor House, 1975.
          Manhattan magazine publisher faces the end of
     a marriage and is party to and witnesses the new
     lifestyles.

731. _____. Nicolette. New York: Arbor House, 1976.
          A husband in his middle-age crisis returns to
     his wife after an affair with a gentile woman.

732. Katz, H. W. No. 21 Castle Street. Translated by
     Norbert Guterman. New York: Viking, 1940.
          Family chronicle of tragic experiences of Galician
     Jews in Germany from 1914 to 1933.

733. Katz, Leo. Seedtime. Translated by Joel Ames.
     New York: Knopf, 1947.
          Jews in Bukovina become scapegoats during Ru-
     manian peasant uprising in 1907.

734. Ka-Tzetnick, 135633. Atrocity. New York: Stuart,
     1963.
          Eleven-year-old boy becomes sexual toy for block
     chiefs in Auschwitz camp.

735. _____. House of Dolls. Translated by Moshe M.
     Kohn. New York: Simon & Schuster, 1955
          Nazi cruelty revealed in diary of young Polish-
     Jewish schoolgirl caught on a school excursion to
     Cracow in 1939.

736. _____. Phoenix over the Galilee. Translated by
     Nine de Nur. New York: Harper & Row, 1969.
          Holocaust survivor marries Sabra and is involved
     in hope for friendship with Arabs during period
     prior to the Six Day War.

737. Kaufelt, David A. The Bradley Beach Rumba. New
     York: Putnam, 1974.
          Overprotective mother fails to shield Jewish
     princess daughter from affair with wealthy Syrian
     during summer spent at New Jersey resort.

738. _____ . Late Bloomer. New York: Harcourt, 1979.
     Widow resists marriage to husband's younger brother and runs off with Southern artist.

739. _____ . Six Months with an Older Woman. New York: Putnam, 1973.
     Bachelor publisher has affair with older liberated divorcee while seeking freedom from mother.

740. Kaufman, Myron S. Remember Me to God. Philadelphia: Lippincott, 1957.
     Snobbish son of Boston judge who seeks escape from Judaism at Harvard and is in pursuit of a Boston debutante.

741. _____ . Thy Daughter's Nakedness. Philadelphia and New York: Lippincott, 1968.
     Story of rabbi in small town near Boston and his daughter's love affair with young intern.

742. Kaufman, Sue. The Happy Summer Days. New York: Scribner's, 1959.
     Teenaged mother's helpers involved in activities of young married couples vacationing on island near New York.

743. Kavinoky, Bernice. Honey from a Dark Hive. New York: Rinehart, 1955.
     Conflicts in Pennsylvania town caused by love of Jewish teacher and Catholic coal miner.

744. _____ . The Mother. New York: Rinehart, 1958.
     Dominating widow seeks to have her son become a doctor and wrecks his potential chance for marriage when he becomes a clothing-store clerk.

745. _____ . All the Young Summer Days. Indianapolis: Bobbs-Merrill, 1952.
     Adolescence and love affairs of young people of two families who summer at lake cottages.

746. Kay, Teresa. A Crown for Ashes. Milwaukee: Bruce, 1952.
     During World War II, Jewish musician loves Hungarian aristocrat who dies, and he embraces Catholicism.

747. Keil, Rose Kluger. <u>A Woman Named Chaye</u>. New
     York: Exposition, 1952.
         Polish-Jewish girl rebels against a marriage ar-
     ranged for her before her birth.

748. Keller, Beverly. <u>The Baghdad Defections</u>. Indianap-
     olis: Bobbs-Merrill, 1973.
         Bigoted Arab involved with American woman as
     both cross paths with Israeli and American agents
     who search for a German gas-warfare expert.

749. Kellner, Esther. <u>The Promise</u>. New York: West-
     minster, 1956.
         The story of Abraham and Sarah from their mar-
     riage in Ur to their arrival in the Promised Land.

750. Kemmelman, Harry. <u>Monday the Rabbi Took Off</u>.
     New York: Putnam, 1972.
         Rabbi Small solves incident concerning Arab mil-
     itants and a relative of the Rabbi who replaces him
     while he is visiting Israel.

751. _____. <u>Friday the Rabbi Slept Late</u>. New York:
     Crown, 1964.
         First in a series about rabbi in Massachusetts
     suburb whose Talmudic training enables him to
     solve a murder.

752. _____. <u>Saturday the Rabbi Went Hungry</u>. New
     York: Crown, 1966.
         Burial of apparent suicide threatens bequest to
     Rabbi Small's congregation.

753. _____. <u>Sunday the Rabbi Stayed Home</u>. New York:
     Putnam, 1969.
         Problems of rabbi-congregational relationships
     woven into murder mystery.

754. _____. <u>Thursday the Rabbi Walked Out</u>. New
     York: Morrow, 1978.
         Rich, anti-Semitic Yankee is murdered and the
     Rabbi solves the case in his usual wise way.

755. _____. <u>Tuesday the Rabbi Saw Red</u>. New York:
     Fields, 1974.
         Rabbi Small teaches at a Christian college, is
     involved in student activism and faculty policies,
     and solves a murder.

756.   _____. Wednesday the Rabbi Got Wet. New York:
        Morrow, 1976.
            The mysterious death of an old man leads Rabbi
        Small into real-estate intrigue and mysticism, re-
        treats, and modern cults.

757.   Keneally, Thomas. Moses the Lawgiver. New York:
        Harper & Row, 1975.
            The familiar story of Moses and the Exodus is
        given new insights and is lavishly illustrated with
        scenes from the CBS-TV six-part spectacular.

758.   Kent, Madeleine. The Corsair. New York: Double-
        day, 1956.
            Jean Lafitte, hero of the Battle of New Orleans,
        becomes aware of his Jewish ancestry.

759.   _____. Island of the Innocent. New York: Harper,
        1945.
            English intellectuals depicted in period between
        Munich and Polish invasion and warm relationship
        between German-Jewish violinist and unhappily mar-
        ried girl.

760.   Kent, Malcolm. Plotkin's Pyramid. New York: Lad-
        din, 1970.
            Wealthy, lonely, and aged man seeks to memor-
        ialize himself through a pyramid crypt in a Brook-
        lyn cemetery.

761.   Kern, Louisa. The Wife of Mahlon. New York:
        Pageant, 1954.
            The Biblical Ruth described from the death of
        her husband to her marriage to Boaz.

762.   Kersh, Gerald. The Thousand Deaths of Mr. Small.
        Garden City: Doubleday, 1950.
            Psychological novel with flashbacks of life of son
        of Polish immigrants in London who is frustrated in
        desire to marry non-Jew.

763.   Kessler, Jascha. An Egyptian Bondage and Other
        Stories. New York: Harper & Row, 1967.
            Stories about the American-Jewish theme include
        resort hotel steward, UJA money-raiser, and se-
        duction of young errand boy.

764. Kesten, Hermann. Ferdinand and Isabella. New
      York: Wyn, 1946.
         Early childhood through death of Queen Isabella
      and, incidentally, King Ferdinand with Inquisition-
      period portrayal and abuse of human rights.

765. Keyes, Frances Farkinson. Joy Street. New York:
      Messner, 1950.
         Boston's Beacon Hill locale for lawyer and his
      family who number Jews, Italians and Irish as
      junior members of firm.

766. Kidel, Boris. A Flawed Escape. St. Martin's,
      1974.
         A German Jew goes underground to survive in
      Nazi Germany and holds on to phial of cyanide as
      escape clause.

767. Kiefer, Warren. The Pontius Pilate Papers. New
      York: Harper & Row, 1976.
         Scholar at Israeli museum is murdered after he
      claims to have discovered papyri that put a new
      complexion on the Synoptic gospels.

768. Kieve, Rudolph S. The Sorcerers. Boston: Hough-
      ton Mifflin, 1949.
         Interrelationships between Prussian Junker fam-
      ily and wealthy Rhinish-Jewish family prior to rise
      of Hitler.

769. King, Harold. Closing Ceremonies. New York:
      Coward, McCann & Geoghegan, 1979.
         Former SS major threatens assassination of a
      world leader by the time of close of the 1976 Mon-
      treal Olympics unless an urn with ashes stolen from
      a mausoleum in Paraguay is returned.

770. Kirst, Hans Hellmut. The Nights of the Long Knives.
      Translated by J. Maxwell Brownjohn. New York:
      Coward, McCann & Geoghegan, 1976.
         A select group of six SS men are trained for
      special assignments as aged Jew is used to teach
      them the nature of their enemy.

771. Kis, Danilo. Garden, Ashes. Translated by William
      Hannaher. New York: Harcourt, 1975.
         The boyhood of the author in Yugoslavia and Hung-
      ary in the 40s is recreated in this narrative.

772. _____. A Tomb for Boris Davidovich. Translated
by Duska Mikic. New York: Harcourt Brace Jovanovich, 1978.
A portrait of Jews suffering during the Stalin
period in the Soviet Union.

773. Kishon, Ephraim. Noah's Ark, Tourist Class. Translated by Yohanan Goldman. New York: Atheneum,
1963.
Present-day Israeli life sketched in satirical and
humorous fashion through vignettes.

774. Kissin, Rita. This Precious Dust, a Novel. Chicago:
Ziff-Davis, 1948.
Small-town German rabbi's daughter, married to
Nazi, flees to the United States and to a happier
second marriage.

775. Klane, Robert. Fire Sale. New York: Atheneum,
1975.
Department-store owner seeks to have an arson-
ist solve his business failure.

776. _____. The Horse Is Dead. New York: Random
House, 1969.
Young Jew seeks to escape Jewish identity after
he becomes aware of anti-Semitism.

777. _____. Where's Poppa? New York: Random
House, 1970.
Bachelor lawyer who lives with eighty-seven-year-
old mother seeks ways to have an affair with a non-Jew.

778. Klein, Abraham M. The Second Scroll. New York:
Knopf, 1951.
Canadian Jew searches for uncle in travels across
European continent and finally to Israel, to discover him
murdered by Arabs.

779. Klein, Norma. It's OK if You Don't Love Me. New
York: Dial, 1977.
Seventeen-year-old daughter of divorcee explores
love with her gentile virgin lover in this sexual
coming-of-age novel.

780. Klein-Haparash, J. He Who Flees the Lion. Translated by Richard and Clara Winston. New York:
Atheneum, 1963.

Wealthy Jews caught in Soviet Poland sovietized as workers on farm, unable to flee to the United States.

781. Kline, Terry. Death Knell. New York: Putnam, 1977.
A woman who is obsessed by the Holocaust becomes involved with a survivor of Auschwitz.

782. Kluger, Richard. Members of the Tribe. New York: Doubleday, 1977.
Northern Jew, first merchant and then lawyer in Savannah, becomes involved in murder trial reminiscent of the Leo Frank case.

783. Kober, Arthur. Bella, Bella Kissed a Fella. New York: Random House, 1951.
Short stories about Bronx heroine whose life revolves around meeting marriageable men.

784. _____. That Man Is Here Again: The Adventures of a Hollywood Agent. New York: Random House, 1946.
Incidents in the life of a Hollywood agent who is a hustler and uses a humorous dialect.

785. Koestler, Arthur. Thieves in the Night: Chronicle of an Experiment. New York: Macmillan, 1946.
Half-Jewish Englishman in Palestine becomes deeply involved with Jews during the period of 1937 to 1939 and their struggle against the British and Arabs.

786. Kolb, Leon. Berenice: Princess of Judea. New York: Twayne, 1959.
The princess of Judea is torn between her love for the Roman conquerer Titus and her duty to her country.

787. _____. Moses, the Near Easterner: A Novel. San Francisco: Genuart, 1956.
The life of Moses from childhood to death.

788. _____. The Sage. San Francisco: Genuart, 1965.
Rabbi Jochanan ben Zakkai's leadership in Palestine prior to the final destruction of Jerusalem.

789. Kollek, Amos. <u>Don't Ask Me if I Love</u>. New York:
   Evans, 1971.
   Generation gap evident in Israeli who questions
   values of family, state, and religion and whose love
   for American girl ends in tragedy.

790. Kolpacoff, Victor. <u>The Raid</u>. New York: Atheneum,
   1971.
   An Al Fatah terrorist is followed through one
   day of his life, which includes a raid on an Israeli
   power station.

791. Komaiko, S. B. <u>Here to Stay</u>. New York: Bloch, 1949.
   Almost one hundred short tales reflecting American Jewish life, immigrants, assimilation, and rise
   up economic ladder.

792. Konecky, Edith. <u>Allegra</u>. New York: Harper &
   Row, 1976.
   Daughter of unfulfilled marriage reaches adolescence without need for psychiatric help, unlike her
   brother.

793. Koperwas, Sam. <u>Westchester Bull</u>. New York: Simon & Schuster, 1976.
   A Jewish college football star is unable to play
   in pro football and links himself to a semi-pro team
   in New York.

794. Kops, Bernard. <u>By the Waters of Whitechapel</u>. New
   York: Norton, 1970.
   London youth rebels against middle-class conform-
   ity of his parents and becomes symbolic antihero.

795. _____. <u>The Dissent of Dominick Shapiro</u>. New
   York: Coward-McCann, 1966.
   London youth rebels against middle-class con-
   formity of his parents and becomes symbolic antihero.

796. _____. <u>The World Is a Wedding</u>. New York:
   Coward-McCann, 1963.
   Autobiographical novel of British poet-playwright
   born in London slums, who lives through Blitz, wanders
   through Paris and Tangiers, and returns to Soho.

797. Kosinski, Jerzy. <u>The Painted Bird</u>. Boston: Houghton Mifflin, 1965.

Polish-Jewish boy separated from parents at beginning of World War II wanders through Poland and
encounters bestiality.

798. Kossak-Szczucka, Zofia. The Covenant: A Novel of
      the Life of Abraham, the Prophet. New York: Roy,
      1951.
          Abraham as mystic and tribal chief is followed
      from Euphrates valley to desert to Egypt.

799. Kossoff, David. A Small Town Is a World: The
      "Rabbi Stories" of David Kossoff. New York: St.
      Martin's, 1979.
          This series of vignettes of an East European
      rabbi and his wife are outgrowths of scripts used
      in the author's one-man shows.

800. _____. The Voices of Masada. New York: St.
      Martin's, 1973.
          Cousin of Eleazar, the leader of the Zealots,
      survives mass suicide on Masada and tells the
      story.

801. Kotker, David. Herzl the King. New York: Scrib-
      ner's, 1972.
          The last ten years of Theodor Herzl's life are
      covered in this novel based on Herzl's diaries.

802. Kotlowitz, Robert. The Boardwalk. New York:
      Knopf, 1977.
          In the summer of 1939, a budding teenaged pian-
      ist and his family spend a two-week vacation at an
      Atlantic City resort hotel.

803. _____. Somewhere Else. New York: Charter-
      house, 1972.
          Polish rabbi's son migrates from Warsaw to
      London, works in a diamond shop, and becomes
      involved with Socialists, Zionists, and liberated
      women.

804. Kramer, Larry. Faggots. New York: Random
      House, 1978.
          New York's gay community is revealed through
      a forty-year-old Jew who seeks love and a bakery
      heir who tries to kidnap himself and collect a mil-
      lion from his father.

805. Krantz, Judith. Scruples. New York: Crown, 1978.
Wealthy widow, owner of a chic store in Beverly
Hills, marries a movie producer and learns the in-
side story of the Academy Awards.

806. Krasner, William. The Gambler. New York: Har-
per, 1950.
Rise and fall of petty gambler from East Side of
New York.

807. Kravitz, Nathan. Zaquta, the Seer. Translated by
William Shure. New York: Vantage, 1952.
Ethical history of humankind seen through eyes
of a seer.

808. Krech, Hilda Sidney. To Wake in the Morning. New
York: Macmillan, 1954.
Realities of wartime living mature girl in her
relationships with two men, one of whom is Jewish
and through whom she encounters anti-Semitism.

809. Kumin, Maxine. The Abduction. New York: Harper
& Row, 1972.
Director of inner-city educational project abducts
black boy as protest against her failures in life.

810. _____. Through Dooms of Love. New York:
Harper & Row, 1965.
Relationship described between New Jersey Jewish pawnbroker and Radcliffe Bolshevik daughter,
and sons, one a rabbi and the other a surgeon.

811. Kurtz, Irma. The Grand Dragon. New York: Dutton, 1979.
Female Jewish reporter attracted to KKK leader
and decides to emigrate to Israel when she realizes
the depth of his anti-Semitism.

812. Kutnick, Aaron A. In Search of Happiness. Detroit:
Harlo, 1970.
Eastern European Jew emigrates to the United
States in this autobiographical novel.

813. Kuznetsov, Anatoly. Babi Yar. New York: Dial,
1967.
Eye-witness account of Babi Yar massacre on
the outskirts of Kiev in 1941.

814. La Farge, Christopher. The Sudden Guest. New
      York: Coward-McCann, 1946.
          Spinster recollects, during period of hurricane
      warning, her niece, whom she had driven away be-
      cause of refusal to permit marriage to Jew.

815. Lambert, Derek. The Yermakov Transfer. New
      York: Saturday Review/Dutton, 1974.
          Russian-Jewish activist plots to kidnap Soviet
      premier to permit Jewish scientists with hydrogen
      bomb to exit to Israel.

816. Landon, Joseph. Angle of Attack. Garden City:
      Doubleday, 1952.
          Psychological conflict of Jew who strikes a bar-
      gain for his life with three Nazi pilots.

817. Lange, Monique. A Little Girl Under a Mosquito Net.
      Translated by Patsy Southgate. New York: Viking,
      1973.
          The growing up during World War II of a French
      girl who wrestles with God in Paris and Saigon and
      experiences anti-Semitism.

818. Lange, Suzanne. The Year. New York: Philipps,
      1970.
          A year is described in the life of an American
      Jew on an Israeli kibbutz.

819. Langley, Lee. From the Broken Tree. New York:
      Dutton, 1978.
          A three-generation chronicle, beginning in Polish
      ghetto and culminating in Israel, of a family that
      achieves wealth and status in England and the U.S.

820. Lamport, Felicia. Mink on Weekdays (Ermine on Sun-
      day). Boston: Houghton Mifflin, 1950.
          Wealthy middle-class sisters of New York City
      family and their adventures as adolescents.

821. Lamson, Peggy. The Charmed Circle. Philadelphia:
      Lippincott, 1950.
          Intermarriage between wealthy girl and Jewish
      GI Bill of Rights student on college campus where
      fraternity discrimination exists.

822. Langfus, Anna. The Lost Shore. Translated by Peter
      Wiles. New York: Pantheon, 1963.

Polish refugee in Paris after World War II re-
covers her self-esteem through liaison with older
man.

823. _____. The Whole Land Brimstone. Translated
by Peter Wiles. New York: Pantheon, 1962.
Warsaw ghetto survivor wanders through Europe
and is denounced as Russian spy.

824. Langgasser, E. The Quest. New York: Knopf,
1953.
Postwar pilgrimage by Germans seeking absolu-
tion for their sins and crimes of Nazis.

825. Lapatine, Kenneth A. The Trials and Tribulations of
Aaron Amsted. New York: Walker, 1974.
A greeting-card poet covertly follows pretty ladies and is drawn into trouble involving the FBI and
leftist radicals.

826. Lapham, Arthur. Justus. St. Louis: Concordia,
1973.
The Sanhedrin trial is interesting scene in plod-
ding story of the life of Jesus.

827. Larner, Jeremy. Drive, He Said. New York: Delacorte, 1964.
All-American Jewish basketball star perceives
hollowness of education and respectability and awaits
the end.

828. Latham, Aaron. Orchids for Mother. New York:
Little, Brown, 1977.
A former CIA agent, fired by the new Director,
gets a clever revenge and is later involved in the
1973 Arab-Israeli war.

829. Laurents, Arthur. The Way We Were. New York:
Harper & Row, 1972.
Dissolution of marriage is caused by revelation
of wife's Communist background during the 1950s
witch-hunting days.

830. Lawrence, Josephine. Let Us Consider One Another.
New York: Appleton-Century, 1945.
Socially prominent Boston girl marries Jew and
causes anti-Semitic backlash.

831. Lea, Tom. Wonderful Country. New York: Little,
     Brown, 1952.
         Emphasis on people who built the town of Puerto
     in Texas during 1880, including Jewish storekeepers.

832. Leahy, Surell Rogovin. A Book of Ruth. New York:
     Simon & Schuster, 1975.
         Brooklyn-born Jewish teacher meets Catholic
     priest in Boston, and the two break off their ties
     with the past because of their love for each other.

833. Lebowitz, Albert. Laban's Will. New York: Ran-
     dom House, 1966.
         Southern Jewish lawyer enjoys reading different
     versions of his will to his children during summer
     at home.

834. LeDrew, F. R. (pseud.). The Kissinger Complex.
     New York: Stonehill, 1975.
         Kissinger plots to kill Nixon, who seeks to brand
     him a traitor in order to justify his shift away from
     Israel, and is rewarded with Secretaryship.

835. Lee, Marjorie. On You It Looks Good. New York:
     Morrow, 1963.
         Romantic encounters of career girl in world of
     fashion in New York garment trade.

836. Lees, Hannah. Till the Boys Come Home. New
     York: Harper, 1944.
         American wife, with husband's medical unit in
     Africa, engages in promiscuous relationship with
     Jewish scientist.

837. Leftwich, Joseph. Yisroel: The First Jewish Omni-
     bus: 1st rev. ed. New York: Yoseloff, 1963.
         Collection of stories divided into countries and
     languages of origin, English, American, German,
     Yiddish, Hebrew, French, Russian, and Dutch.

838. Leibert, Julius Amos. The Lawgiver: A Novel
     About Moses. New York: Exposition, 1953.
         Psychiatric interpretation of Moses and fictitious
     characters of his time.

839. Lelchuck, Alan. American Mischief. New York:
     Farrar, Straus and Giroux, 1973.

A young militant scholar is hero of novel dealing
with student activism in Cambridge, Massachusetts.

840.   . Miriam at Thirty-Four. New York: Farrar, Straus and Giroux, 1974.
A photographer divorcee finds that her freedom
results in disenchantment as she is adrift among
artists in Cambridge, Massachusetts.

841. Lempel, Blanche. Storm over Paris: A Novel. New
York: Philosophical Library, 1954.
Polish-Jewish refugee in Paris falls in love with
German who joins Nazi party.

842. Leokum, Arkady. The Temple. New York: World,
1969.
Reform Rabbi in New York suburb stirs up en-
mity because of civil-rights stand and prod against
conservatism.

843. Lerman, Rhoda. The Girl That He Marries. New
York: Holt, Rinehart and Winston, 1976.
Outrageously funny account of a thirty-year-old
woman's mating game with a very adroit son of an
adoring mother.

844. Leroux, Etienne. One for the Devil. Translated by
Charles Eglington. Boston: Houghton Mifflin, 1968.
Second in trilogy of South African family in which
abnormal child is suspected of murder.

845.   . Seven Days at the Silbersteins. Translated by Charles Eglington. Boston: Houghton Mifflin, 1967.
Non-Jewish fiancee learns much of Jewish family life as he meets future wife for the first time
on her parents' South African estate.

846. Leslie, Warren. The Starrs of Texas. New York:
Simon & Schuster, 1978.
Department-store family beset by rivalries and
diverse ambitions as head of clan expands his power and control.

847. Lessner, Erwin Christian. At the Devil's Booth.
Garden City: Doubleday, 1953.
Anti-Nazi Austrian nobleman forced to flee from
country to country as German army is victorious.

848. Lev, Igal. <u>Jordan Patrol</u>. New York: Doubleday, 1970.
Arab-Israeli war depicted in account of six Sabras fighting on West Bank of Jordan.

849. Levi, Primo. <u>The Reawakening</u>. Boston: Little, Brown, 1965.
Survivors of the Auschwitz concentration camp seek new lives in Europe.

850. Leviant, Curt. <u>The Yemenite Girl</u>. New York and Indianapolis: Bobbs-Merrill, 1977.
Author and literary critic is infatuated with a Yemenite beauty both real and fictional as conceived by his hero, a Nobel-prize winning author.

851. Levin, Beatrice. <u>The Lonely Room</u>. New York and Indianapolis: Bobbs-Merrill, 1950.
Rhode Island college student in conflict with parents' objection to her scholastic ambitions marries non-Jew.

852. Levin, Ira. <u>The Boys from Brazil</u>. New York: Random House, 1975.
Unreconstructed Nazis meet in restaurant in Brazil and are assigned murders to cover up Dr. Mengele's experiments to preserve Aryan race.

853. Levin, Meyer. <u>Compulsion</u>. New York: Simon & Schuster, 1956.
Psychoanalytical account of Leopold-Loeb murder in Chicago in the 1920s.

854. _____. Eva. New York: Simon & Schuster, 1959.
Young Polish-Jewish girl masquerades as non-Jew among Nazis and escapes from them.

855. _____. <u>The Fanatic: A Novel</u>. New York: Simon & Schuster, 1964.
Fictionalization of author's obsession with <u>The Diary of Anne Frank</u> through characters of an army chaplain and Czech refugee.

856. _____. <u>Gore and Igor</u>. New York: Simon & Schuster, 1968.
Eccentric characters find refuge in Israel and become joyous fighters in 1967 war.

857. _____. The Harvest. New York: Simon & Schuster, 1978.
   The settlers in Palestine are viewed in the twenty
years prior to the establishment of the State of Israel.

858. _____. My Father's House. New York: Viking,
1947.
   Illegal immigration into Palestine background for
Polish-Jewish boy's search for his father.

859. _____. The Settlers. New York: Simon & Schuster, 1972.
   Russian-Jewish family emigrates to Palestine at
turn of century and develops roots as novel moves
to post-World War I British mandate.

860. _____. The Spell of Time: A Tale of Love in
Jerusalem. New York: Praeger, 1974.
   Older biochemist in Faustian experiment changes
roles with young American student to win the love
of his apprentice.

861. _____. The Stronghold. New York: Simon &
Schuster, 1965.
   Jewish leader joins imprisoned political leaders
jailed by Germans at close of World War II.

862. Levin, Samuel. The Turning of the Tide. Translated
by Joseph Leftwich. South Brunswick, N.J.: Barnes,
1978.
   A Hasidic shtetl is transformed into an industrial
town as Socialism and Zionism replace faith in God.

863. Lewis, Jerry D. Tales of Our People. New York:
Geis, 1969.
   Jewish acculturation process in America revealed
in short stories contained in earlier anthologies.

864. Lewis, Robert. Michel, Michel. New York: Simon
& Schuster, 1967.
   French-Jewish child, saved by Catholic and then
baptized, is object of struggle between Israeli aunt
and Catholic church.

865. Lewisohn, Ludwig, ed. Among the Nations. New
York: Farrar, Straus; Philadelphia: Jewish Publication Society of America, 1948.

French, English, and Biblical Jews illuminated
in stories by Somerset Maugham, Jacques de La-
cretelle, John Galsworthy, and Thomas Mann.

866. _____. Breathe upon These. Indianapolis: Bobbs-
Merrill, 1944.
Jewish-refugee scientist and his doctor wife re-
tell story of Nazi brutality, British treatment of
Zionists in Palestine, and the Struma incident.

867. _____. The Case of Mr. Crump. New York:
Farrar, Straus, 1947.
Young musician from South Carolina driven to
murder by horrors of marriage to older New York
woman.

868. _____. The Island Within. Philadelphia: Jewish
Publication Society, 1968.
Reissue of classic novel of Southern American
Jew's alienation from Judaism and his eventual re-
turn to Judaism.

869. _____. Renegade. Philadelphia: Jewish Publication Society; New York: Dial, 1942.
Wealthy Jew buys a title, marries a noblewoman,
and does not find inner peace in eighteenth-century
France.

870. Levitt, Saul. The Sun Is Silent. New York: Harper,
1951.
Jews are members of an American bomber crew
flying over Germany from English base.

871. Ley-Piscator, Maria. Lot's Wife. Indianapolis and
New York: Bobbs-Merrill, 1954.
Biblical setting of Abraham, his nephew Lot, and
their wanderings from Tyre to Egypt and Sodom.

872. L'Heureux, John. Family Affairs. New York: Doubleday, 1974.
A collection of short stories depicting individuals
on the brink of destruction or despair, including a
young Jew and senile old man.

873. Liben, Meyer. Hunger, Justice. New York: Dial,
1967.
Short stories of Jewish life in New York during
the Depression years.

874. Lichtman, William. Between the Star and the Cross.
      New York: Citadel, 1957.
          Former American World War II flyer finds new
      meaning in life by service in Israeli Air Force.

875. Lieber, Joel. The Chair. New York: McKay, 1969.
          Oklahoma dentist frustrated by anti-Semitism in
      his advocacy of fluoridation.

876. _____. The Circle Game. New York: Simon &
      Schuster, 1970.
          Drug culture in literary circle draws professor
      into circle of sexual and psychological adventures.

877. _____. How the Fishes Live. New York: McKay,
      1967.
          Former Israeli war fighter one of seven survi-
      vors of Atlantic shipwreck.

878. _____. Move! New York: McKay, 1968.
          Apostate Jew turned Zoroastrian eventually finds
      redemption after hilarious adventures.

879. _____. Two-way Traffic. New York: Doubleday,
      1972.
          Autobiographical novel of suicidal tendencies of
      writer whose marriage collapsed and whose talent
      had become diffused.

880. Lieberman, Herbert. The Climate of Hell. New
      York: Simon & Schuster, 1978.
          American businessman, Auschwitz survivor, in-
      volved in plot to unmask former SS men and SS doc-
      tor in Paraguay.

881. Liederman, Judith. The Moneyman. Boston: Hough-
      ton Mifflin, 1979.
          Saga of self-made millionaire rising from Brook-
      lyn ghetto to financial empire on fringe of enter-
      tainment industry.

882. Lieferant, Sylvia and Henry. The Gentile: A Novel.
      Philadelphia: Muhlenberg, 1948.
          Reverse discrimination story of gentile dress de-
      signer from Jewish firm who finds herself to be an
      outsider.

883. Lind, Jakob. Soul of Wood and Other Stories. New
York: Grove, 1964.
Gothic tales of Jewish victims of Nazi terror in
Central Europe.

884. Linetski, Isaac Joel. The Polish Lad. Translated
by Moshe Spiegel. Philadelphia: Jewish Publication Society, 1975.
A hundred-year-old Yiddish novel that satirizes
Hasidic life and depicts Polish lad's attraction to
the Haskalah movement.

885. Link, William, and Levinson, Richard. Fineman.
New York: Laddin, 1972.
Grief caused by death of a friend begins flash-
backs into life of a Jew married to a gentile and
into the family conflicts.

886. Linklater, Eric. Husband of Delilah. New York:
Harcourt, 1963.
The epic Biblical story of Samson and the Philis-
tines.

887. Lippincott, David. Salt Mine. New York: Viking,
1979.
Dissident Soviet Jews plot to hold foreign tourists hostage in Kremlin museum and threaten to
blow up Lenin's tomb.

888. Lipsky, Eleazar. The Scientists. New York: Appleton-Century-Crofts, 1959.
Patent lawsuit between former teacher and student
over the development of a new medical breakthrough.

889. Lipsky, Louis. Tales of the Yiddish Rialto. New
York: Yoseloff, 1963.
Sketches of actors and theater personnel of the
New York Yiddish theater of the early 1900s.

890. Lipton, Lawrence. Brother, the Laugh Is Bitter: A
Novel. New York: Harper, 1942.
Ex-bootlegger and racketeer loses out to forces
of anti-Semitism and corruption.

891. _____. In Secret Battle. New York: Appleton-
Century, 1944.
Jewish industrialist joins forces to combat organ-
ized fascism in the United States.

892. Liptzin, Sam. In Spite of Tears. Translated by
      S. P. Rudens, New York: Amcho, 1946.
          Translation of short pieces by Yiddish humorist
      depicting life of immigrants to America.

893. List, Shelley Steinman. Did You Love Daddy When I
      Was Born? New York: Saturday Review, 1972.
          Four generations of females are depicted while
      young matron's marriage is breaking up and her
      grandmother is dying.

894. Lister, Stephen. By the Waters of Babylon. New
      York: Dodd, Mead, 1945.
          Wealthy Jew in England reveals his life story,
      Moroccan birth, school days in England, World War
      I service, and wanderings in Europe.

895. Littell, Blaine. The Dolorosa Deal. New York:
      Saturday Review, 1973.
          A black-American spy is featured in Arab and
      Israeli intrigues in Jerusalem in which urban de-
      velopment is used as cover.

896. Littell, Robert. Mother Russia. New York: Har-
      court Brace Jovanovich, 1978.
          A brazen Jewish operator battles against Soviet
      bureaucracy.

897. Litvinoff, Emanuel. The Lost Europeans: A Novel.
      New York: Vanguard, 1959.
          English-reared Berliner returns to Germany to
      obtain financial restitution and falls in love with
      native girl.

898. _____. The Penguin Book of Jewish Short Stories.
      Harmondsworth, England: Penguin, 1979.
          Along with Malamud, Oz, Spark, and Roth are
      works translated from the Yiddish, sixteen authors
      in all.

899. Litwack, B. H. The Last Shiksa. New York: Put-
      nam, 1978.
          Park Avenue millionaire, contemptuous of his
      fellow Jewish associates, driven to seek affair with
      gentile wife of his psychiatrist.

900. Litwack, Leo. Waiting for the News. New York:
      Doubleday, 1969.

American Jewish helplessness against Nazi crimes
is coupled with account of Detroit labor leader who
is killed.

901.   Livingston, Harold. The Coasts of the Earth. Boston: Houghton Mifflin; New York: Ballantine, 1954.
American airmen volunteer to fight in 1948 Israeli war and ferry arms and ammunition from
Prague to Tel Aviv.

902.   Llewellyn, Richard. Bride of Israel, My Love. New
York: Doubleday, 1973.
Electronics engineer sets up specialty shop to
aid Israeli defense and is involved with spies and
beautiful women.

903.   _____. A Hill of Many Dreams. New York:
Doubleday, 1974.
New York art dealer, disillusioned with art world,
creates a kibbutz in Israel for artists as a retreat.

904.   Lobel, Brana. The Revenant. New York: Doubleday,
1979.
Jewish career girl attracted to scion of old
Brooklyn family moves with him into a spooky house,
where he is transported into the past.

905.   Lofts, Norah. Esther. New York: Macmillan, 1950.
Retelling of the life of Esther, Queen of Persia,
follows Biblical account.

906.   Longstreet, Stephen. God and Sarah Pedlock. New
York: McKay, 1976.
Brilliant pianist of the Pedlock clan seeks inner
peace through tortuous process of self-probing and
exotic experiences.

907.   _____. The Pedlock Inheritance. New York: Mc-
Kay, 1972.
In this novel in the Pedlock series, the main
focus is on Judge Pedlock's nomination to the Su-
preme Court.

908.   _____. The Pedlocks: A Family. New York:
Simon & Schuster, 1951.
Narrative of Jewish family from Confederate army
officer to grandson who seeks his own way of life
as American Jew.

909. _____. Pedlock Saint: Pedlock Sinner. New
     York: Delacorte, 1969.
          Concluding novel in trilogy concerned with gener-
     ational conflict between Orthodox Judaism and mod-
     ern Jewish community through persons of two rab-
     bis.

910. _____. Pedlock & Sons. New York: Delacorte,
     1966.
          Pedlock family, department-store magnates, now
     in third and fourth generation of Jews with weakened
     heritage.

911. _____. She Walks in Beauty. New York: Arbor
     House, 1970.
          Executive with cosmetic firm has affair with
     daughter of Italian Jewish contessa who is engaged
     in bitter rivalry for control of industry.

912. Lothar, Ernst. Angel with the Trumpet. Translated
     by Elizabeth Reynolds. New York: Doubleday, Dor-
     an, 1944.
          Austrian locale, from Mayerling to Ostmark,
     story of Catholic woman of Jewish ancestry and the
     Alt Family, royal purveyors.

913. _____. The Prisoner. Translated by James A.
     Galston. Garden City: Doubleday, Doran, 1945.
          Aged refugee a teacher of literature, learns
     from German prisoner-of-war of his youth in Vienna
     and his disillusionment with Nazism.

914. Lowenstein, Ralph Lynn. Bring My Sons from Far.
     New York: World, 1966.
          Virginia youth from middle-class background
     finds fulfillment through illegal entry into Pales-
     tine and role in war.

915. Lowry, Robert. The Big Cage. New York: Double-
     day, 1950.
          Young writer is encouraged by older patroness
     who succeeds in seduction.

916. Ludlum, Robert. The Holcroft Covenant. New York:
     Marek, 1978.
          Secret fund set up by Nazis to compensate Holo-
     caust victims is really a front to establish a Fourth
     Reich.

917. Ludwig, Jack. Confusions. Greenwich, Conn.:
      Graphic Society, 1963.
          Harvard Ph.D. from Boston area finds his way
      to small California college after slapstick episodes.

918. Lukas, Susan Reis. Fat Emily. New York: Stein
      and Day, 1974.
          Southern Californian Jewish girl, in rebellion
      against her parents, has affairs with Israeli ex-
      change student and becomes self-supporting.

919. Lund, Roslyn Rosen. The Sharing. New York: Mor-
      row, 1978.
          Battle over husband's estate leads widow to new
      understanding with mother-in-law.

920. Lurie, Morris. Rappaport. New York: Morrow,
      1967.
          Australian antique dealer daydreams with friend,
      who decides abruptly to travel to Russia.

921. Lustig, Arnost. Darkness Casts No Shadow. Trans-
      lated by Jeanne Nemcova. Washington, D.C.: In-
      scape, 1976.
          Story of the escape of two teenagers from a Ger-
      man death train and their attempt to return to
      Prague.

922. _____. Diamonds of the Night. Translated by
      Jeanne Nemcova. Washington, D.C.: Inscape,
      1978.
          Nine short stories of children in Warsaw up-
      rising, concentration camps, and liberation of
      Prague.

923. _____. Dita Saxova. Translated by Jeanne Nem-
      cova. New York: Harper & Row, 1979.
          Czech survivor of concentration camp seeks hap-
      piness in Switzerland but experiences disillusion-
      ment and tragic death.

924. _____. Night and Hope. Translated by George
      Theiner. New York: Dutton, 1962.
          Stories of life in Terezin, the Auschwitz recep-
      tion center, by a Czech survivor.

925. _____. A Prayer for Katerina Horovitzova. Trans-

lated by Jeanne Nemcova. New York: Harper &
Row, 1973.
    Young girl and other Americans promised free-
dom by Nazis but the hoax leads them to the gas
chambers.

926.   McDuffie, Laurette. The Stone in the Rain.   Garden
       City: Doubleday, Doran, 1946.
           North Carolina self-made man builds "restricted"
       beach resort to block Jews and Negroes.

927.   McGivern, William P. Caprifoil. New York: Dodd,
       Mead, 1972.
           Retired American and British espionage agents
       marked for death seek former French colleague and are
       led to Algiers and Arab guerrillas out to destroy
       Israel.

928.   McHale, Tom. Alinsky's Diamond.   Philadelphia:
       Lippincott, 1974.
           American-born Israeli organizes pilgrimage from
       France to Jerusalem in order to have priest smug-
       gle a diamond in a cross.

929.   McHugh, Arona. A Banner with a Strange Device:
       A Novel. New York: Doubleday, 1964.
           Young Bostonians, including rebel from Orthodox
       Jewish background, seek meaning after World War
       II.

930.   _____. The Luck of the Van Meers. New York:
       Doubleday, 1969.
           Saga of Sephardic family, from Holland in the
       eighteenth century to Russia, Germany, and the
       United States in 1906.

931.   _____. The Seacoast of Bohemia. New York:
       Doubleday, 1965.
           Search for personal security and love of Boston
       girl in rebellion against Orthodox Jewish father.

932.   McLaughlin, Robert. The Side of the Angels.   New
       York: Scribner's, 1947.
           Conflict between conservative officer in OSS and
       liberal brother who falls in love with Jewish girl.

933.   McMenamin, Thomas. Call Me Manneschewitz.   New
       York: Scribner's, 1971.

Humorous story of courtship, marriage and ethnic complications of Irishman and his Jewish wife.

934. Mailer, Norman. <u>The Naked and the Dead</u>. New York: Rinehart, 1948.
World War II novel of reactions of Americans in occupation of Japanese held island in Pacific with allusions to anti-Semitism.

935. Malamud, Bernard. <u>The Assistant</u>. New York: Farrar, Straus & Cudahy, 1957.
Non-Jewish assistant to poor New York shopkeeper converts to Judaism out of love for his daughter.

936. _____. <u>Dubin's Lives</u>. New York: Farrar, Straus and Giroux, 1977.
Middle-aged prize-winning biographer seeks to find his secret self apart from the lives of those he has created.

937. _____. <u>The Fixer</u>. New York: Farrar, Straus and Giroux, 1966.
Blood-libel case in Czarist Russia holds victim in prison for over two years.

938. _____. <u>Idiots First</u>. New York: Farrar, Straus & Cudahy, 1963.
Short stories in New York Jewish settings include love of storekeeper for Negro woman and concern of dying man for imbecile son.

939. _____. <u>The Magic Barrel</u>. New York: Farrar, Straus & Cudahy, 1958.
Thirteen short stories reveal lives of poorer Jews in New York, their misfortunes, pathos, and humor.

940. _____. <u>Pictures of Fidelman</u>. New York: Farrar, Straus and Giroux, 1969.
Six stories of middle-aged Jewish artist seeking self-discovery in Italy.

941. _____. <u>Rembrandt's Hat</u>. New York: Farrar, Straus and Giroux, 1973.
Collection of short stories reflecting human dilemmas relating to death, sex, search for identity.

942. _____. The Tenants. New York: Farrar, Straus and Giroux, 1971.
Interracial conflict pits Jewish and black writer against each other in New York East Side tenement-house setting.

943. Malaquais, Jean. World Without Visa. Garden City: Doubleday, 1948.
German Jewish refugees and French Jews are victims of Nazi occupation of Marseilles.

944. Maletz, David. Young Hearts. New York: Schocken, 1950.
Life on kibbutz in Israel and the problems facing a young married couple.

945. Malin, Irving, and Stark, Irwin, eds. Breakthrough: A Treasury of Contemporary American-Jewish Literature. Philadelphia: Jewish Publication Society; New York: McGraw-Hill, 1964.
In addition to poetry and essays, contains representative collection of fiction by Roth, Bellow, Gold, Mailer and others.

946. Maloff, Saul. Happy Families. New York: Scribner's, 1968.
Divorced Jew searches for runaway daughter in Greenwich Village and through her boyfriend, an atheistic rabbinical student.

947. _____. Heartland. New York: Scribner's, 1973.
New York intellectual involved with non-Jewish woman on lecture tour to the West and winds up in pagan rites in sacred groves.

948. Malvern, Gladys. The Foreigner. New York: Longmans, Green, 1954.
Ruth overcomes stigma of being a foreigner in this retelling of Biblical story.

949. Mamis, Justin. Love. New York: Stein and Day, 1964.
Problems of Jewish family in Vermont town in attempts to integrate into non-Jewish community.

950. Mand, Ewald. The Unfaithful. Philadelphia: Muhlenberg, 1954.
Biblical story of the prophet Hosea and his unfaithful wife.

951. Mandel, George. The Breakwater. New York: Holt,
      Rinehart and Winston, 1960.
           Young Jew searches for identity in carnival world
      of Coney Island during Depression years.

952. Manger, Itzik. The Book of Paradise. Translated
      by Leonard Wolf. New York: Hill & Wang, 1965.
           Fantasy of life in Paradise much like East Euro-
      pean villages.

953. Mankowitz, Wolf. A Kid for Two Farthings. New
      York: Dutton, 1954.
           London's East Side Jewish community includes
      boy who dreams of return of his father from Africa.

954. _____. The Mendelman Fire, and Other Stories.
      Boston: Little, Brown/Atlantic, 1957.
           Includes tales set in Russian village and England
      with lower-class Jewish families.

955. Mann, Mendel. At the Gates of Moscow. Translated
      by I. R. Lask and Christopher Derrick. New York:
      St. Martin's, 1964.
           Polish Jew distrusted by official Soviet apparatus
      after he joins Army in 1941 following his escape to
      Russia.

956. Mann, Thomas. Joseph, the Provider. New York:
      Knopf, 1944.
           Last of tetralogy about Joseph covering his im-
      prisonment in Egypt through his death.

957. _____. The Tables of the Law. Translated by
      H. T. Lowe-Porter. New York: Knopf, 1945.
           Novelette following Moses from Hebrew back-
      ground in Egypt to Mt. Sinai.

958. Manoff, Arnold. Telegram from Heaven. New York:
      Dial, 1942.
           Bronx Jewish stenographer looks for job and
      boyfriend and is assisted in both by beginning of
      World War II.

959. Manus, Willard. Mott the Hoople. New York: Mc-
      Graw-Hill, 1966.
           Adventures of young Socialist Jew from the Bronx
      who finally chooses to marry rich Jewish girl.

960.   Marcus, Alan.   Straw to Make Brick.   Boston: Little,
        Brown, 1948.
            Jewish corporal in American occupation forces
        in Bavaria in conflict between hatred of Germans
        and love for German girl.

961.   Marcus, David.   To Next Year in Jerusalem.   New
        York: St. Martin, 1954.
            Irish Jew falls in love with Catholic girl and is
        in conflict with support of Zionist drive for a Jew-
        ish State.

962.   Margolian, Abraham.   A Piece of Blue Heaven.   Fred-
        ericton, N.B., Canada: New Elizabethan, 1956.
            Dutch surgeon hides Jews during Nazi occupation
        of Amsterdam.

963.   Mark, David.   The Neighborhood.   New York: Double-
        day, 1959.
            Coming-of-age book set in poverty section of
        Brooklyn's Jews in the 1930s.

964.   Markfield, Wallace.   Teitlebaum's Window.   New
        York: Knopf, 1970.
            Brooklyn setting for adolescent growing up in the
        midst of family security touched by emerging war.

965.   _____.   To an Early Grave.   New York: Simon &
        Schuster, 1964.
            Jewish intellectuals review their lives during
        trip to Brooklyn to attend funeral of writer.

966.   _____.   You Could Live if They Let You.   New
        York: Knopf, 1974.
            A dead Jewish comedian, like Lenny Bruce, is
        revealed through transcripts of interviews as angry
        with the vulgarization of the American Jewish com-
        munity.

967.   Markish, David.   A New World for Simon Ashkenazy.
        Translated by Michael Glenny.   New York: Dutton,
        1976.
            A Soviet émigré's account of the exile of a fifteen-
        year-old and his family from Moscow to a village
        in Asia.

968.   Markowitz, Arthur.   The Daughter.   New York: Far-
        rar, Straus and Young, 1951.

Daughter of Polish émigrés in South Africa returns to respectability through arranged marriage
after early promiscuous affairs.

969. Markson, Elaine. Home Again, Home Again. New
      York: Morrow, 1978.
         A widow in Miami is about to remarry when her
      son and daughter, each with a broken marriage,
      descend upon her.

970. Markus, Julia. Uncle; A Novel. Boston: Houghton
      Mifflin, 1978.
         Jersey City youngster emerges from Depression
      as successful camp operator and serves as support
      to motley group of characters.

971. Marshall, Effie Lawrence. Queen Esther. Portland,
      Me.: Falsmouth, 1950.
         Queen Esther's role in saving her people is de-
      veloped in this Biblically-based novel.

972. Marshall, Paule. Soul Clap Hands and Sing. New
      York: Atheneum, 1961.
         Novellas of four men's relationships with women
      include one of frustrated Jewish Brooklyn teacher.

973. Marshall, William Leonard. The Age of Death. New
      York: Viking, 1970.
         Auschwitz is an incident in antiwar novel that be-
      gins in Belgium in World War I and ends with Rus-
      sians entering Berlin in World War II.

974. Martin, Bernard. That Man from Smyrna. New
      York: Jonathan David, 1978.
         A fictionalized biography of the seventeenth-
      century pseudo-Messiah Sabbatai Zevi.

975. Martin, Burton E. Unpromised Land, A Novel. New
      York: Washburn, 1948.
         Struggle between American UNRRA officer in
      Italian displaced-persons camp and black mar-
      keteers.

976. Martin, Peter. The Building. Boston: Little, Brown,
      1960.
         Four sons of Russian immigrants search for
      roots in upper New York State community.

977. _____. The Landsmen. Boston: Little, Brown,
      1952.
            Stories of nineteen families in tiny Czarist village;
      includes musician, water-carrier, and outcast.

978. Masters, Dexter. The Accident. New York: Knopf,
      1955.
            Implications of Atomic Age through death of
      young scientist from experiment in Los Alamos
      laboratory.

979. Matmor, Yoram. Who? Me? New York: Simon &
      Schuster, 1970.
            Absurdity of war underscored in humorous fashion
      in present-day Israeli setting.

980. Maugham, Robin. The Sign. New York: McGraw-
      Hill, 1974.
            A wealthy member of the Sanhedrin is physically
      attracted to a new prophet--Caleb, who claims to
      be the Messiah--and steals his body from the cross
      before he dies.

981. Maximov, Vladimir. Farewell from Nowhere. Trans-
      lated by Michael Glenny. New York: Doubleday,
      1979.
            A portrait of a young Jewish poet growing up in
      the Soviet Union who is torn between his homeland
      and family, who wish to leave for Israel.

982. Maxwell, James A. I Never Saw an Arab Like Him.
      Boston: Houghton Mifflin, 1948.
            Thirteen stories of experiences of American in-
      telligence agent in Tripoli touching upon Zionists,
      Arabs, and British.

983. Mayer, Frederick. Web of Hate. New York: Whit-
      tier, 1961.
            Former Nazi, disillusioned by war, witnesses re-
      birth of German nationalist spirit in son.

984. Mayrant, Drayton. Lamp in Jerusalem. New York:
      Appleton-Century-Crofts, 1957.
            Two lovers torn by family feuds in Jerusalem
      during period of division of the kingdom.

985. Mazzetti, Lorenza. The Sky Falls. Translated by
      Marguerite Waldman. New York: McKay, 1963.

War experiences of two sisters living with uncle
in small Italian village near front lines.

986. Megged, Aron. *Fortunes of a Fool*. Translated by
Aubrey Hodes. New York: Random House, 1962.
Chronicles of a lonely outsider in Israeli society
who considers himself the only good man in a society of the wicked.

987. _____. *Living on the Dead*. Translated by Misha
Louvish. New York: McCall, 1971.
Israeli author receives advance to write novel
about hero of liberation of Palestine.

988. Meisels, Andrew. *Son of a Star*. New York: Put-
nam, 1969.
The final rebellion against the Romans in 132
C. E. stresses the Messianic hopes in Bar Kochba.

989. Meites, Irving, ed. *The Marriage Broker*. Based
on stories of Shulem the Shadchan by Tashnak. New
York: Putnam, 1960.
East European Jewish marriage broker and his
attempts to arrange betrothals.

990. Memmi, Albert. *The Pillar of Salt*. Translated by
Edouard Roditi. New York: Criterion, 1955.
Struggle of native North African of Italian-Jewish
and Berber descent to escape from life of Tunisian
ghetto.

991. _____. *Strangers*. Translated by Brian Rhys.
New York: Orion, 1960.
Disintegration of marriage between Tunisian-
Jewish doctor and Alsatian-Catholic after return
to Tunis from Paris.

992. Menaker, Daniel. *Friends and Relations: A Collection of Stories*. New York: Doubleday, 1977.
Most of the characters in these stories are "lib-
erals" who experience loneliness, senility, and the
usual human tragedies.

993. Mende, Robert. *Spit and the Stars*. New York:
Rinehart, 1949.
Growth to manhood of Brooklyn boy in New York
garment trade with trade-union association.

994. Mendele Mocher Seforim. Fishke the Lame. Trans-
      lated by Gerald Stillman. New York: Yoseloff,
      1960.
           Jewish life in Eastern Europe in the late 1900s
      illustrated in humorous adventures of travelers who
      encounter beggar group.

995. _____. The Nag. Translated by Moishe Spiegel.
      New York: Beechhurst, 1954.
           Allegory of impoverished scholar and his adven-
      tures with his horse in East Europe during last cen-
      tury.

996. _____. The Parasite. Translated by Gerald
      Stillman. New York: Yoseloff, 1956.
           Early Yiddish novel of Haskalah movement de-
      picting power and poverty in East European village.

997. Mendelssohn, Peter. Across the Dark River. New
      York: Doubleday, Doran, 1940.
           Fifty Jews, trapped by Nazis in Austrian hamlet,
      are loaded on barge on Danube river.

998. Merochnik, Minnie. Celeste and Other Stories. New
      York: Arrowhead, 1950.
           Short stories include one of love affair between
      Jew and non-Jew.

999. _____. Essence of Life. New York: Storm,
      1956.
           Unhappily married woman involved with young
      Jew active in movement to create State of Israel.

1000. Mezvinsky, Shirley. The Edge. New York: Double-
       day, 1965.
            Nervous breakdown suffered by wife in upper-
       middle-class New York Jewish family.

1001. Michaels, Leonard. Going Places. New York: Far-
       rar, Straus and Giroux, 1969.
            Short stories include Manhattan characters illus-
       trating themes of sexual conflict, old age, slum life.

1002. _____. I Would Have Saved Them if I Could.
       New York: Farrar, Straus and Giroux, 1975.
            Stories, vignettes, and fragments sketch the New
       York Jewish milieu of the growing-up of a boy.

1003. Michener, James A. <u>Caravans</u>. New York: Random House, 1963.
    U.S. Jewish embassy official sent to Afghanistan in 1946 to investigate disappearance of American woman married to native.

1004. _____, ed. <u>Firstfruits</u>. Philadelphia: Jewish Publication Society, 1973.
    Fifteen short stories by Israeli authors depict life situations ranging from childhood to old age.

1005. _____. <u>The Source</u>. New York: Random House, 1965.
    12,000 years in Jewish life recreated through archaeological excavations in Israel that reveal various levels of culture.

1006. Miller, Arthur. <u>I Don't Need You Any More</u>. New York: Viking, 1967.
    Nine stories include allusions to search for Jewish identity and early years of writer.

1007. _____. <u>Focus</u>. New York: Reynal and Hitchcock, 1945.
    American of English descent is mistaken for a Jew and becomes victim of anti-Semitism in Queens, New York.

1008. Miller, David. <u>The Chain and the Link</u>. Cleveland and New York: World, 1951.
    Jewish scholar in Lithuanian town rises to leadership of community during Napoleonic period.

1009. Miller, Jimmy. <u>Some Parts in the Single Life</u>. New York: Knopf, 1970.
    Stories revolve around "single" Jewish women, divorcees, widows, bachelor girls, and their frustrations and affairs.

1010. Miller, Merle. <u>The Sure Thing</u>. New York: Sloane, 1949.
    FBI investigates Jewish Communist in loyalty probe in Washington.

1011. _____. <u>That Winter</u>. New York: Sloane, 1948.
    Jewish veteran seeking readjustment in New York driven to suicide after he tries to pass as non-Jew and courts an anti-Semitic girl.

1012. Millstein, Gilbert. The Late Harvey Grosbeck.
New York: Doubleday, 1974.
An arrogant New York newspaper editor is the
victim of a nearly fatal beating by the Mafia.

1013. Milton, Edith. Corridors. New York: Delacorte,
1967.
Survivor of holocaust in New York mental institution
relives German childhood in an American setting
troubled by violence and killing.

1014. Minkin, Jacob S. Gabriel Da Costa. New York:
Yoseloff, 1970.
Biographical novel of Marrano Jew who fled to
Holland and was banished by the Jewish community
for his radical thinking.

1015. Mirsky, Mark. Blue Hill Avenue. Indianapolis:
Bobbs-Merrill, 1972.
Orthodox Rabbi in Dorchester, Massachusetts is
unable to counsel a distraught mother and comes to
accept reality of evil and suffering.

1016. _____. The Secret Table. New York: Braziller,
1975.
Several short stories depict modern-day Jews in
Boston beset by ethnic conflicts, culture heroes,
and supported by life-affirming faith.

1017. Misheiker, Betty. Wings on Her Petticoat. New
York: Morrow, 1952.
Daughter tells of mother's journey with children
from Lithuanian town to join husband in South Africa.

1018. Misrock, Henry. God Had Seven Days. Garden City:
Doubleday, 1950.
Miracle heals disabled war veterans in hospital.

1019. Mitchell, Paige. The Covenant. New York: Athen-
eum, 1973.
Mississippi setting of Jewish attorney faced with
KKK, anti-Semitism, marital problems, and murder.

1020. Moll, Elick. Memoir of Spring. New York: Putnam, 1960.
Successful Hollywood composer recalls boyhood
life in Brooklyn after return to New York.

1021. _____. The Perilous Spring of Morris Seidman.
Boston: Houghton Mifflin, 1972.
A semiretired dress manufacturer emerges from
depression with the aid of a psychiatrist and a top-
less waitress.

1022. _____. Mr. Seidman and the Geisha. New York:
Simon & Schuster, 1972.
Middle-aged New York dress manufacturer intro-
duced to Japanese cafe society by geisha girl.

1023. _____. Seidman and Son. New York: Putnam,
1958.
Successful dress manufacturer reveals his life
to Hollywood writer who wishes to make him hero
of movie.

1024. Molnár, Ferenc. Farewell My Heart. Translated
by Elinor Rice. New York: Simon & Schuster,
1945.
Middle-aged Hungarian journalist and his marriage to young dancer after he comes to America
in 1939.

1025. Moosdorf, Johanna. Next Door. Translated by
Michael Glenny. New York: Knopf, 1964.
Head of pharmaceutical firm revealed as doctor
who engaged in experiments in concentration camp.

1026. Morgan, Thomas B. This Blessed Shore. New
York: Shorecrest, 1966.
New York editor concerned with problem of
mercy-killing in visiting dying father in Midwest.

1027. Morgenstern, Soma. In My Father's Pastures.
Philadelphia: Jewish Publication Society; New York:
Farrar, Straus, 1948.
Austrian Jew discovers his Jewish heritage in
visiting uncle in Galacia prior to World War II.

1028. _____. The Son of the Lost Son. Translated by
Joseph Leftwich and Peter Gross. New York: Rinehart; Philadelphia: Jewish Publication Society, 1946.
Galacian landowner journeys to Vienna for Jewish
conference and encounters son of his apostate brother.

1029. _____. The Testament of the Lost Son. Trans-

lated by Jacob Sloan and Maurice Samuel.   Phila-
delphia: Jewish Publication Society, 1950.
 Last of trilogy tracing return of young Viennese
Jew to his father's East European heritage.

1030. _____. The Third Pillar.   Translated by Ludwig
 Lewisohn.   New York: Farrar, 1955.
 Nazi crimes against Jews in Poland symbolized
in slaughter of children.

1031. Morgulas, Jerrold.   The Accused.   New York:
 Doubleday, 1967.
 Nazi survivors in Manhattan's Washington Heights
prepare for judgment on High Holy Days.

1032. Morris, Ira Victor.   Liberty Street.   New York:
 Harper, 1944.
 Red tape and cynical American minister frustrate
European refugees in Central America.

1033. Morris, Wright.   The Huge Season.   New York:
 Viking, 1954.
 Effects of jazz age on generation from college
days to exploits in Paris.

1034. Morrison, Lester M., and Hubler, Richard G.
 Trial and Triumph.   New York: Crown, 1965.
 The life career of Maimonides is traced from
Spain to Egypt and Palestine.

1035. Morton, Frederic.   Asphalt and Desire.   New York:
 Harcourt, Brace, 1951.
 Confusion and yearnings of Hunter College student
during summer following her graduation.

1036. _____. The Schatten Affair.   New York: Atheneum, 1965.
 Austrian-American Jewish PR man in Berlin after World War II in project to open a luxury hotel.

1037. Moss, Rose.   The Family Reunion.   New York:
 Scribner's, 1974.
 Three generations of a South African Jewish family, now scattered over three continents, hold reunion in Nice while concerned about the end of the
world.

1038. Mossinsohn, Igal. Judas. Translated by Jules Bar-
       low. New York: St. Martin's, 1963.
          Fearful of revenge by Christians following the
       Crucifixion, Judas lives in exile.

1039. Motley, Willard. We Fished All Night. New York:
       Appleton-Century-Crofts, 1951.
          Three young men in Chicago political and labor
       circles; includes Jew who was discharged from army
       as psychoneurotic.

1040. Murdock, James. Ketti Shalom. New York: Ran-
       dom, 1953.
          Jewish Joan of Arc leader of imprisoned Jews
       in British prison in Acre.

1041. Mure, Pierra La. Beyond Desire: A Novel Based
       on the Life of Felix and Cecile Mendelssohn. New
       York: Random, 1955.
          Biographical account of life of Felix Mendelssohn,
       his Jewish antecedents, and his assimilation.

1042. Murray, Audrey Alison. Anybody's Spring. New
       York: Vanguard, 1960.
          South African scion of Johannesburg family con
       dones infidelity of non-Jewish wife.

1043. Musil, Robert. The Man Without Qualities. Trans-
       lated by Eithne Wilkins and Ernst Kaiser. New
       York: Coward-McCann, 1953.
          Viennese life in 1913 reveals importance of Jews
       in that community.

1044. Myers, Martin. The Assignment. New York: Har-
       per & Row, 1971.
          Jewish junkman, who is a reincarnation of famous
       personages, involved with financiers and lawyers in
       comic tale.

1045. Nahman of Bratzlav. The Tales of Nahman of Brat-
       zlav. Translated by Arnold J. Band. New York:
       Paulist, 1978.
          Volume 3 in the series Classics of Western Spir-
       ituality is a translation of thirteen stories of the
       mystic dealing with the attributes of God.

1046. Nathan, Robert. A Star in the Wind. New York:
       Knopf, 1962.

American Jewish newspaper correspondent sent from Rome on refugee ship to cover 1948 Arab-Israeli war recaptures identity.

1047. Neagoe, Peter. No Time for Tears. New York: Kamin, 1958.
Difficulties in adjustment of Polish Jewess who emigrated to Brooklyn.

1048. Neider, Charles. Naked Eye. New York: Horizon, 1965.
Son reviews love-hate relationship with father during latter's terminal illness.

1049. _____. The White Citadel. New York: Twayne, 1954.
Jewish banker in Bessarabia finally emigrates to America with his family leaving parents behind.

1050. Nemerov, Howard. The Homecoming Game: A Novel. New York: Simon & Schuster, 1957.
Jewish professor fails star football player on eve of important game.

1051. Neshamit, Sarah. The Children of Mapu Street. Philadelphia: Jewish Publication Society, 1970.
Experiences of Jewish family trapped in Kovno during World War II.

1052. Neugeboren, Jay. Corky's Brother. New York: Farrar, Straus and Giroux, 1969.
Adolescent tells stories of Jews, Puerto Ricans, and other ethnic groups in Brooklyn, with emphasis on sports.

1053. _____. Listen Reuben Fontanez. Boston: Houghton Mifflin, 1968.
Elderly Jewish teacher's experiences with Puerto Ricans and Hasidic Jews in New York's ghettos.

1054. _____. An Orphan's Tale. New York: Holt, Rinehart and Winston, 1976.
Thirteen-year-old runaway from a Jewish boys' home seeks father amidst group of former orphans of the home.

1055. _____. Sam's Legacy. New York: Holt, Rinehart and Winston, 1974.

A father and son are pictured in their relationships in Brooklyn environment.

1056. Neugroschel, Joachim, ed. Yenne Velt: The Great
       Works of Jewish Fantasy and Occult. New York:
       Stonehill, 1976.
          Mysticism, fantasy, and the irrational are at
       the center of this collection, which spans all of
       Jewish literature.

1057. Neumann, Robert. By the Waters of Babylon. New
       York: Simon & Schuster, 1940.
          Life stories of Jewish passengers on bus bombed
       on Palestine border.

1058. _____. Children of Vienna, a Novel. New York:
       Dutton, 1947.
          Negro chaplain in American occupation army aids
       doomed refugee children in Austria.

1059. _____. The Inquest. New York: Dutton, 1945.
          Inquest into death of Jewish refugee of Russian
       and Italian parents found after night with aged Eng-
       lish writer.

1060. Newby, P. H. Something to Answer For. New York:
       Lippincott, 1969.
          Friend of Jewish widow in Port Said seeking to
       settle her affairs becomes involved with Egyptian
       Jewess.

1061. Newman, Alfred. Six of Them. Translated by Ana-
       tol Murad. New York: Macmillan, 1945.
          Trial in Munich of six accused of distribution of
       anti-Nazi literature.

1062. Newman, Sally. No, My Darling Daughter. New
       York: Harper & Row, 1975.
          Law student escapes from domineering mother by
       having her own apartment and seeking foreign lovers.

1063. Nissenson, Hugh. My Own Ground. New York:
       Farrar, Straus and Giroux, 1976.
          Memoir by a sixty-year-old of his teenage years
       as an orphaned immigrant on New York's East Side
       and his involvement with Marxists, whores, and
       pimps.

1064. _____. A Pile of Stones. New York: Scribner's, 1965.
       Short stories depicting search for meaning set in
       Poland in 1900s, in Israel in the 1950s, and in
       modern-day America.

1065. _____. In the Reign of Peace. New York: Far-
       rar, Straus and Giroux, 1972.
       Six of the eight short stories are set in Israel
       at the time of the Six Day War and reflect clash
       of secularism and traditional Judaism.

1066. Obletz, Rose Meyerson. The Long Road Home.
       New York: Exposition, 1958.
       Refugees from Nazi experience in Europe find
       refuge in Israel.

1067. Oboler, Arch. House on Fire. New York: Bar-
       tholomew, 1969.
       Two children are possessed by their dead grand-
       mother in this demonic thriller.

1068. Offit, Sidney. He Had It Made. New York: Crown, 1959.
       New York college student earns tuition as waiter
       in Catskill Mountain hotel.

1069. Olbracht, Ivan. The Bitter and the Sweet. Trans-
       lated by Iris Urwin. New York: Crown, 1967.
       Trials of lives of Jews in small Carpathian village
       told in three novellas.

1070. Oldenbourg, Zoe. The Awakened. Translated by
       Edward Hyans. New York: Pantheon, 1957.
       Converted German Jew leaves Russian officer
       husband after death of her father in war.

1071. _____. The Chains of Love. Translated by
       Michael Bullock. New York: Pantheon, 1959.
       Personal conflicts of Jewish émigrés in postwar
       Paris include characters from The Awakened.

1072. Oleck, Jack. The Villagers. New York: Lyle Stu-
       art, 1971.
       Included in assorted characters in Greenwich Vil-
       lage is Jew who seeks independence from his wealthy,
       garment-center family.

1073. Olivier, Stefan. Rise Up in Anger. New York:
       Putnam, 1963.

German officer in occupied Athens sent to concentration camp for helping Jews and exposing army
black marketeers.

1074. O'Neal, Cothburn. Hagar. New York: Crown, 1958.
Life of Abraham's concubine Hagar from childhood until giving birth to Ishmael.

1075. Opatoshu, Joseph. A Day in Regensburg. Translated by Jacob Sloan. Philadelphia: Jewish Publication Society, 1968.
Short stories include scenes in Regensburg ghetto,
revenge against Nazis, ruins of Warsaw ghetto, and
Hasidic rabbi in decaying American synagogue.

1076. _____. The Last Revolt: The Story of Rabbi
Akiba. Translated by Moishe Spiegel. Philadelphia: Jewish Publication Society, 1952.
Story of Akiba's role in the Bar Kochba rebellion against the Romans.

1077. Oppenheim, Edward Phillips. Last Train Out. New
York: Little, 1940.
Viennese philanthropist evades Nazis and escapes
with his art treasures on last train out of Vienna
before invasion.

1078. Orde, Lewis. Rag Trade. New York: St. Martin's,
1978.
A three-generation saga that starts with an immigrant tailor whose son builds a network of men's
clothing stores and whose children fight over the
family business.

1079. Oren, Uri. Loving Strangers. Translated by Irem
Goldstein and Yigal Shenkman. New York: Avon,
1975.
Israeli soldier falls in love with Jordanian student
through love letters found in the Sinai campaign and
is nursed by her during the Six Day War.

1080. Orlovitz, Gil. Milkbottle H. New York: Delacorte,
1968.
Philadelphia Jew enmeshed in family and love relationships in shifting patterns of behavior.

1081. Ormonde, Czeni. Solomon and the Queen of Sheba.
New York: Farrar, 1954.

Sheba joins forces with Adonijah to force Solomon off throne.

1082. Ornitz, Samuel. Bride of the Sabbath. New York: Rinehart, 1951.
Second-generation New York social worker in identity search while married to non-Jew and seeking meaning in Christianity.

1083. Orpaz, Yitzhak. The Death of Lysanda. Translated by Richard Flint. New York: Grossman, 1970.
Russian-born Israeli is author of novella revolving around a newspaper proofreader, amateur taxidermist, and writer who is beguiled by a real and phantasized woman.

1084. Osborne, Letitia Preston. They Change Their Skies. Philadelphia: Lippincott, 1945.
Boarders in pension in Honduras include several Jewish refugees whose fate affects others.

1085. Osgood, Phillips Endicott. The Sinner Beloved: A Novel of the Life and Times of Hosea the Prophet. New York: American, 1956.
Enemies of the prophet Hosea corrupt his wife, whom he continues to love.

1086. Oxenhandler, Bernard. A Song Is Borne. New York: Clarendon Press, 1963.
Rise to world fame of boy cantor from New York's East Side.

1087. Oxenhandler, Neal. A Change of Gods. New York: Harcourt, Brace, 1962.
Difficulties in marriage of St. Louis Jew to Chicago Catholic girl.

1088. Oz, Amos. Elsewhere, Perhaps. Translated by Nicholas de Lange. New York: Harcourt Brace Jovanovich, 1973.
The complexities of personal relationships on a kibbutz are laid bare in midst of threat of Jordanian attack.

1089. _____. The Hill of Evil Counsel. Translated by Nicholas de Lange. New York: Harcourt Brace Jovanovich, 1976.
The close of the British mandate is the link between three stories of Jerusalem inhabitants.

1090. _____. My Michael. Translated by Nicholas de
       Lange. New York: Knopf, 1972.
           Israel in the 50s is background for alienated Jew
       who, turned off by unimaginative husband, seeks
       sexual adventures with Arabs.

1091. _____. Touch the Water, Touch the Wind. Trans-
       lated by Nicholas de Lange. New York: Harcourt
       Brace Jovanovich, 1974.
           Allegory based on escape from Poland to Israel
       of hero who reveals a mathematical answer to in-
       finity.

1092. _____. Unto Death. New York: Harcourt Brace
       Jovanovich, 1975.
           Two novellas, one depicting band of Crusaders
       journeying to Jerusalem, the second set in con-
       temporary Israel and the paranoiac concern for the
       fate of Soviet Jews.

1093. Ozick, Cynthia. Bloodshed and Three Novellas. New
       York: Knopf, 1976.
           Ghost of poet Tcherniknovsky appears in collec-
       tion of stories with heroes coming to terms with
       Judaism.

1094. _____. The Pagan Rabbi and Other Stories. New
       York: Knopf, 1971.
           Eight short stories of Jewish characters seeking
       self-realization laced with supernatural elements.

1095. Pace, Eric. Saberlegs. New York: World, 1970.
           Nazi hunters search for German chemist who
       plans to sell poison gas to Egyptian commando unit
       in current Arab-Israeli war.

1096. Packer, Bernard. The Second Death of Samuel Auer.
       New York: Harcourt Brace Jovanovich, 1979.
           Philadelphia grocer faces losing battle in chang-
       ing neighborhood and recalls his days in World War
       II.

1097. Paley, Grace. Enormous Changes at the Last Minute.
       New York: Farrar, Straus and Giroux, 1974.
           Seventeen short stories of New York life, old-
       folks home, subway settings, changing neighborhood,
       and people's failures.

1098. _____. The Little Disturbances of Man. New
York: Doubleday, 1959.
    Short stories in New York setting includes Jewish
children in Christmas play.

1099. Papier, Judith Barnard. The Past and Present of
Solomon Sorge. Boston: Houghton Mifflin, 1967.
    In attempt to find missing wife, political science
professor discovers reasons for failure of marriage.

1100. Parent, Gail. David Meyer Is a Mother. New York:
Harper & Row, 1975.
    A male chauvinist TV executive pursues prosti-
tute, who had ridiculed him as a researcher, and
mothers their child.

1101. _____. Sheila Levine Is Dead and Living in New
York. New York: Putnam, 1972.
    Overweight, anxious Jewish girl is a born loser
and botches up her suicide attempt, the last straw
in her humorous adventures.

1102. Parker, Norton S. Table in the Wilderness. Chicago: Ziff-Davis, 1947.
    Account of Joseph and his brothers retold.

1103. Parrish, Anne. Pray for a Tomorrow. New York:
Harper, 1941.
    Allegory based on betrayal of Jewish refugee by
friend on Cornwall island.

1104. Patai, Irene Steinman. The Valley of God. New
York: Random House, 1956.
    Explores marriage of the prophet Hosea and his
unfaithful wife.

1105. Patterson, James. The Jericho Commandment. New
York: Crown, 1979.
    Prominent Westchester Jewish family is mur-
dered in what appears to be a plot by Jewish ex-
tremists to avenge victims of the Holocaust by killing athletes at the 1980 Moscow Olympics.

1106. Paul, Louis. Dara, the Cypriot. New York: Simon
& Schuster, 1959.
    Cypriot charm maker witnesses ninth-century
B.C. struggles of Ahab, Jezebel, and Elijah.

1107.   Pawel, Ernst. From the Dark Tower. New York:
        Macmillan, 1957.
            Suicide of employer brings rebellion of insurance
        man against Long Island Jewish life and move to
        Colorado.

1108.   _____. The Island in Time. Garden City: Doub-
        leday, 1951.
            Reaction of Jews interned on island off Italy
        while awaiting passage to Palestine.

1109.   Pearlman, Ronny. The Monday Man. New York:
        Stein and Day, 1970.
            Impotent man seeks help from psychiatrist and
        after adventures with his wife takes refuge in san-
        atorium.

1110.   Pell, Franklyn. Hangman's Hill. New York: Dodd,
        Mead, 1946.
            American war correspondent in Alsace suspected
        of crimes because of anti-Nazi hatred and mistaken
        identity as Jew.

1111.   Penfield, Wilder. No Other Gods. Boston: Little,
        Brown, 1954.
            Abram searches for the one God in Ur and leaves
        with followers for Canaan.

1112.   Perera, Victor. The Conversion. Boston: Little,
        Brown, 1970.
            American graduate student in Spain, of Sephardic
        heritage, is beset by dreams, fantasies, and latter-
        day inquisitor.

1113.   Peretz, I. L. The Book of Fire. Translated by
        Joseph Leftwich. New York: Yoseloff, 1960.
            Collection of stories by master Yiddish writer
        includes vignettes of young lovers, village idiot,
        Hasidic rabbis in East European villages.

1114.   _____. Selected Stories. Edited by Irving Howe
        and Eliezer Greenberg. New York: Schocken,
        1974.
            Eighteen short stories covering life of East Euro-
        pean Jews in the late nineteenth century.

1115.   _____. In This World and the Next. Translated by
        Moshe Spiegel. New York: Yoseloff, 1958.

Polish Jewry in prewar Warsaw depicted in classic short stories.

1116. Perman, Morris. Man's Heart Is Evil, a Novel.
New York: Field/Doubleday, 1947.
Difficulties in adjustment to America of Russian-Jewish immigrants and their family in New York's East Side.

1117. Picard, Jacob. The Marked One and Other Stories.
Translated by Ludwig Lewisohn. Philadelphia:
Jewish Publication Society, 1956.
Jewish life in villages in Germany beginning in the eighteenth century portrayed in vignettes of local characters in Orthodox environment.

1118. Pick, Robert. The Terhoven File. Philadelphia:
Lippincott, 1944.
Gestapo agents search for file of Viennese lawyer who defended German refugee in extradition case in 1934 seeking information harmful to Hitler.

1119. Pilpel, Robert H. To the Honor of the Fleet. New
York: Atheneum, 1979.
American-Jewish naval officer assigned to German fleet prior to World War I to learn as much as possible in preparation for U.S. entry into the war.

1120. Pincus, Oscar. Friends and Lovers. New York:
World, 1963.
Jewish-refugee physicist from Warsaw finds solace in woman in Cambridge, Massachusetts, academic setting.

1121. Pitzer, R. Daughter of Jerusalem. New York:
Liveright, 1956.
Love story woven into account of times of Jeremiah.

1122. Plain, Belva. Evergreen. New York: Delacorte,
1978.
Polish-immigrant girl center of three-generational story of family, fortune, deceits, and triumphs.

1123. Pollack, Harry. Gabriel. Toronto: McGraw-Hill
Tyerson, 1975.

The coming to age of the son of Polish-Jewish
immigrants in the 30s in Toronto.

1124.   Pollack, James S.   The Golden Egg.   New York:
        Holt, 1946.
            Rise and fall of Hollywood dynasty established by
        two Jews from New York's Lower East Side.

1125.   Popkin, Zelda.   Dear Once.   New York: Lippincott,
        1975.
            The narrator covers a fifty-year period in the
        life of a family, which includes marriage to a Hol-
        lywood actor who is destroyed by the Communist
        blacklist.

1126.   _____.   Herman Had Two Daughters.   Philadel-
        phia: Lippincott, 1968.
            From beginnings in Pennsylvania town, protag-
        onists move on to wealth, Broadway, Jewish propa-
        ganda, and fund raising.

1127.   _____.   Quiet Street.   Philadelphia and New York:
        Lippincott, 1951.
            Boston-bred mother sees daughter become fighter
        for Israel in Jerusalem in 1948.

1128.   _____.   Small Victory.   Philadelphia: Lippincott,
        1947.
            American Jewish college professor in postwar
        Germany commits suicide after unsuccessful at-
        tempts to re-educate German youth.

1129.   _____.   Walk Through the Valley.   Philadelphia:
        Lippincott, 1949.
            Readjustment of wife following sudden death of
        husband reveals problems of other widows.

1130.   Posy, Arnold.   Messiah's Chains.   Translated by
        Joseph Leftwich.   New York: Bloch, 1963.
            Fanciful epic with Messianic themes from Bible
        and Rabbinic lore.

1131.   Potok, Chaim.   In the Beginning.   New York: Knopf,
        1975.
            Gifted boy becomes a Biblical scholar in Ortho-
        dox setting in the Bronx spanning period of Depres-
        sion to the Holocaust.

1132.   _____ . My Name Is Asher Lev. New York:
        Knopf, 1972.
            Hasidic youth from Brooklyn seeks career as
        painter defying family's religious abhorrence of
        representational art.

1133.   _____ . The Chosen. New York: Simon & Schus-
        ter, 1967.
            Orthodox Hasidic and non-Hasidic families in
        Brooklyn with views on child rearing, education,
        contemporary religious and Zionist life.

1134.   _____ . The Promise. New York: Knopf, 1969.
            Sequel to The Chosen follows careers of two
        boys, one as an Orthodox rabbi with rationalist
        foundation and the second a clinical psychologist.

1135.   Pressner, Jacob. Breaking Point. Translated by
        Barrows Mussey. Cleveland and New York: World,
        1958.
            Plight of Jews in German-occupied Holland re-
        solved in deportation to Auschwitz concentration
        camp.

1136.   Price, Anthony. The Alamut Ambush. New York:
        Doubleday, 1972.
            Death of British intelligence agent leads to Pal-
        estinian terrorist groups and Middle East intrigues.

1137.   Prose, Francine. Judah the Pious. New York:
        Atheneum, 1973.
            Hasidic rabbi seeks to win toleration for Jews
        from Polish prince through device of storytelling
        revolving around a pious, saintlike Jew.

1138.   Rabikovitz, Dalia. The New Israeli Writers. New
        York: Sabra, 1969.
            Fourteen stories by Israeli writers, including
        Shamir, Megged, and Shaham, on themes of kib-
        butz life, war, personal dislocation.

1139.   Ralston, Gilbert, and Newnafer, Richard. The
        Frightful Sin of Cisco Newman. Englewood Cliffs,
        N.J.: Prentice-Hall, 1972.
            Three Chicagoans--Jew, Arab, and Italian--kid-
        nap the Pope and take him to Israel while the ran-
        som is being collected.

1140. Ramati, Alexander. Rebel Against the Light. New
       York: Farrar, Straus & Cudahy, 1960.
           Difficulty of adjustment to Israeli life by refugee
       who recalls level of living in Europe.

1141. Raphael, Frederic. Lindmann: A Novel. New York:
       Holt, Rinehart and Winston, 1964.
           British civil servant takes identity of Austrian
       refugee as sole survivor in wreck of ship bound
       from Rumania to Palestine in 1942.

1142. _____. The Limits of Love. New York: Lip-
       pincott, 1961.
           Search of three children of Orthodox shopkeeper
       in London after World War II for personal fulfill-
       ment.

1143. _____. Orchestra & Beginners. New York:
       Viking, 1968.
           Intermarriage of British-Jewish magnate and
       American wife provides plot for problems of son
       prior to World War II.

1144. Raskin, Barbara. Loose Ends. New York: Bantam,
       1973.
           Both husband and lover have abandoned a mother
       of four who now is on her own.

1145. Raskin, Saul. Go Back and Tell. New York: Whit-
       tier, 1958.
           Autobiographical novel of artist recalling child-
       hood days, family, and struggle to achieve recog-
       nition.

1146. Rawicz, Piotr. Blood from the Sky. Translated by
       Peter Wiles. New York: Harcourt, Brace & World,
       1964.
           Survivor of massacre of Jewish community in the
       Ukraine finds temporary haven in Paris.

1147. Rayner, William. The Last Days. New York: Mor-
       row, 1969.
           The siege of Masada ending the Jewish rebellion
       against Rome in the first century.

1148. Rees, Barbara. Try Another Country. New York:
       Harcourt, 1967.

In one of the three short stories, neurotic young Jew victimizes girl who trusts him.

1149. Rees, Jean A. Jacob Have I Loved. Grand Rapids: Eerdmans, 1963.
The Biblical Jacob is portrayed in a reverential manner.

1150. Reich, Tova. Mara. New York: Farrar, Straus and Giroux, 1978.
Rabbi proprietor of nursing-home empire beset by daughter married to hippy Israeli and by his own financial manipulations.

1151. Remarque, Erich Maria. The Night in Lisbon. New York: Harcourt, Brace & World, 1964.
Two survivors of Nazi terror meet in Lisbon in 1942 and exchange tales of their escapes.

1152. _____. Shadows in Paradise. Translated by Ralph Manheim. New York: Harcourt, 1972.
Non-Jewish refugee from Nazis thrown in with Jewish refugees in New York at close of World War II and world of art dealers, collectors, and Hollywood frenzy.

1153. _____. Spark of Life. Translated by James Stern. New York: Appleton-Century-Crofts, 1952.
Horrors in Nazi concentration camp seen in slow death of inmates through exhaustion and hunger.

1154. _____. A Time to Love and a Time to Die. Translated by Denver Lindley. New York: Harcourt, 1954.
German soldier marries during furlough at close of World War II and returns to guard Russian prisoners, only to be killed.

1155. Renek, Morris. Las Vegas Strip. New York: Knopf, 1975.
Brooklyn boy makes good in the world of the casinos and gamblers and runs afoul of the Syndicate.

1156. Reznikoff, Charles. The Lionhearted: A Story About the Jews in Medieval England. Philadelphia: Jewish Publication Society, 1944.

The twelfth-century persecution of Jews in England focuses on trials of young medical student during the York massacre.

1157.   Rhodes, Evan H.   An Army of Children.   New York: Dial, 1978.
        Jew and Christian teenagers center of recreation of the Children's Crusade in 1212, which moved from England to Jerusalem.

1158.   Ribalow, Harold U., ed.   The Chosen.   New York: Abelard-Schuman, 1959.
        Twenty-three short stories reflecting American-Jewish life with themes of intermarriage, Hasidic rabbis, army life, and old age.

1159.   _____.   My Name Aloud.   New York: Yoseloff, 1969.
        Thirty-eight short stories by American-Jewish authors ranging from Jewish holidays, search for identity, refugees, Bar Mitzvah, and impact of Israel.

1160.   _____.   These Your Children.   New York: Beechhurst, 1952.
        Jewish life in immigrant generations in America and Europe portrayed in these twenty-five short stories.

1161.   _____.   This Land, These People.   New York: Beechhurst, 1950.
        Problems of acculturation, generational conflict depicted in twenty-four short stories by American-Jewish writers.

1162.   _____.   Treasury of American Jewish Stories.   New York: Yoseloff, 1958.
        Personalities, adjustment problems, anti-Semitism, urban living, Jewish-Negro relations among themes in these fifty short stories.

1163.   Rice, John R.   Seeking a City: A Novel Based on the Biblical Story of Abraham.   Grand Rapids: Eerdmans, 1957.
        A portrayal of Abraham and his relationships with Sarah and Isaac.

1164. Richardson, Anne. Digging Out. New York: Mc-
Graw-Hill, 1967.
Three-generation saga of Russian immigrants
from Czarism who founded a fortune in America.

1165. Richler, Mordecai. The Apprenticeship of Duddy
Kravitz. Boston: Atlantic/Little, Brown, 1959.
Canadian-Jewish boy seeks escape from ghetto
and success at any price.

1166. _____. Cocksure. New York: Simon & Schuster,
1969.
Jewish personalities in Hollywood film industry
delineated in portrayal of distasteful promoter.

1167. _____. St. Urbain's Horseman. New York:
Knopf, 1971.
Canadian-Jewish film and TV director faces
trial in Old Bailey on sodomy and assault charges.

1168. _____. The Street. Washington, D.C.: New
Republic, 1975.
Semiautobiographical stories and memoirs of the
author's boyhood years in the Jewish ghetto of Mon-
treal.

1169. Richter, Hans Werner. They Fell from God's Hands.
Translated by Geoffrey Saintsbury. New York:
Dutton, 1956.
Stories of ten displaced persons in the camp near
Nuremberg in 1950.

1170. Rigadon, Charles. The Last Ball. New York: Trident, 1972.
An unscrupulous Jew intermarries in order to be
accepted into better families of New York.

1171. Riley, Frank. Jesus II. New York: Sherbourne,
1972.
A Sephardic Jew from Boston is convinced that
he is Jesus in his Second Coming, flies to Rome,
stays in New York with William Buckley, and is
spied upon by the Vatican.

1172. Robbins, Harold. The Dream Merchants. New
York: Knopf, 1949.

Rise of motion-picture industry in Hollywood includes Jewish role in its development.

1173. _____. Never Love a Stranger. New York: Knopf, 1948.
New York racketeer of partly-Jewish origins killed in World War II.

1174. _____. The Pirate. New York: Simon & Schuster, 1974.
Mideast Arab tycoon, a Jewish foundling, involved in jet set, terrorists, high finance, and dramatic denouement.

1175. _____. A Stone for Danny Fisher. New York: Knopf, 1952.
Flatbush son of druggist develops into boxer and gangster and is killed by cohorts.

1176. Robbins, Lawrence. A Certain Protocol. New York: Harper & Row, 1975.
Brooklyn Jewish boy claims he is the world's greatest flamenco guitarist in freewheeling world of Madrid.

1177. Roberts, Mary Carter. Little Brother Fate. New York: Farrar, Straus & Cudahy, 1957.
Reconstruction of Snyder-Grey, Halls-Mills, and Loeb-Leopold crimes.

1178. Roberts, Thomas A. The Heart of the Dog. New York: Random House, 1972.
The Arab-Israeli conflict is the heart of a thriller which takes an ex-CIA operative to the Mideast as a pawn in the intelligence operation.

1179. Robertson, Minns S. To God Alone: A Novel. Daytona Beach, Fla.: College, 1956.
Thinly veiled recreation of journey of Jesus and disciples to Jerusalem for Passover.

1180. Robinson, Armin, ed. The Ten Commandments. New York: Simon & Schuster, 1943.
Ten short novels illustrating Nazi perversion of moral codes written by authors including Werfel, Mann, Romain, and Bromfield.

1181. Robinson, Henry Morton. The Cardinal. New York: Simon & Schuster, 1950.
    Sister of cardinal dies in childbirth after marriage to Jew.

1182. Roeburt, John. Seneca, U.S.A. New York: Curl, 1947.
    Newspaperman crusades against anti-Semitism after murder of his crooked publisher.

1183. Rogers, Barbara. The Doomsday Scroll. New York: Dodd, Mead, 1979.
    CIA agent and Biblical scholar and woman they love search for Arab raiders who have kidnapped an Israeli boy they believe to be the Messiah.

1184. Rogin, Gilbert. What Happens Next? A Novel. New York: Random House, 1971.
    Editor and writer in mid-30s and early 40s reveals the sadness and absurdity of life in New York.

1185. Roiphe, Anne. Long Division. New York: Simon & Schuster, 1972.
    New York City Jewish mother travels across the States in a station wagon with her ten-year-old daughter on her way to Mexico for a divorce.

1186. _____. Torch Song. New York: Farrar, Straus and Giroux, 1977.
    Rebellious product of upper-class New York Jewish family falls in love with teenage alcoholic who is Byronesque in his failings.

1187. Roman, Eric. A Year As a Lion. New York: Stein and Day, 1978.
    College professor, a Holocaust Jew, is recruited as undercover agent to play role of an anti-Communist poet and authentic hero.

1188. Romanowicz, Zofia. Passage Through the Red Sea. Translated by Virgilia Peterson. New York: Harcourt, 1962.
    Two former female inmates of Nazi prison labor camp are reunited in Paris after war.

1189. Ronch, Isaac E. The Awakening of Motek: A Novel.

Translated from the Yiddish. New York: Bunt-
ing, 1953.
  Jewish boy growing up in Lodz prior to World
War I departs for new life in America.

1190. Rose, Louise Bleicher. The Launching of Barbara
       Fabrikant. New York: McKay, 1974.
         Dieting college student regains all her weight af-
       ter abortive affair with professor.

1191. Rosen, Isidore. Will of Iron. New York: Crown,
       1950.
         Brooklyn matriarch dominates family during the
       Depression years.

1192. Rosen, Norma. Green: A Novella and Eight Stories.
       New York: Harcourt, Brace & World, 1967.
         Stories of West Side Jewish family and struggle
       between material wants and artistic expression.

1193. Rosenberg, Ethel. Go Fight City Hall. New York:
       Simon & Schuster, 1949.
         Brooklyn Jewish family includes uncle who dab-
       bles in cemetery real estate and mother-daughter
       conflicts.

1194. _____. Uncle Julius and the Angel with Heart-
       burn. New York: Simon & Schuster, 1951.
         Sequel to Go Fight City Hall focusing on Julius's
       meeting with an angel with similar heartburn con-
       dition.

1195. Rosenberg, Theresa Abeles. Stolen Waters Are
       Sweet: A Novel of a Woman's Faith in a Man's
       Weakness. New York: William-Frederick Press,
       1946.
         Woman's religious faith enables her to rescue
       husband from a reckless infatuation.

1196. Rosenfeld, Isaac. Passage from Home. New York:
       Dial, 1946.
         Adolescent Chicago boy breaks from family to
       live for a time with modern aunt and her lover.

1197. Rosenfeld, Max, ed. Pushcarts and Dreams. Trans-
       lated by Max Rosenfeld. New York: Yoseloff, 1969.
         Short stories of ten Yiddish authors reflecting

immigrant experiences in New York, sweatshops, unionism, unemployment in the early 1900s.

1198. Ross, Fran. Oreo. New York: Greyfalcon House, 1974.
Child of Jewish father and black mother searches for her father when she grows up by looking at entries in Manhattan telephone book.

1199. Ross, Frank (pseud.). Dead Runner. New York: Atheneum, 1977.
Israelis want Arab killer of Jewish military hero in London delivered to them while Palestinians park hijacked jet with atomic bomb at Heathrow Airport.

1200. Ross, Sam. Port Unknown. Cleveland and New York: World, 1951.
World War II navy officer on tanker recalls his Jewishness during Atlantic crossing.

1201. _____. The Sidewalks Are Free. New York: Farrar, Straus, 1950.
Americanization of Chicago boy in Jewish ghetto before World War I.

1202. _____. Solomon's Palace. New York: Delacorte, 1973.
Small-time Jewish gangster from Chicago makes deal with Capone's mob and attempts to take over West Coast organization.

1203. Rossner, Judith. To the Precipice. New York: Morrow, 1966.
East Side girl, ambitious for money and status, denies love for childhood friend to accept unhappy marriage.

1204. Rossner, Robert. A Hero Like Me; A Hero Like You. New York: Saturday Review, 1972.
Teenaged Jewish student, a Nazi, is confronted by his teacher, an ex-copywriter, in urban high school setting.

1205. Rosten, Leo. O K*A*P*L*A*N! My K*A*P*L*A*N! New York: Harper & Row, 1976.
A completely rewritten account of the students in adult evening classes in New York's East Side.

1206.   _____ . The Return of Hyman Kaplan. New York:
        Harper, 1959.
            Sequel to The Education of Hyman Kaplan brings
        together at a reunion the adults from an English
        night-school class.

1207.   Rosten, Norman. Under the Boardwalk. Englewood
        Cliffs, N.J.: Prentice-Hall, 1968.
            Adolescent struggles of Jewish boy in Coney Is-
        land in fifteen vignettes of associations with parents,
        denial of God, realization of sex.

1208.   Rostov, Mara. Eroica. New York: Putnam, 1977.
            Daughter of former Nazi who is threatening to
        destroy Israel through blackmail of underdeveloped
        nations seeks to subvert his plan.

1209.   Roth, Henry. Call It Sleep. New York: Pageant,
        1960.
            Reissue of classic story of Brooklyn boy whose
        father suspected that he was another man's son.

1210.   Roth, Philip. The Ghost Writer. New York: Far-
        rar, Straus and Giroux, 1979.
            Young writer's search for a father image leads
        him to obscure writer, sex triangle, and resolution
        of integrity and independence.

1211.   _____ . Goodbye, Columbus, and Five Short Stor-
        ies. Boston: Houghton Mifflin, 1959.
            Modern-day American Jewish life illustrated in
        love affair of Radcliffe girl with Newark librarian,
        Jewish army sergeant, and Hasidic rabbi in suburbs.

1212.   _____ . Letting Go. New York: Random House,
        1962.
            Problems of interpersonal relationships of college
        instructor and colleagues beset by guilt, money cri-
        sis, and problems of intermarriage.

1213.   _____ . My Life As a Man. New York: Holt,
        Rinehart and Winston, 1974.
            Quasiautobiographical account of novelist whose
        energies have been sapped by possessive women
        and who seeks psychiatric help.

1214.   _____ . Portnoy's Complaint. New York: Random
        House, 1969.

New York lawyer communicates to his analyst
his hatred of mother, self, and Judaism.

1215.   . Professor of Desire. New York: Farrar,
Straus and Giroux, 1977.
After summer romp, graduate student becomes
professor, marries, is divorced, and finally meets
his wholesome woman.

1216. Rothberg, Abraham. The Heirs of Cain. New York:
Putnam, 1966.
Survivor of Polish ghetto assigned to eliminate
two German scientists in his new role as Israeli
secret agent.

1217.   . The Sword of the Golem. New York:
McCall, 1970.
The sixteenth-century Prague legend of the Golem
is transformed into a humanized person who becomes symbolic of humanity's brute spirit.

1218.   . The Song of David Freed. New York:
Putnam, 1968.
Boy cantor in Brooklyn loses religious faith as
he comes of age.

1219. Rothschild, Sylvia. Sunshine and Salt. New York:
Simon & Schuster, 1964.
Generational conflict develops when elderly moth-
er comes to live with married daughter's family.

1220. Routtenberg, Max J. Once in a Minyan and Other
Stories. New York: KTAV, 1977.
The American Jewish scene is portrayed in ten
stories reflecting the clash between tradition and
contemporary life.

1221. Rovit, Earl. A Far Cry. New York: Harcourt,
Brace & World, 1967.
Parallel lives of Jewish usurer in sixteenth-
century Venice and twentieth-century metaphysician
dying of cancer in Catholic hospital.

1222.   . The Player King. New York: Harcourt,
Brace & World, 1965.
Boston Jewish professor searches for wife while
undergoing strange adventures in New York.

1223.   Rowe, John.   The Aswan Solution.   New York:
        Doubleday, 1979.
            Israel's moral credibility is damaged when it
        blows up Aswan Dam in attempt to limit nuclear-
        armament race.

1224.   Rubens, Bernice.   Chosen People.   New York:
        Atheneum, 1969.
            London rabbi cared for by spinster daughter
        while son is sent to mental institution and second
        daughter is estranged because of intermarriage.

1225.   Rubenstein, S. Leonard.   The Battle Done.   New
        York: Morrow, 1954.
            Jewish master sergeant in charge of German
        prisoners of war in South Carolina camp prison.

1226.   Rubin, Louis D.   The Golden Weather.   New York:
        Atheneum, 1961.
            Thirteen-year-old son of fine old Charleston,
        South Carolina, Jewish family enjoys his summer
        of 1936.

1227.   Rubin, Michael.   An Absence of Bells.   New York:
        McGraw-Hill, 1972.
            Jewish wife of psychologist and Irish Catholic
        teacher throw off family ties to seek life together.

1228.   _____.   Whistle Me Home.   New York: McGraw-
        Hill, 1967.
            Family in Brooklyn and intergenerational con-
        flicts, relationships with Negroes, search for es-
        cape.

1229.   Rudnicki, Adolf.   Ascent to Heaven.   Translated by
        H. C. Stevens.   New York: Roy, 1951.
            Precarious existence of Warsaw Jews under Ger-
        man occupation told in fourteen short stories.

1230.   Rudolph, Marguerita.   The Great Hope.   New York:
        Day, 1948.
            Ukrainian-Jewish parents of Soviet student killed
        by bandits as second daughter emigrates to America.

1231.   Ruskay, Sophie.   The Jelly Woman.   New York:
        Barnes, 1970.
            Collection of short stories and other pieces,

mainly autobiographical in nature, about Jewish
girl's move toward maturity.

1232.   Russcol, Herbert, and Banai, Margalit.   Kilometer
        95.   Boston: Houghton Mifflin, 1958.
        Member of Stern gang falls in love with rational
        girl in Gaza border kibbutz and changes his ideas
        about retribution.

1233.   Rutherford, Douglas.   Kick Start.   New York: Walk-
        er, 1974.
        A motorcyclist is recruited by an international
        agency to spy in the Israel-Arab conflict and locate
        a secret object hidden in a spa.

1234.   Sahl, Hans.   The Few and the Many.   Translated
        by Richard and Clara Winston.   New York: Har-
        court, 1962.
        Refugee who escapes Nazis tries to make new
        life in Prague, Amsterdam, and France and final-
        ly emigrates to America.

1235.   St. John, Robert.   The Man Who Played God.   New
        York: Doubleday, 1963.
        Trial of Hungarian Jewish community executive
        on charges of collaboration with Nazis in attempt
        to save Jews.

1236.   Salaman, Esther Polianowsky.   The Fertile Plain.
        New York: Abelard-Schuman, 1957.
        Family life portrayed in Ukrainian village in
        years preceding the Russian Revolution.

1237.   Salinger, J. D.   Franny and Zooey.   Boston: Little,
        Brown, 1961.
        Stories of New York family with daughter en-
        couraged to become actress by her brother.

1238.   _____.   Raise High the Roof Beam, Carpenters
        and Seymour: An Introduction.   Boston: Little,
        Brown, 1963.
        Two stories of the New York Glass family where
        Seymour leaves bourgeois bride at altar and then
        develops himself as major poet and holy man.

1239.   Samuel, Edwin H.   A Coat of Many Colours.   New
        York: Abelard-Schuman, 1960.

Short stories of Jews in many lands include por-
trayals of fund raisers, gamblers, stamp-collectors,
and problems in Israel.

1240. _____. A Cottage in Galilee. New York: Abelard-Schuman, 1958.
Personal experiences in Palestine from World
War I to 1948 sketching kibbutz life, Arab-Jew relationships, role of British.

1241. _____. The Cucumber King and Other Stories.
New York: Abelard-Schuman, 1965.
Short stories about Jews in Shanghai, Dublin,
Canada, London, and Israel.

1242. _____. His Celestial Highness. New York: Abelard-Schuman, 1968.
Tales of Jews in Cambodia, Japan, Israel focus-
ing on theme of conflicts within individuals.

1243. _____. My Friend Musa and Other Stories. New
York: Abelard-Schuman, 1963.
Short stories of tensions between Arabs and Jews
in Israel.

1244. Samuel, Maurice. The Second Crucifixion. New
York: Knopf, 1960.
Emergence of Christianity in first century under
Roman rule with story of rejection of wife by Roman
husband with revelation of her Jewish background.

1245. Samuels, Gertrude. Of David and Eva: A Love
Story. New York: Signet, 1978.
Israeli physician falls in love with a Lebanese
nurse through their relationship in the northern
border town that services the wounded.

1246. _____. Mottele: A Partisan Odyssey. New
York: Harper & Row, 1976.
Twelve-year-old Jewish orphan joins Polish resistance group to battle the Nazis and experiences
the Warsaw ghetto uprising and the revolt of Jews
at Lodz.

1247. Samuelson, William. All Lie in Wait. Englewood
Cliffs, N.J.: Prentice-Hall, 1969.
Jewish resistance to Nazi terror and annihilation
of Polish- and Russian-Jewish communities.

1248. Sanders, Ed. Shards of God. New York: Grove,
       1970.
           Abbie Hoffman and Jerry Rubin are at center of
       confrontation between the Yippies and the Establish-
       ment and the emergence of a new society.

1249. Sandmel, Samuel. Alone atop the Mountain. New
       York: Doubleday, 1973.
           First-person narrative of the life of Moses with
       modern scholarship applied to familiar stories.

1250. Sara. Where Mist Clothes Dream and Song Runs
       Naked. New York: McGraw-Hill, 1965.
           Russian immigrant family in Boston seeks to find
       future out of poverty-stricken background.

1251. Saroyan, William. Rock Wagram. Garden City:
       Doubleday, 1951.
           Relationships between Jewish movie producer
       and bartender who becomes Hollywood actor.

1252. Sarton, M. Faithful Are the Wounds. New York:
       Rinehart, 1955.
           Impact of suicide of Harvard English professor
       on colleagues and family.

1253. Sartre, Jean-Paul. The Reprieve. Translated by
       Eric Sutton. New York: Knopf, 1947.
           German refugees and French Jews react to
       events in days preceding Munich agreement.

1254. _____. Troubled Sleep. Translated by Eric Sut-
       ton. New York: Knopf, 1951.
           The fall of France in June 1940 has impact on
       native Jews as well as refugees from Germany and
       Poland.

1255. Satz, Mario. Sol. Translated by Helen R. Lane.
       New York: Doubleday, 1979.
           The problem of Jewish identity in Latin America
       is explored through conflicting cultural traditions
       besetting a love affair.

1256. Saunders, Jake, and Waldrop, Howard. The Texas-
       Israeli War: 1999. New York: Ballantine, 1974.
           Israeli agents attempt to rescue the kidnapped
       President of the U.S.

1257. Sayre, Joel. The House Without a Roof. New York: Farrar, Straus, 1948.
      Fictional account of anti-Nazi German family and their acceptance of guilt following World War II.

1258. Schaeffer, Susan Fromberg. Anya. New York: Macmillan, 1974.
      Polish Jew survives horrors of Warsaw ghetto and concentration camps and finds haven in America.

1259. _____. Falling. New York: Macmillan, 1973.
      Graduate student near suicide finds life worthwhile after probing her past with wise analyst.

1260. Scharlemann, Dorothy Hoyer. My Vineyard. St. Louis: Concordia, 1946.
      Jerusalem is the "main character" in events at time of Jesus.

1261. Schechtman, Elya. Erev. Translated by Joseph Singer. New York: Crown, 1967.
      Pogroms, conversion, and army-service themes in account of Jewish family prior to the Russian Revolution of 1905.

1262. Schmitt, Gladys. Alexandra. New York: Dial, 1947.
      Jewish friend of famous actress reminisces about their lifelong relationship and her rise in theater.

1263. Schoonover, Lawrence. Key of Gold. Boston: Little, Brown, 1968.
      Three Sephardic Jewish doctors minister to needs of Torquemada, Spinoza, and Peter Stuyvesant.

1264. Schrobsdorff, Angelika. The Men. Translated by Michael Bullock. New York: Putnam, 1963.
      Return from Bulgaria of girl of mixed German-Jewish marriage and her discovery of Nazi horrors and heavy hand of occupying forces.

1265. Schulberg, Budd W. The Disenchanted. New York: Random House, 1950.
      Jewish movie producer involved in disintegration of literary genius fashioned after F. Scott Fitzgerald.

1266.   _____.   What Makes Sammy Run.   New York:
         Random House, 1941.
            Ambitious copy boy on New York newspaper rises
         to top in Hollywood through harsh means.

1267.   Schulz, Bruno.   Sanatorium Under the Sign of the
         Hourglass.   Translated by Celina Wieniewska.   New
         York: Walker, 1978.
            A high school art teacher, murdered by the SS
         in 1942, produced these stories of his family and
         the small Polish town in which they lived.

1268.   _____.   The Street of Crocodiles.   Translated by
         Celina Wieniewska.   New York: Walker, 1963.
            Boyhood in Polish-Jewish village before Nazi in-
         vasion recounted in nostalgic manner.

1269.   Schwartz, Delmore.   In Dreams Begin Responsibil-
         ities.   New York: New Directions, 1978.
            Eight short stories reflecting the generational
         gap between Jewish immigrants and their middle-
         class intellectual children.

1270.   _____.   The World Is a Wedding.   Norfolk, Conn.:
         New Directions, 1948.
            Short stories of griefs and dreams of young peo-
         ple during the Depression.

1271.   _____.   Shenandoah.   Norfolk, Conn.: New Di-
         rections, 1941.
            A dramatic tale in prose and verse examining
         the meaning of Jewish destiny in events around cir-
         cumcision ceremony of Bronx child.

1272.   Schwartz, Irving.   Every Man His Sword.   Garden
         City: Doubleday, 1951.
            Violence and reprisals in Southern town where
         young Jewish soldier protests lynching of a Negro.

1273.   Schwartz, Jonathan.   Almost Home: Collected Stor-
         ies.   New York: Doubleday, 1970.
            The central character in most of the stories is
         a thirty-year-old Jew; themes of marriage, divorce,
         and family relationships.

1274.   Schwartz-Bart, Andre.   The Last of the Just.   Trans-
         lated by Stephen Becker.   New York: Atheneum,
         1960.

Jewish martyrdom begins in twelfth-century England and ends in Nazi gas chamber.

1275. Schweitzer, Gertrude. The Herzog Legacy. New York: Doubleday, 1976.
       A Jewish newspaper publishing dynasty is portrayed in the period from 1844 to 1963.

1276. Schwerin, Doris. Leanna. New York: Morrow, 1978.
       History of past fifty years reflected in marriage of pianist and film director and their inability to truly love each other.

1277. Segal, Albert. Johannesburg Friday. New York: McGraw-Hill, 1954.
       Reminiscences of members of Jewish family in Johannesburg on the day before Day of Atonement.

1278. Segal, Brenda Lesley. Aliya. New York: St. Martin's, 1978.
       Israeli commando paratrooper is killed before his marriage to a Philadelphia WASP, and the pregnant fiancee is taken in by his sister on a kibbutz.

1279. Seide Michael. The Common Thread: A Book of Stories. New York: Harcourt, Brace, 1944.
       Difficulties and mystery of human life displayed in short stories of Jews in Brooklyn.

1280. Selden, Ruth, ed. The Ways of God and Men: Great Stories from the Bible in World Literature. New York: Stephen Daye, 1950.
       Twain, Mann, Werfel, and others are represented in anthology of stories based on Biblical themes.

1281. Seley, Stephen. Baxter Bernstein: A Hero of Sorts. New York: Scribner's, 1949.
       Failure of writer who hopes to run away from world and Jewish identity during World War II.

1282. _____. The Cradle Will Fall. New York: Harcourt, 1945.
       Young boy in New York's East Side reacts emotionally to mother's death.

1283.   Semprun, Jorge. The Long Voyage. New York:
        Grove, 1964.
            Narrative of five-day train trip by prisoners be-
        ing transported to Nazi concentration camp.

1284.   Serge, Victor. The Long Dusk. Translated by
        Ralph Manheim. New York: Dial, 1946.
            Refugees join Frenchmen in underground resis-
        tance movement to Nazi occupation forces.

1285.   Settle, Mary Lee. The Kiss of Kin. New York:
        Harper, 1956.
            Jewish violinist married to granddaughter of
        Southern matriarch joins family in the reading of
        her will.

1286.   Sevela, Efraim. Legend from Invalid Street. Trans-
        lated by Anthony Kahn. New York: Doubleday,
        1974.
            Short stories reveal life of Jews in Vilna, some
        lost in Nazi concentration camp, now facing Soviet
        persecution.

1287.   Seymour, Gerald. The Glory Boys. New York:
        Random House, 1976.
            PLO and IRA agents team up to kill aging Is-
        raeli nuclear physicist on his way to England.

1288.   _____. Kingfisher. New York: Simon & Schus-
        ter, 1978.
            Three Russian Jews hijack a jetliner to go to
        Israel and are forced to land in England for lack
        of fuel.

1289.   Shahar, David. News from Jerusalem. Translated
        by Dalya Bilu and others. Boston: Houghton Mif-
        flin, 1974.
            Fifteen short stories, including selections from
        his novel The Palace of Shattered Vessels, all set
        in the city of Jerusalem.

1290.   _____. The Palace of Shattered Vessels. Trans-
        lated by Dalya Bilu. Boston: Houghton Mifflin,
        1975.
            This is the first in a projected volume series
        with the strange figure of a rationalist and meta-
        physician at its center in a Jerusalem setting.

1291. Shainberg, Lawrence. One on One. New York:
       Holt, Rinehart and Winston, 1970.
            College basketball superstar is beset by voices,
       including his Southern Jewish parents', on the day
       prior to his debut in Madison Square Garden.

1292. Shamir, Moshe. David's Stranger. New York:
       Abelard-Schuman, 1965.
            The love triangle of David, Bathsheba, and
       Uriah.

1293. _____. The King of Flesh and Blood. Translated
       by David Patterson. New York: Vanguard, 1958.
            Alexander Yannai's military conquests and strug-
       gle against Pharisees leads to Roman victory.

1294. Shapiro, Eddie. Strange Gods and the Fighting Rabbi.
       Norwich, N.Y.: Boundary, 1972.
            Former boxer from East Side becomes rabbi in
       upper New York State.

1295. Shapiro, Karl. Edsel. New York: Geis, 1971.
            American-Jewish poet tours Europe under State
       Department auspices and chases women.

1296. Shapiro, Lamed. The Jewish Government and Other
       Stories. Translated by Curt Leviant. New York:
       Twayne, 1971.
            Stories of pre-Revolution Russian shtetl with
       themes of pogroms, inner conflicts, and village
       rabbis.

1297. Shaplen, Robert. A Corner in the World. New
       York: Knopf, 1949.
            Five stories of post-World War II period include
       refugee doctor who flees to Macao and serves the
       downtrodden.

1298. Shankman, Sam. Moulding Forces. New York:
       Philosophical Library, 1954.
            Early 1900 account of Eastern European boy's
       adaptation to America.

1299. Shavelson, Melville. The Eleventh Commandment.
       New York: Arbor House, 1977.
            Father takes daughter to live in Israel, digs a
       well, discovers oil and upsets Arab plan to destroy
       Israel.

1300. _____. Lualda. New York: Arbor House, 1975.
       The story of a twenty-year affair between a Jew-
       ish Hollywood film director and an Italian sex sym-
       bol.

1301. Shaw, Irwin. Act of Faith, and Other Stories. New
       York: Random House, 1946.
       Short stories with themes of anti-Semitism in
       American army and attraction to Palestine by Jew-
       ish soldier.

1302. _____. Mixed Company. New York: Random
       House, 1950.
       Short stories reflect superstition in religion and
       Arab-Jewish conflict in Palestine.

1303. _____. The Troubled Air. New York: Random
       House, 1951.
       Period of anti-Communist blacklist, which forces
       dismissal of Jewish staff member of radio network.

1304. _____. Voices of a Summer Day. New York:
       Delacorte, 1965.
       Reflections of middle-aged man on his childhood,
       the political conflicts of the 1920s, and his relation-
       ships with his son.

1305. _____. The Young Lions. New York: Random
       House, 1948.
       World War II novel of American soldiers, brutal
       officers, anti-Semitism, cynicism, and idealism.

1306. Shaw, Robert. The Man in the Glass Booth. New
       York: Harcourt, Brace & World, 1967.
       Recreation of the Eichmann trial and the preced-
       ing Nazi horrors in Europe.

1307. Sheffield, Herman B. A Unique Heritage. New York:
       Bloch, 1941.
       Jewish family escapes terrors of Nazi forces in
       Germany and emigrates to America.

1308. Shem, Samuel. House of God. New York: Marek,
       1978.
       The first year as intern in a prestigious Jewish
       hospital in New York is filled with politics, women,
       and depressing patients.

1309. Shenhar, Yitzhak, ed. Tehilla and Other Israeli
       Tales. Translated by I. M. Lask, Israel Schen,
       and Lea Ben-Dor. New York: Abelard-Schuman,
       1956.
            Anthology of Israeli writers includes themes of
       kibbutz life, war, emigration from Europe.

1310. Schneider, Isidor. The Judas Time. New York:
       Dial, 1947.
            Communist professor informs on faculty cell for
       promise of professorship.

1311. Sherman, Dan. Riddle. New York: Arbor House,
       1977.
            International mercenary returns home to collect
       his inheritance and begin a gentleman's life.

1312. Shneour, Zalman. Song of the Dnieper. Translated
       by Joseph Leftwich. New York: Roy, 1945.
            Life in Jewish village along the river Dnieper in
       pre-Soviet times.

1313. _____. Downfall. New York: Roy, 1944.
            Jewish-gentile relationships developed in story
       of merchant family in Warsaw during German oc-
       cupation in 1915.

1314. Shohet, Jacqueline. Jacob's Ladder. New York:
       Roy, 1953.
            Egyptian-Jewish mother in Cairo determined to
       Europeanize daughter with use of English governess.

1315. Sholom Aleichem. The Adventures of Menahem-
       Mendl. Translated by Tamara Kahana. New York:
       Putnam, 1969.
            The classic Schlemiel of Yiddish literature por-
       trayed in the character of a man who never suc-
       ceeds.

1316. _____. Adventures of Mottel, the Cantor's Son.
       Translated by Tamara Kahana. New York: Henry
       Schuman, 1953.
            Cantor's sons emigrate from Kasrilova to Amer-
       ica and seek quick rise up ladder of fortune.

1317. _____. The Old Country. Translated by Julius
       and Frances Butwin. New York: Crown, 1946.

Twenty-seven short stories of humorous characters in East European shtetl including Tevye and
his daughters.

1318.   _____. The Great Fair: Scenes from My Childhood. Translated by Tamara Kahana. New York:
Noonday, 1955.
Autobiographical novel of life of Jewish boy in
small East European village.

1319.   _____. Old Country Tales. Translated by Curt
Leviant. New York: Putnam, 1966.
Collection of stories of village Jews in Eastern
Europe.

1320.   _____. Some Laughter, Some Tears. Translated
by Curt Leviant. New York: Putnam, 1968.
Stories of peddlers, rabbis, small shopkeepers
in East European villages.

1321.   _____. Stories and Satires. Translated by Curt
Leviant. New York: Yoseloff, 1959.
More short stories and a playlet describing vil-
lage personalities in Eastern Europe.

1322.   _____. Selected Stories of Sholom Aleichem.
New York: Random House, 1956.
Tales of poverty-stricken Jews in Eastern Europe
enriched by their religion.

1323.   _____. Wandering Star. Translated by Francis
Butwin. New York: Crown, 1952.
Cantor's daughter and her boyfriend flee from
East European village and emigrate to America and
the Yiddish theater.

1324.   Shorris, Earl. The Boots of the Virgin. New York:
Delacorte, 1968.
Detroit Jew gains fame as Spanish bullfighter.

1325.   Shubert, Hilda. They Came from Kernitza. Mon-
treal: Chateau Books, 1972.
Three stories of Jews from Russia who emigrated
to Canada.

1326.   Shulman, Irving. Amboy Dukes. New York: Doubleday, 1947.

Brooklyn gangs of juvenile delinquents roam
streets during World War II years.

1327. _____. The Big Brokers. New York: Dial, 1951.
New York and Los Angeles gangster mobs grad-
uated from ranks of Brooklyn ghetto gangs.

1328. _____. Cry Tough! New York: Dial, 1949.
Jewish delinquent out of reform school slips into
old patterns after try for respectability with Brooklyn family.

1329. _____. The Devil's Knee. New York: Trident,
1973.
A sequel to The Amboy Dukes, this follows the
characters to Hollywood and includes underworld
figures.

1330. _____. Saturn's Child. New York: Saturday Re-
view/Dutton, 1976.
Sociology professor finds his way out of a broken
marriage and identity crisis to a new awakening.

1331. Sidney, William. The Good Tidings. New York:
Farrar, Straus, 1950.
Couple turn to teachings of John the Baptist dur-
ing days of Herod and Rome.

1332. Siegel, Benjamin. A Kind of Justice. New York:
Harcourt, Brace, 1960.
Sixteenth-century Marrano seeks revenge in Lon-
don on sailor who betrayed his wife to Inquisition.

1333. _____. The Sword and the Promise. New York:
Harcourt, Brace, 1959.
Greek physician, enslaved by Romans, joins
Jews to fight against oppressions of Hadrian.

1334. Sigal, Clancy. Zone of the Interior. New York:
Crowell, 1976.
An American writer in the 60s is introduced by
psychiatrist to Jewish mysticism, LSD, and a
whole variety of mind-boggling alternatives.

1335. Silberstang, Edwin. Nightmare of the Dark. New
York: Knopf, 1967.

Twelve-year-old Austrian boy witnesses death of
mother and others in concentration camp and escapes.

1336. Silman, Roberta. Blood Relations. Boston: Little,
       Brown, 1977.
       A majority of the stories in this collection deal
       with second-generation family, success in stock
       market, social workers, and family relationships.

1337. Silva-Coronel, Paul. The Birth of Ludwig Kleinst.
       Translated by Lowell Blair. New York: Harper
       & Row, 1971.
       A Jewish concert pianist seeks out Nazi physician
       who engaged in experiments and is now in hiding in
       South America.

1338. Silver, Lily Jay. Shadow on the Sun. New York:
       Duell, Sloan and Pearce, 1958.
       Wife and daughter leave occupied France after
       death of husband and find new life in Cuba as mis-
       tress and nun.

1339. Silver, Warren A. The Green Rose. New York:
       Dial, 1977.
       Eleventh-century Spain is setting for novel of
       life of the poet-philosopher Ibn Gabirol and Moslem-
       Christian enmity.

1340. Simcles, L. S. Seven Days of Mourning. New York:
       Random House, 1963.
       East Side family refuses to accept death of son
       and is forced into mourning by stranger.

1341. Simonhoff, Harry. The Chosen One. New York:
       Yoseloff, 1964.
       Marranos of sixteenth-century Portugal misled
       by messianic pretensions of Solomon Molko and
       David Reubeni.

1342. Simpson, Robert. April's There. New York: Har-
       per & Row, 1973.
       A London Jewish reporter, up from the slums,
       has romance with daughter of wealthy manufacturer
       and is involved in Nazi espionage during World War
       II.

1343. Sinclair, Jo. Anna Teller. New York: McKay, 1960.
       Elderly woman fights Russians in Hungarian revolt of 1956 and emigrates to America to dominate life of her son.

1344. _____. The Changelings. New York: McGraw-Hill, 1955.
       Conflicts in first and second generation of Irish and Jewish immigrants as neighborhood turns black.

1345. _____. Wasteland. New York: Harper, 1946.
       Re-identification of Jewish newspaperman with family and heritage which he had rejected.

1346. Singer, Isaac Bashevis. A Crown of Feathers, and Other Stories. New York: Farrar, Straus and Giroux, 1973.
       The grotesque and absurd, the supernatural and metaphoric are typical themes in this collection reflecting human irrationality.

1347. _____. The Estate. New York: Farrar, Straus and Giroux, 1969.
       Sequel to The Manor follows lives of Polish family of nineteenth century emerging from ghetto to Zionism, anti-Semitism, and emigration to America.

1348. _____. Enemies: A Love Story. New York: Farrar, Straus and Giroux, 1972.
       Survivor of Holocaust, a book salesman in Brooklyn, is entangled in web of his second wife, a Pole who saved him, a mistress, and his first wife, whom he thought dead.

1349. _____. The Family Moskat. Translated by A. H. Gross. New York: Knopf, 1950.
       Polish-Jewish family and community face disintegration on brink of German occupation.

1350. _____. A Friend of Kafka and Other Stories. New York: Farrar, Straus and Giroux, 1970.
       Over twenty short stories peopled by actors, writers, demons, and the varied characters of a master storyteller.

1351. _____. Gimpel the Fool, and Other Stories. Trans-

lated by Saul Bellow and others.   New York: Noonday, 1957.
    Nineteenth-century Polish ghetto setting of sacred
fool who is completely open to suffering.

1352. _____.   The Isaac Bashevis Singer Reader.   New
York: Farrar, Straus and Giroux, 1971.
    Includes selections from novels and short stories
including The Magician of Lublin and In My Father's
Court.

1353. _____.   The Magician of Lublin.   Translated by
Elaine Gottlieb and Joseph Singer.   New York:
Noonday, 1960.
    Magician and escape-artist flees wife and family
but returns in penitence after misadventures.

1354. _____.   The Manor.   Translated by Joseph Singer.
New York: Farrar, Straus and Giroux, 1967.
    Deceitful wife and apostate daughter plague head
of Jacoby family of Poland as secular world in-
trudes.

1355. _____.   Old Love.   New York: Farrar, 1979.
    This collection of stories includes demented wom-
an in Brazil, aged scholar whose first manuscript
is returned, and selfish and unselfish loves.

1356. _____.   Passions, and Other Stories.   New York:
Farrar, Straus and Giroux, 1975.
    Twenty stories portraying life of Jews in Amer-
ica and Europe, including Holocaust victims, suicide, and dabblers in magic.

1357. _____.   Satan in Goray.   Translated by Jacob
Sloan.   New York: Noonday, 1955.
    Seventeenth-century world of dybbuks and fiends
witnesses effect of Sabbatai Zevi on Jewish community after Chmielnicki massacres.

1358. _____.   The Seance and Other Stories.   New York:
Farrar, Straus and Giroux, 1968.
    Sixteen stories dealing with murder, rabbis,
dybbuks, mediums, moneylenders in European, New
York, and Canadian settings.

1359. _____.   Short Friday and Other Stories.   New
York: Farrar, Straus and Giroux, 1964.

Short stories with characters like widows, Yeshiva students, village shohet, and also holiday ob-
servances.

1360. _____. Shosha. New York: Farrar, Straus and
Giroux, 1978.
Ghetto life in Poland in the 1930s is heart of
search of novelist for a bride who finally emigrates
to America after the Holocaust.

1361. _____. The Slave. Translated by Cecil Hemley.
New York: Farrar, Straus, 1962.
Polish Jew escapes from Chmielnicki pogroms
and falls in love with daughter of peasant for whom
he is a cowherd.

1362. _____. The Spinoza of Market Street. New York:
Farrar, Straus, 1961.
Chief librarian of Warsaw synagogue removed
from post by superstition-ridden group because of
rationalist bent.

1363. Singer, I. J. The Family Carnovsky. Translated
by Joseph Singer. New York: Vanguard, 1969.
Three generations of Polish Jews followed to intermarriage, emigration to America, tension of
German and Jewish identity.

1364. _____. Steel and Iron. Translated by Joseph
Singer. New York: Funk & Wagnalls, 1969.
Jewish soldier deserts from Russian army in
1915 and attempts to assist refugees in Warsaw.

1365. _____. Yoshe Kalb. Translated by Joseph Singer.
New York: Harper & Row, 1965.
Reissue of classic Yiddish novel of pious Polish
Jew who wanders through country as beggar.

1366. Singer, Jeanne Florence. This Festive Season. New
York: Harcourt, Brace, 1943.
Non-Jewish professor concerned for former stud-
ent who is refused an instructorship because he is
Jewish.

1367. Singer, Philip E. They Did Not Fear. New York:
Beechhurst, 1952.
Viennese Jews join partisan group to fight for

Israel after imprisonment in concentration camp
in Poland.

1368.   Singer, Sally M.   For Dying You Always Have Time.
New York: Putnam, 1970.
Bronx schoolteacher leaves Hadassah tour in Israel and becomes involved with spies and counter-
espionage activities.

1369.   Sklovsky, Max.   Dynasty: A Novel of Chicago's Industrial Revolution.   Chicago: Americana House,
1959.
Jewish immigrant seeks future during Chicago's
industrial revolution.

1370.   Skvorecky, Josef.   Miss Silver's Past.   Translated
by Peter Kussi.   New York: Grove, 1974.
A novel by a Czech author strips bare the corruption and censorship in the publishing field centering around a former Terezin victim who murders an official.

1371.   Slaughter, Frank Gill.   The Curse of Jezebel: A
Novel of the Biblical Queen of Evil.   New York:
Doubleday, 1961.
The fortunes of Jezebel and Ahab linked with her
ties to Canaanites.

1372.   _____.   East Side General.   New York: Double-
day, 1952.
Hospital superintendent maintains ties with East
Side orthodox parents in spite of his intermarriage.

1373.   _____.   God's Warrior.   New York: Doubleday,
1967.
Saul of Tarsus center of conflict between Jewish
sects and emerging Christianity.

1374.   _____.   Road to Bithynia: A Novel of Luke, the
Beloved Physician.   New York: Doubleday, 1951.
Luke joins followers of Jesus and is befriended
by Paul.

1375.   _____.   The Scarlet Cord: A Novel of the Woman
of Jericho.   New York: Doubleday, 1956.
Rahab dominates Jericho during siege by Joshua.

1376. _____. The Song of Ruth: A Love Story from
the Old Testament. New York: Doubleday, 1954.
       Story of the Biblical Ruth and her love affair with
Boaz.

1377. Slavitt, David. Feel Free. New York: Delacorte,
1968.
       Middle-class married Jewish businessman seeks
escape from business trap through affair with woman.

1378. Smith, Bert Kruger. A Teaspoon of Honey. Nashville, Tenn.: Aurora, 1970.
       Russian pogrom causes young man to escape to
America where he loses a fortune made in Texas
oil wells.

1379. Smith, Godfrey. Caviare. New York: Coward,
1976.
       Jewish scientist defects to Russia with one of
her father's coscientists to deliver him in exchange
for an uncle who helped her escape from the Nazis.

1380. Smith, Martin. Flora's Dream. New York: Dutton,
1972.
       Aunt helps family supress boy who becomes a
college teacher of English obsessed with sex.

1381. Smith, Robert Kimmel. Sadie Shapiro in Miami.
New York: Simon & Schuster, 1977.
       The famed knitting grandmother is used in Miami
to publicize a real-estate development for senior
citizens that turns out to be an embezzlement scheme.

1382. _____. Sadie Shapiro's Knitting Book. New York:
Simon & Schuster, 1973.
       Resident of senior citizen "hotel" becomes author
of a best-seller of knitting patterns and national ce-
lebrity.

1383. Smith, Valerie Kohler. The Rape of the Virgin Butterfly. New York: Dial, 1973.
       Wildly liberal Jewish high school teacher involved
with macho WASP and anti-Communist mood of the
50s.

1384. Smith, Wilbur. Eagle in the Sky. New York: Doubleday, 1974.

World-renowned author, blinded in Arab terrorist
attack, and photographer, former fighter pilot, are
lovers who cannot find happiness.

1385. Snitzer, J. L. The Story of the Baal Shem: Life,
Love and Teachings of the Founder of Chassidism
and Jewish Mysticism. Translated by Samuel Ro-
senblatt. New York: Pardes Pub. House, 1946.
Novel based on the life of the Baal Shem Tov
and his creation of the Hasidic movement.

1386. Snow, Charles Percy. The Conscience of the Rich.
New York: Scribner's, 1958.
Wealthy Jewish family in England opposed to
son's desire to become a doctor and witnesses intermarriage of daughter.

1387. Sobel, Irwin Philip. The Hospital Makers. New
York: Doubleday, 1973.
A doctor describes the varied cast in the development of a charitable hospital in the 30s to a
great medical complex in the 50s.

1388. Sobel, Samuel. A Treasury of Jewish Sea Stories.
New York: Jonathan David, 1965.
Short stories of Jews and the sea from Biblical
to modern times.

1389. Solomon, Ruth Freeman. The Candlesticks and the
Cross. New York: Putnam, 1968.
Distinguished Jewish family falls from security
to exile during the Rasputin period in Russia.

1390. _____. The Eagle and the Dove. New York:
Putnam, 1971.
The second in the Pirov family saga of the ro-
mance between the Jewish heiress and her Tartar
husband in Russia under Czar Nicholas II.

1391. _____. Two Lives, Two Lands. New York:
Putnam, 1975.
The third in a trilogy about the Pirov family
taking them from Russia to San Francisco, and
two half-brothers involved in ridding Palestine of
the Turks to prepare for the Jewish State.

1392. Southron, Arthur Eustace. On Eagle's Wings. New
York: McGraw-Hill, 1954.

Life of Moses from early life in Egypt to leadership in the Exodus.

1393. Spacks, Barry. Orphans. New York: Harper &
       Row, 1972.
       A successful cartoonist looks back upon earlier
       failures as soldier in Korea, attempts to befriend
       a Korean orphan, and desires to set a seduction
       record.

1394. _____. The Sophomore. New York: Prentice-
       Hall, 1968.
       Sophomore flees school because of love affair
       and returns to face responsibilities.

1395. Spark, Muriel. The Mandelbaum Gate. New York:
       Knopf, 1965.
       Half-Jewish Englishwoman crosses from Israel
       into Jordan and is rescued by British foreign-ser-
       vice officer.

1396. Sperber, Manes. The Abyss. Translated by Con-
       stantine Fitzgibbon. Garden City: Doubleday,
       1952.
       Jews in partisan groups in Poland fighting the
       Nazis to prevent destruction of Jewish village.

1397. Spicehandler, Daniel. Burnt Offering. New York:
       Macmillan, 1961.
       Battle around Stella Montis Monastery between
       Arabs and Jews during the 1948 war.

1398. Spicehandler, Ezra, and Arnson, Curtis. New Writ-
       ing in Israel. New York: Schocken, 1977.
       Thirteen Israeli poets and five prose writers are
       featured in this anthology.

1399. Spigelgass, Leonard. A Majority of One. New
       York: Random House, 1959.
       Adventures of Jewish widow who accompanies
       son and his wife to his government post in Japan.

1400. Spiraux, Alain. Time Out. Translated by Frances
       Keene. New York: Times Books, 1978.
       An old cobbler in Paris helps a nine-year-old
       rid himself of his Hitler demon as the real Hitler
       moves on the city.

1401.   Stebel, S. L.   The Collaborator.   New York: Ran-
        dom House, 1968.
            Israeli economist accused of collaboration with
        Nazis during occupation of Europe.

1402.   Stegner, Wallace.   Second Growth.   Boston: Hough-
        ton Mifflin, 1947.
            New England town ultimately accepts young Jew-
        ish couple as residents after initial rebuff.

1403.   Stein, Hana.   The Wedding.   New York: Wyn, 1950.
            East Side Jewish family prepares for wedding of
        younger daughter faced with the desertion of the
        older daughter's husband.

1404.   Steinberg, Milton.   As a Driven Leaf.   Indianapolis:
        Bobbs-Merrill, 1940.
            Tale of Elisha ben Abuyah of the second century,
        who became an apostate.

1405.   Steiner, Moses J.   Satan in the Woods.   New York:
        Shengold, 1978.
            A Polish Jew embraces Zionism in this story of
        survival between the two World Wars.

1406.   Stern, Chaim.   Isaac: The Link in the Chain.   New
        York: Speller, 1977.
            A fictionalized biography of the Biblical Isaac
        highlights his relationship with Ishmael and Rebecca.

1407.   Stern, Daniel.   The Girl with the Glass Heart.   In-
        dianapolis: Bobbs-Merrill, 1952.
            Attractive girl rebels against Orthodox immigrant
        parents and their parochial views.

1408.   _____.   The Rose Rabbi.   New York: McGraw-
        Hill, 1971.
            Former rabbinical student now with ad agency
        seeks to understand his past and the reasons for
        his failure in life.

1409.   _____.   The Suicide Academy.   New York: Mc-
        Graw-Hill, 1968.
            Allegory of institution headed by Jew where in-
        mates decide whether they should live or die.

1410.   _____.   Who Shall Live, Who Shall Die.   New
        York: Crown, 1963.

Former inmate of concentration camp produces Broadway play about Nazi death camps.

1411.   Stern, Gladys B.   Young Matriarch.   New York: Macmillan, 1942.
Sequel to The Matriarch carries the story of the Viennese Jewish family, the Rakonitz clan, to London and problems of intermarriage.

1412.   Stern, Karl.   Through Dooms of Love.   New York: Farrar, Straus & Cudahy, 1960.
Former Czech glassworks owner and daughter escape Nazis in 1939 and emigrate to America from Holland.

1413.   Stern, Lucille.   The Midas Touch: A Novel.   New York: Citadel, 1957.
Prosperous businessman develops estrangement from Orthodox family after rise to success.

1414.   Stern, Selma.   The Spirit Returneth ... A Novel. Translated by Ludwig Lewisohn.   Philadelphia: Jewish Publication Society, 1946.
Fourteenth-century German-Jewish communities experience pogroms and martyrdom during period of Black Death.

1415.   Stettin, Alma.   Don't Ask Too Much of Love.   New York: Vantage, 1954.
Jew suffers self-doubts and denial of heritage through intermarriage.

1416.   Stilman, Abram.   Healer of All Flesh: A Novel. New York: Whittier, 1959.
Ghetto Jew escapes from Czarist Russia to America and becomes noted surgeon.

1417.   Stilwell, Hart.   Campus Town.   New York: Doubleday, 1950.
Jewish professor at Southern university assists students to understand danger of Ku Klux Klan.

1418.   Stirling, Monica.   Sigh for a Strange Land.   Boston: Little, Brown, 1959.
Teenager describes attempts of refugees from Soviet tyranny to rebuild their lives.

1419.   Stone, Irving. The Passions of the Mind.   New
        York: Doubleday, 1971.
            Biographical novel of Sigmund Freud reveals
        enormous research into Vienna of the nineteenth
        and twentieth century and development of psycho-
        analysis.

1420.   Strassova, Helena. The Path.   Translated by Peter
        Freixa. New York: Orion/Grossman, 1969.
            Jewish girl in occupied France during World War
        II loses mother and brother, has child by English
        captain in the Maquis, and finds haven in America.

1421.   Street, James. Velvet Doublet. New York: Double-
        day, 1953.
            Clashes of Jew, Christian, and Moslem mirrored
        in Columbus's voyages to Tangiers and America.

1422.   Strick, Ivy. Scot Free. New York: Taplinger,
        1979.
            New York Jew is married to a Midwestern
        WASP and concludes that the union is a disaster
        after an abortion and spending Christmas with his
        family.

1423.   Stryjkowski, Julian. The Inn. Translated by Celina
        Wieniewska. New York: Harcourt Brace Jovano-
        vich, 1972.
            Pogrom, rape, and pillage of Jewish town in
        Austria during World War I by Cossacks.

1424.   Styron, William. Lie Down in Darkness. Indian-
        apolis and New York: Bobbs-Merrill, 1951.
            Jewish husband of Southern girl victim of anti-
        Semitism and aggravates wife's neurotic tendencies.

1425.   _____ . Sophie's Choice. New York: Random
        House, 1979.
            Aspiring novelist becomes confidant of two lov-
        ers, a Polish-Catholic girl who had been in a con-
        centration camp and a Brooklyn Jewish intellectual.

1426.   Suhl, Yuri. Cowboy on a Wooden Horse. New York:
        Macmillan, 1953.
            Sequel to One Foot in America finds hero as up-
        holsterer and involved with unionism and love affair.

1427. _____. One Foot in America. New York: Macmillan, 1950.
Polish-Jewish boy emigrates to Brooklyn and re-
quires adjustment to American ways.

1428. Sukenick, Ronald. The Death of the Novel and Other
Stories. New York: Dial, 1969.
Lower East Side milieu of Jewish characters,
holidays, and adjustment of immigrants.

1429. _____. UP. New York: Dial, 1968.
Brooklyn Jewish boy achieves goal as teacher of
English.

1430. Sultan, Stanley. Rabbi: A Tale of the Waning Year.
Massachusetts: Morning Star, 1977.
Sephardic Jewish family in New York finds problems in relating to other Jews and experiences usual generational problems.

1431. Sulzberger, C. L. The Tallest Liar. New York:
Crown, 1977.
An eight-footer who is black, Jewish, and a
Nazi becomes star with Harlem Globetrotters,
focus of incident in the Mideast, and is visited
by sorceress.

1432. _____. The Tooth Merchant. New York: Quad-
rangle, 1973.
An amoral Armenian spy attempts to sell im-
probable secret weapons to leaders including Stalin,
Nasser, Ben Gurion, Eisenhower.

1433. Suslov, Ilya. Here's to Your Health, Comrad Shif-
rin! Translated by Maxine Bronstein. Blooming-
ton: Indiana University Press, 1977.
Satiric account of career of Soviet Jew in his
attempt to become a journalist during the post-
Stalin days.

1434. Swados, Harvey. Celebration. New York: Simon
& Schuster, 1975.
The aged Jewish founder of a progressive school,
a kind of culture hero, is caught between his establishment friends and his radical grandson.

1435. _____. Nights in the Gardens of Brooklyn. Boston: Little, Brown, 1961.

Fables set in Brooklyn, Provence, South Pacific,
of men emasculated by women who are bored and
frustrated.

1436. _____. Out Went the Candle. New York: Viking,
1955.
Garment-center executive who builds network of
war industries destroyed by Senate investigating
committee.

1437. _____. Standing Fast. New York: Doubleday,
1970.
Sweeping story of anti-Stalinist Marxists covering
period from World War II through the Kennedy ad-
ministration.

1438. Swiggett, Howard. The Power and the Prize: A
Novel. New York: Ballantine, 1954.
London and New York business executive dis-
suaded from marriage to Viennese refugee by chairman of the board.

1439. Sylvester, Harry. Moon Gafney. New York: Holt,
1947.
Irish-Catholic politician driven from power because of refusal to play anti-Negro, anti-Semitic
role.

1440. Tabor, Paul. They Came to London. New York:
Macmillan, 1943.
Twelve national types personify refugees who try
to reach England to fight Nazis, including Viennese
professor drowned as he tries escape from North
African prison camp.

1441. Taft, Allen Robert. American Story. New York:
Arco, 1947.
Friendships of Catholic, Protestant, and
Jew traced from childhood with attendant con-
flicts.

1442. Tammuz, Benjamin. Castle in Spain. Translated
by Joseph Schachter. Indianapolis: Bobbs-Merrill,
1973.
A young Israeli journalist falls in love with an
older Scandinavian embassy worker and affair ends
in tragedy.

1443.   Tanous, Peter, and Rubinstein, Paul. The Petro-
        dollar Takeover. New York: Putnam, 1975.
            Tentative Arab-Israeli peace leads Arabs to at-
        tempt to buy General Motors to guarantee tanks
        needed for impending Iran-Saudi Arabia conflict.

1444.   Tarr, Herbert. The Conversion of Chaplain Cohen.
        New York: Geis, 1963.
            Humorous portrayal of Jewish chaplain in U.S.
        Air Force.

1445.   _____. Heaven Help Us! New York: Random
        House, 1968.
            Bachelor rabbi in first pulpit in New York sub-
        urb encounters slum landlords, Sisterhood leaders,
        and country-club Jews.

1446.   _____. So Help Me God! New York: Times
        Books, 1979.
            Non-Jew attempts to evade draft by enrolling in
        a rabbinical school and becomes involved as coun-
        selor for family problems.

1447.   _____. A Time for Loving. New York: Random
        House, 1973.
            At the close of his life, King Solomon, with the
        help of Shulamith, attempts to regain his powers to
        thwart Jeroboam.

1448.   Taube, Herman. Empty Pews. Translated by Sarah
        Chodosh Lesser. Baltimore: Grossman, 1959.
            Refugees from Nazi Europe find new life in Amer-
        ica after pains of adjustment.

1449.   Taube, Herman and Suzanne. Remember. Translat-
        ed by Helena Frank. Baltimore: Grossman, 1951.
            Short stories of harrowing experiences of men
        and women in German concentration camps.

1450.   Taylor, Daniel. They Move with the Sun. New
        York: Farrar, Straus, 1948.
            Psychiatrist tells of his boyhood in Indiana and
        his choice of vocation to understand anti-Semitism.

1451.   Teilhet, Hildegarde. The Terrified Society. New
        York: Doubleday, 1947.
            Jewish girl in love with head of native fascist

movement who flees to Guatemala after attack upon
her violinist brother in Atlanta.

1452.   Templeton, Charles. Act of God. Boston: Little,
        Brown, 1977.
            A Roman Catholic cardinal murders an American
        archaeologist who claims to have found the bones
        of Jesus in Israel.

1453.   Tennenbaum, Silvia. Rachel, the Rabbi's Wife.
        New York: Morrow, 1978.
            Suburban New York rabbi's wife involved in
        struggle to express her individuality in midst of
        community's expectations of her.

1454.   Tennyson, Hallam. The Wall of Dust, and Other
        Stories. New York: Viking, 1948.
            Six stories of individuals coping with new en-
        vironments including English Jew in postwar Pal-
        estine.

1455.   Terrall, Robert. The Steps of the Quarry. New
        York: Crown, 1951.
            American occupation forces in Austria near a
        concentration camp and their relationships to sev-
        eral Jewish survivors.

1456.   Terrot, C. The Angel Who Pawned Her Harp. New
        York: Dutton, 1953.
            Visit of a Very Heavenly Person to the East End
        of London and the effects upon the life of a pawn-
        broker and others.

1457.   Thomas, Leslie. Come to the War. New York:
        Scribner's, 1970.
            Concert pianist has affairs and adventures prior
        to and during the '67 Israeli-Arab war.

1458.   Thompson, Francis J. Abraham's Wife. New
        York: Vanguard, 1954.
            Problems of black laborers in Florida and Cuba
        told in parallel fashion to Biblical account of Abra-
        ham and Sara.

1459.   Thompson, Morton. Not as a Stranger. New York:
        Scribner's 1953.
            Portrait of successful doctor befriended in med-

ical school by Jewish professor embittered by anti-Semitism.

1460.   Tidyman, Ernest. Shaft Among the Jews. New York: Dial, 1972.
Hassidic diamond merchants enlist aid of black private detective disguised as janitor to penetrate world of jewelers and end scandal.

1461.   Tigay, Betty S. Rich People, and Other Stories. Chicago: Stein, 1942.
Short stories of lives of Jews in Midwestern city.

1462.   _____. Rock of Refuge. New York: Vantage, 1954.
Girl engaged to rabbi influences her mother to return to Judaism.

1463.   Todd, Ian. Ghosts of the Assassins. Miami: Seeman, 1976.
Today's Arab terrorists are linked to ancient sect of Moslem assassins and are hunted by international group of secret agents.

1464.   Todrin, Boris. Out of These Roots. Caldwell, Idaho: Caxton, 1944.
Son of Russian-Jewish immigrants on East Side of New York achieves small success as poet.

1465.   Torday, Ursula. Young Lucifer. New York: Lippincott, 1960.
Jewish boy in Paris hostel for concentration-camp survivors falls in love with Irish girl in neighboring fashionable finishing school.

1466.   Torres, Tereska. The Golden Cage. Translated by Meyer Levin. New York: Dial, 1959.
Three refugee families from Warsaw, Belgium, and Lyons await visas to Palestine in Portuguese coastal village in 1940.

1467.   _____. The Open Doors. New York: Simon & Schuster, 1968.
Ex-GI assists Jewish underground to help refugees from France and Italy to arrive in Palestine.

1468. Trachtenberg, Inge. An Arranged Marriage. New
       York: Norton, 1975.
            German-Jewish couple from Berlin are persuaded
       to seek help from Freud for husband's epilepsy,
       return in seeming recovery, and wife takes lesbian
       lover after mate's death.

1469. _____. So Slow the Dawning. New York: Norton,
       1973.
            Through eyes of teenager, a middle-class Berlin
       Jewish family is viewed from the 1920s through
       their emigration in 1939.

1470. Traub, Barbara Fishman. The Matrushka Doll.
       New York: Marek, 1979.
            Former inmate of Auschwitz is betrayed by sur-
       viving Jews of her town and Russian soldier lover.

1471. Trew, Andrew. Ultimatum. New York: St. Mar-
       tin's, 1976.
            Old nuclear warheads are hijacked by Palestinian
       terrorists who demand land and money from Israeli
       agents.

1472. Trumbo, Dalton. Night of the Aurochs. New York:
       Viking, 1979.
            Trumbo's unfinished novel is the life of an unre-
       pentant Nazi from his birth to Auschwitz and Nurem-
       burg and prison term.

1473. Twersky, Jacob. The Face of the Deep. Cleveland:
       World, 1953.
            Lives of former residents of home for blind bab-
       ies now an executive, a college professor, and a
       beggar.

1474. _____. A Marked House. New York: Yoseloff,
       1968.
            Hasidic rabbinical family in America faces con-
       flicts in tensions and attractions of secular environ-
       ment.

1475. Uhnak, Dorothy. Law and Order. New York: Sim-
       on & Schuster, 1973.
            Former policewoman depicts three generations of
       New York policemen, corruption, violence, and Irish
       anti-Semitism.

1476. Uhlman, Fred. Reunion. New York: Farrar,
Straus and Giroux, 1977.
An adult émigré from Nazi Germany recreates
his friendship with son of German nobility.

1477. Ujvari, Peter. By Candlelight. Translated by Andrew Handler. New Jersey: Fairleigh Dickinson,
1977.
A Hungarian rabbinical student is attracted to
the secular studies of the German Enlightenment
and is expelled from the Yeshiva.

1478. Unruh, Fritz von. The End Is Not Yet. New York:
Storm, 1947.
Polish dancer commanded to perform for Hitler
reveals the corruption of Nazi movement.

1479. Updike, John. Bech: A Book. New York: Knopf,
1970.
Short stories about a middle-aged Jewish writer
on State Department cultural exchange and lecture
circuit.

1480. Uris, Leon. Exodus. New York: Doubleday, 1958.
Widowed American nurse joins Jewish illegal
forces to assist refugees to enter Palestine.

1481. _____. Mila 18. New York: Doubleday, 1961.
Warsaw-ghetto freedom fighters die at post fighting German forces.

1482. _____. QBVII. New York: Doubleday, 1970.
Jewish journalist defends himself in British court
against libel action brought by Polish doctor once
in concentration camp.

1483. Van Aerde, Rogier. Cain. Translated by I. and E.
Graham-Wilson. Chicago: Regnery, 1954.
Recreation of pre-patriarchal Biblical times with
tragedy of the Sons of Adam and Eve.

1484. Van Dyke, Henry. Ladies of the Rachmaninoff Smile.
New York: Farrar, Straus and Giroux, 1965.
Nephew tells of relationship between elderly Jew
and her Negro maid, and a seance to communicate with
aunt's son.

1485. Van Praag, Van. <u>Day Without End</u>. New York:
       Sloane, 1949.
          Ordeal of platoon in Normandy causes breakdown
       of officer and reveals strength of Jewish scout.

1486. Van Rjndt, Philippe. <u>The Trial of Adolf Hitler</u>. New
       York: Summit Books/Simon & Schuster, 1978.
          Hitler lives secretly in Beyrouth, supported by
       fortune of gold, and after twenty-five years de-
       mands a UN trial to vindicate his philosophy.

1487. Van Slyke, Helen. <u>All Visitors Must Be Announced</u>.
       New York: Doubleday, 1972.
          A Jewish couple is faced with discrimination in
       their attempt to buy an apartment-house cooperative
       unit in New York.

1488. Veen, Adriaan Van Der. <u>The Intruder</u>. Translated
       by James S. Holmes and Hans van Marle. New
       York: Abelard-Schuman, 1958.
          Dutch journalist falls in love with Jewish refugee
       in New York after lecture to a synagogue group.

1489. Vicas, Victor, and Haim, Victor. <u>The Impromptu
       Imposter</u>. New York: Abelard-Schuman, 1971.
          American killer of French policeman escapes to
       Israel using stolen passport of Jew and is black-
       mailed into working for former SS members.

1490. Vidal, Nicole. <u>Emmanuel</u>. Translated by Eric Earn-
       shaw Smith. New York: Viking, 1965.
          Mother in Egyptian ghetto convinced that son is
       the Messiah, whom she ultimately brings to Pales-
       tine at age seventeen in time for its move to inde-
       pendence.

1491. Viertel, Joseph M. <u>The Last Temptation</u>. New
       York: Simon & Schuster, 1955.
          Refugees from Vienna and Prague find refuge in
       Israel and are confronted by charge that husband be-
       trayed the Haganah.

1492. Viertel, Peter. <u>Bicycle on the Beach</u>. New York:
       Delacorte, 1971.
          Fifteen-year-old son of German-Jewish family
       has affair with wife of British actor in California
       just prior to Hitler's attack on England.

1493. Vinokur, Gregory. The Commissar. New York:
       Twayne, 1965.
          Soviet-Jewish writer realizes truth of Stalin's
       anti-Jewish madness and escapes Soviet tyranny.

1494. Wager, Walter. Time of Reckoning. New York:
       Playboy, 1977.
          CIA superstar tracks down murders in West
       Germany by a New York Jewish pathologist, a child
       victim of Dachau.

1495. Wagner, Eliot. Better Occasions. New York: Cro-
       well, 1974.
          Freelance house painter in Bronx, beset by wife
       and daughters, is attracted by widow who is his
       client.

1496. _____. Grand Concourse. Indianapolis and New
       York: Bobbs-Merrill, 1954.
          Bronx family seeks better life as symbolized in
       the Grand Concourse, the boulevard near their side
       street.

1497. Walden, Daniel, ed. On Being Jewish: American
       Jewish Writers from Cahan to Bellow. Greenwich,
       Conn.: Fawcett, 1974.
          Walden's anthology of Jewish writers covers the
       period from 1896 to 1973 with over thirty writers.

1498. Walden, David. The Season. New York: Grey-
       stone, 1942.
          Proprietor of hotel in Catskills seeks profit
       through exploitation of summer help.

1499. Waldman, Adele. My Enemy, My Brother. New
       York: Yoseloff, 1963.
          Jewish professor of philosophy in Munich resists
       Nazis and escapes to Switzerland with family.

1500. Wallace, Irving. The Word: A Novel. New York:
       Simon & Schuster, 1972.
          Public-relations man promotes newly discovered
       gospel by brother of Jesus, which claims that he
       survived the crucifixion for nineteen years.

1501. Wallant, Edward Lewis. The Children at the Gate.
       New York: Harcourt, Brace & World, 1964.

Jewish orderly in New England hospital convinces
skeptical Catholic worker of worth of compassion
and concern.

1502. _____ . The Human Season. New York: Harcourt, 1960.
Plumber in New Haven, grief-stricken by wife's
death, experiences loneliness in refusal to live with
daughter.

1503. _____ . The Pawnbroker. New York: Harcourt,
Brace & World, 1961.
Polish refugee college instructor, now pawnbroker in Harlem, faces up to life's responsibilities
after murder of Negro assistant.

1504. _____ . The Tenants of Moonbloom. New York:
Harcourt, Brace & World, 1963.
Rent collector for slum landlord brother shows
concern for tenants of apartment houses.

1505. Wallenrod, Reuben. Dusk in the Catskills. New
York: Reconstructionist, 1957.
Hotel setting in the Catskills reveals lives of
Jewish vacationers, the college help, and the own-
ers.

1506. Wallis, James Harold. The Niece of Abraham Pein.
New York: Dutton, 1943.
German refugee in New Hampshire village ac-
cused of murder of niece by anti-Semitic residents.

1507. Wander, Fred. The Seventh Well. Translated by
Marc Linder. New York: International Publishers,
1977.
Twelve short stories each deal with a different
personage in concentration camps in Germany and
France.

1508. Ward, Mary Jane. The Professor's Umbrella. New
York: Random House, 1948.
Jewish instructor in English in Midwestern university fired on false charge of moral turpitude by
anti-Semitic president.

1509. Waren, Helen. Out of the Dust. New York: Crown,
1952.

American Jew and sabras establish kibbutz in Negev just prior to War of Independence.

1510. Warren, Robert Penn. Wilderness: A Tale of the Civil War. New York: Random House, 1961.
Crippled Bavarian Jew joins Union Army in search for meaning of life and freedom.

1511. Wartofsky, Victor. Meeting the Pieman. New York: Day, 1971.
Jewish carpenter buys family grocery store in Washington, D.C., in the black ghetto and faces robbery, rape of wife, and riots.

1512. Waten, Judah. So Far No Further. Melbourne: David & Charles, 1973.
Immigrant Jewish and Catholic families in Australia are intertwined through love affairs of their children.

1513. Watkins, Shirley. The Prophet and the King. New York: Doubleday, 1956.
The prophet Samuel and King Saul engage in struggle against the Philistines when young David emerges as hero.

1514. Wechsberg, Joseph. The Self-Betrayed. New York: Knopf, 1955.
Ruthless Jewish Communist official purged and executed in shift of doctrinal policy.

1515. Weidman, Jerome. The Center of the Action. New York: Random House, 1969.
New York auditor moves to top of publishing business through devious means.

1516. _____. The Enemy Camp: A Novel. New York: Random House, 1958.
East Side Jew marries Philadelphia socialite and experiences uneasiness in gentile world of Connecticut.

1517. _____. A Family Fortune. New York: Simon & Schuster, 1978.
Aged and physically infirm tycoon of liquor industry threatened by exposure of the nature of his rise from immigrant status to power.

1518. _____ . Fourth Street East: A Novel on How It
Was. New York: Random House, 1970.
    New York East Side setting of a boy's growing
up in the 1920s and the family move to the Bronx.

1519. _____ . Last Respects. New York: Random
House, 1972.
    New York East Side saga of reflections on mother-
son relationship and ghetto characters.

1520. _____ . Other People's Money. New York: Random House, 1967.
    Anti-Semitic tycoon raises orphan who loves his
daughter but is rebuffed because of Jewish ancestry.

1521. _____ . The Sound of Bow Bells. New York:
Random, 1962.
    Popular writer reasserts Jewish identity through
son's Bar Mitzvah after compromises in search for
success.

1522. _____ . The Temple. New York: Simon & Schuster, 1975.
    Former GI who entered Buchenwald, now wealthy,
encourages the building of a Jewish enclave and
synagogue in anti-Semitic section of Westchester,
N.Y.

1523. _____ . Tiffany Street. New York: Random
House, 1974.
    In this sequel to Fourth Street East and Last Re-
spects, Benny Kramer is a successful attorney faced
with a conscientious-objector son in Vietnam war.

1524. _____ . Your Daughter, Iris. New York: Doubleday, 1955.
    Bronx stenographer's letters to her mother from
England where husband is to perform important operation.

1525. Weinberg, Marcel. Spots of Time. New York:
Macmillan, 1972.
    Teenaged boy tells of incarceration in DP camp,
stay in orphanage, and new life in America with
aunt.

1526. Weinberg, Norbert. Beyond the Wall. New York:
Bloch, 1978.

The Western Wall in Jerusalem is the scene of light stories of doubt and faith.

1527. Weingarten, Violet. Mrs. Beneker. New York: Simon & Schuster, 1968.
        Middle-aged suburbanite faced with pregnant daughter, college son involved in civil-rights movement, a straying husband, and swinging Miami parents.

1528. _____. A Woman of Feeling. New York: Knopf, 1972.
        Middle-class mother relives liberal past in confrontation with son facing political difficulties.

1529. Weinreb, Nathaniel Norsen. The Babylonians. New York: Doubleday, 1953.
        Nebuchadnezzar's physician won over to Judaism by Jeremiah's influence.

1530. _____. The Copper Scrolls. New York: Putnam, 1958.
        The Essene cult buries scrolls at Qumran cave before being overcome by Romans.

1531. _____. Esther. New York: Doubleday, 1955.
        Esther's role as wife of Persian king in saving the lives of her kinsmen.

1532. _____. The Sorceress. Garden City: Doubleday, 1954.
        Deborah assists Israelites in their triumph over the Canaanites.

1533. Weinstein, Dr. Alfred A. Barbed-Wire Surgeon. New York: Macmillan, 1948.
        American surgeon captured by Japanese serves in prison camps in Phillipines.

1534. Weiss, David. The Guilt Makers. New York: Rinehart, 1953.
        Buchenwald survivor befriended by ex-GI in America unable to erase memory of German brutality.

1535. _____. I, Rembrandt. New York: St. Martin's, 1979.
        The Jews in Amsterdam are portrayed in this

version of the life of Rembrandt, who uses Spinoza
as his model for Jesus.

1536. Weiss, Ernst. Eyewitness. Translated by Ella R.
       McKee. Boston: Houghton Mifflin, 1977.
           A Jewish psychiatrist has Adolf Hitler as a pa-
       tient in 1918 and is subsequently silenced.

1537. Weiss, Peter. Exile. New York: Delacorte, 1968.
           German half-Jew seeks meaning of self in wan-
       derings in England and Sweden and in refugee cir-
       cles.

1538. Weller, Sheila. Hansel & Gretel in Beverly Hills.
       New York: Morrow, 1978.
           A widow whose hopes for remarriage are dashed
       commiserates with her gay hairdresser, whose af-
       fair with a student is disappointing.

1539. Welles, Patricia. Babyhip. New York: Dutton,
       1967.
           Jewish hippie leaves her middle-class Detroit
       family for sex affairs and drug experiences.

1540. Werfel, Franz. Star of the Unborn. New York:
       Viking, 1946.
           Fantasy predicting future utopia in which only
       Catholic Church and Jews survive.

1541. Wernick, Robert. The Hill of Fortune. New York:
       Scribner's, 1951.
           Jewish girl chooses lover from two non-Jewish
       brothers after their return from army service.

1542. Wertheim, Morits. The Last of the Levanos. New
       York: Yoseloff, 1967.
           Jewish banker recalls death of family at hands
       of Nazis and is unable to find a purpose to life.

1543. Wesker, Arnold. Love Letters on Blue Paper. New
       York: Harper & Row, 1975.
           A collection of stories dealing with aged house-
       wives, retired businessmen, and dying labor leader.

1544. West, Morris L. The Devil's Advocate. New York:
       Morrow, 1959.
           German-refugee doctor in Italy involved in in-

quiry into sainthood status for martyred village priest.

1545.   . The Tower of Babel. New York: Morrow, 1968.
        Israeli intelligence officer, Damascus spy, and Lebanese banker tangle prior to Six Day War.

1546. White, Alan. Possess the Land. New York: Harcourt Brace Jovanovich, 1970.
        Group of kibbutzniks flee from settlement beseiged by Arabs to one that is more protected and create a viable life.

1547. Whittemore, Edward. Jerusalem Poker. New York: Holt, Rinehart and Winston, 1978.
        Second of proposed tetralogy, this one deals with a twelve-year poker game for the control of Jerusalem.

1548.   . Sinai Tapestry. New York: Holt, 1977.
        A forged codex sinaiticus is at the center of intrigue, which culminates in the Smyrna massacre of 1922, this the first in a projected Jerusalem Quartet.

1549. Wibberley, L. The Centurion. New York: Morrow, 1966.
        Roman centurion ordered to supervise crucifixion of Jesus after demonstrating sympathy for him.

1550. Wiesel, Elie. The Accident. Translated by Ann Borchardt. New York: Hill & Wang, 1962.
        Auschwitz survivor, now Israeli newspaperman, attempts suicide in New York City.

1551.   . A Beggar in Jerusalem. Translated by Lily Edelman and Elie Wiesel. New York: Random House, 1970.
        Beggar at Wailing Wall symbolizes search for historic meaning of Jewish experience in aftermath of Six Day War.

1552.   . Dawn. Translated by Frances Frenaye. New York: Hill & Wang, 1961.
        Inner struggle of young Israeli ordered by underground movement to kill British hostage.

1553.   _____. The Gates of the Forest.   New York:
           Holt, Rinehart and Winston, 1966.
                Seventeen-year-old Hungarian-Jewish survivor
           joins partisan forces in forest and finds safety in
           America.

1554.   _____. Night.   Translated by Stella Rodway.
           New York: Hill & Wang, 1960.
                Personal record of teenager in Auschwitz con-
           centration camp who sees father die.

1555.   _____. The Oath. New York: Random House,
           1973.
                Azriel breaks oath of silence concerning a po-
           grom to save life of would-be suicide.

1556.   _____. The Town Beyond the Wall. Translated
           by Stephen Becker. New York: Atheneum, 1964.
                Survivor of concentration camp returns as adult
           to Hungarian birthplace and is captured by Russians.

1557.   Wilchek, Stella. Judith. New York: Harper & Row,
           1969.
                Retelling of Apocryphal tale of Judith, who killed
           Holofernes.

1558.   _____. Tale of a Hero. New York: Harper &
           Row, 1965.
                Clever Viennese Jew establishes new life in
           America after European and South American ad-
           ventures.

1559.   Wilder, Robert. Wait for Tomorrow. New York:
           Putnam, 1950.
                Press agent for exiled king meets Jewish émigrés
           in Mexico and is involved with congressman who re-
           fuses to campaign on anti-Semitic ticket.

1560.   Williams, Jay. Solomon and Sheba. New York:
           Random House, 1959.
                Solomon renounces love for Sheba in favor of a
           united kingdom.

1561.   Wilner, Herbert. Dovisch in the Wilderness, and
           Other Stories. New York: Bobbs-Merrill, 1968.
                Jewish professor in San Francisco lectures to
           literature class on generational conflicts and ethnic
           problems.

1562. Wilson, Dorothy Clarke. The Herdsman. Philadelphia: Westminster, 1946.
      The prophet Amos castigates Jeroboam and the northern kingdom for social injustices.

1563. _____. Jezebel. New York: McGraw-Hill, 1955.
      Ahab's wife, Jezebel, a Phoenician princess, opposes Jewish prophets through her pagan practices.

1564. _____. Prince of Egypt. Philadelphia: Westminster, 1949.
      Moses develops from royal privileges in Egyptian court to become leader of oppressed Hebrews.

1565. Wilson, Mitchell. Live with Lightning. Boston: Little, Brown, 1949.
      Jewish physicist is driven from university post and to suicide because of false charges of subversive activities.

1566. Wilson, S. J. Hurray for Me. New York: Crown, 1964.
      Memories of childhood in Brooklyn during Depression which include death, visit to orphan asylum, and loving mother.

1567. _____. To Find a Man. New York: Viking, 1969.
      Brooklyn youth experiences first stirrings of love and sex in ghetto neighborhood.

1568. Wiseman, Adele. The Sacrifice: A Novel. New York: Viking, 1956.
      Russian immigrant family find freedom in Canada in symbolic framework of story of Abraham and the Sacrifice of Isaac.

1569. Wiseman, Thomas. Journey of a Man. New York: Doubleday, 1967.
      Self-discovery by survivor of Austrian Anschluss who fled with mother to Switzerland, France, and America and to Italian immoral society.

1570. _____. The Quick and the Dead. New York: Viking, 1968.
      Viennese half-Jew stays alive through friendship with Nazi officer and SS man and his mistress.

1571. Wisse, Ruth R. A Shtetl and Other Yiddish Novellas.
       New York: Behrman House, 1973.
           East European Jewry in Czarist Russia is de-
       scribed in these novellas by five Yiddish writers.

1572. Wolfe, Bernard. The Great Prince Died. New
       York: Scribner's, 1959.
           Based on assassination of Leon Trotsky in his
       Mexican retreat.

1573. Wolfert, Ira. An Act of Love. New York: Simon
       & Schuster, 1948.
           Wounded Jewish navy flier nursed to health by
       natives on small Pacific Island.

1574. Wolff, Geoffrey. Bad Debts. New York: Simon &
       Schuster, 1969.
           Self-centered man tries to reunite family at close
       of his life.

1575. Wolpert, Stanley A. Aboard the Flying Swan. New
       York: Scribner's, 1954.
           Young Jew in merchant marine assisted in growth
       to maturity by older sailor.

1576. Wouk, Herman. The Caine Mutiny: A Novel of
       World War II. Garden City: Doubleday, 1951.
           Jewish lawyer defends officer of Pacific mine
       sweeper court-martialed for mutiny.

1577. _____. The City Boy. New York: Simon &
       Schuster, 1948.
           Last summer of Coolidge era evoked in boys' ad-
       ventures in summer camp and in Bronx public
       schools.

1578. _____. Don't Stop the Carnival. New York:
       Doubleday, 1965.
           American-Jewish public-relations man buys hotel
       on Caribbean island and encounters problems with
       natives and guests.

1579. _____. Marjorie Morningstar: A Novel. New
       York: Doubleday, 1955.
           West Side New York Jewish girl has affair with
       playwright and rebels against middle-class parents.

1580.   _____ . War and Remembrance. New York: Little, Brown, 1978.
      This sequel to The Winds of War covers the per-
iod of 1941-1945 and the Jewish family of the son
of Capt. Henry, who are destroyed by the Nazis.

1581.   _____ . The Winds of War; A Novel. Boston:
Little, Brown, 1972.
      U.S. Naval Commander, an attache in Berlin in
1939, on personal relationships with Roosevelt, Hitler, Goering, Churchill, and Stalin finally receives
battleship command at Pearl Harbor.

1582. Yaffe, James. The Good-for-Nothing. Boston: Little, Brown, 1953.
      Elder brother seeks to keep charming no-good
brother out of scandals and difficulties in spite of
widowed, doting mother.

1583.   _____ . Mister Margolies. New York: Random
House, 1962.
      Bachelor vice-president of shoe company forced
out by pressures of nephew.

1584.   _____ . Nothing but the Night. Boston: Atlantic/
Little, Brown, 1957.
      Guilt of affectionate parents emphasized in fic-
tional version of Loeb-Leopold case.

1585.   _____ . Poor Cousin Evelyn. Boston: Little,
Brown, 1951.
      Short stories of upper-class Jews on New York's
West Side.

1586.   _____ . The Voyage of the Franz Joseph. New
York: Putnam, 1970.
      German liner sails from Hamburg with Jewish
refugees and is unable to land passengers at any
port.

1587.   _____ . What's the Big Hurry? Boston: Atlantic/
Little, Brown, 1954.
      Accountant suffers reverses in fall of Chicago
utilities magnate, wanders through Europe, and returns home to realize worth of family love.

1588. Yehoshua, A. B. Early in the Summer of 1970.

Translated by Miriam Arad and Pauline Shrien.
New York: Doubleday, 1977.
     Three stories of war and conflict, a father learn-
ing of his son's death, a military lecturer to soldiers in outpost areas, and Israeli veterans called
back to duty.

1589.   . Three Days and a Child.   Translated by
Miriam Arad.   New York: Doubleday, 1970.
     Five short stories of life and death set in today's
Israel.

1590.   . The Lover.   Translated by Philip Simpson.   New York: Doubleday, 1978.
     Husband, searching for wife's lover during the
Yom Kippur war, is joined by daughter who finds
her own lover, an Arab.

1591. Yellen, Samuel. The Wedding Band.   New York:
Atheneum, 1961.
     Spinster English professor recounts marriage of
her parents, a Jewish second-hand clothes dealer,
and a gentile mother.

1592. Yerby, Frank. The Voyage Unplanned.   New York:
Dial, 1974.
     American lawyer, former French Resistance vol-
unteer, falls in love with Israeli intelligence agent,
the sister of his earlier love in the resistance movement.

1593. Yezierska, Anzia. Bread Givers.   New York: Braziller, 1975.
     A reissue of an autobiographical novel of an im-
migrant girl in the East Side Jewish ghetto of the
20s.

1594. Yglesias, Helen. Family Feeling.   New York: Dial,
1975.
     Left-wing intellectual abhors business-tycoon
brother in complex family saga of move from rags
to riches.

1595. Yglesias, Rafael. The Game Player.   New York:
Doubleday, 1978.
     Shy Jewish boy seeks to learn friends' uncanny
skill and ability to succeed as they move into adulthood.

1596. Yoseloff, Martin. A Time to Be Young. New York:
       Yoseloff, 1967.
            Rebellious youth from middle-class New York
       family seeks answers in Greenwich Village, Iowa,
       and returns to job with finance firm and Jewish
       wife.

1597. _____. Remember Me to Marcie. South Bruns-
       wick, N.J.: Barnes, 1973.
            Iowa girl comes to the big city, has love affairs,
       and marries editor of a Zionist magazine.

1598. Young, George. The Man Called Lenz. New York:
       Coward-McCann, 1955.
            British occupation forces in Palestine seek chief
       leader of Jewish terrorist gang.

1599. Young, I. S. Uncle Herschel, Dr. Padilsky and the
       Evil Eye. New York: Harcourt Brace Jovanovich,
       1973.
            A Russian paramedic immigrates to Brooklyn and
       comes into conflict with doctors, gangsters and su-
       perstitions.

1600. Young, Michael. The Trial of Adolf Hitler. New
       York: Dutton, 1944.
            Survivor of Viennese refugee family creates fan-
       tasy of Germans and trial of Hitler.

1601. Yurick, Sol. The Bag. New York: Trident, 1968.
            Successful novelist finds inner satisfactions in
       working for Welfare Department.

1602. _____. Someone Just Like You. New York:
       Harper & Row, 1972.
            Short stories that include an aged man's fight
       against his caseworker to stay out of Senior Cit-
       izens' Center and boy's determination to build up
       his body.

1603. Zangwill, Israel. The King of Schnorrers. New
       York: Yoseloff, 1960.
            Reprint of classic work portraying Sephardic beg-
       gar in London ghetto at close of eighteenth century
       and his feelings of superiority.

1604. Zara, Louis. Blessed Is the Land. New York:
       Crown, 1954.

Jewish pioneers in New York depicted in diary
of Asser Levy.

1605. _____. This Land Is Ours. Boston: Houghton
Mifflin, 1940.
New York doctor attempts to establish relation-
Eighty-year panoramic sweep of life on the Amer-
ican frontier from time of Braddock's defeat in-
cludes portrait of Jewish trader.

1606. Zehnpfenning, Gladys. Search for Eden. Minneap-
olis: Denison, 1955.
The Biblical Noah is recreated in his struggle
for survival during the Flood.

1607. Zeigerman, Gerald. A Rightful Inheritance. New
York: Atheneum, 1967.
New York doctor attempts to establish relationship with antiestablishment son, who leaves college,
travels in Europe, and dodges military service.

1608. Zeldis, Chayym. The Brothel. New York: Putnam,
1979.
In Judea during the Roman oppression, a brothel
is the center of a plot including a deputy to Pontius
Pilate, a Jewish prostitute, Zealots, and a version
of the Christ story.

1609. _____. Brothers. New York: Random House,
1976.
A recreation of the life of Jesus told by his
brother, who is embittered by the death of their
mother.

1610. _____. Golgotha. New York: Avon, 1974.
A reconstruction of the last days of Jesus and
the treachery of his disciples.

1611. _____. May My Words Feed Others. New York:
Barnes, 1974.
This anthology of short stories and poetry includes the themes of Israel, the Holocaust, Dias-
pora, and America.

1612. Zeno, C. The Four Sergeants. New York: Atheneum, 1977.
A British platoon is dropped into Sicily to blow
up a bridge and is plagued with the problem that

some of the volunteers who are German-Jews cannot be allowed to be taken alive.

1613.   Zuckerman, George. Farewell, Frank Merriwell.
New York: Dutton, 1973.
A successful sportswriter of Irish-Catholic-Jew-
ish background struggles with loss of idealism,
daughter's marriage, wife's attempted suicide,
drinking problem, and Bobby Kennedy's assassination, all on a June weekend.

1614.   Zweig, Arnold. The Axe of Wandsbek. Translated
by Eric Sutton. New York: Viking, 1947.
German butcher in Nazi Hamburg earns extra
money as executioner of Communist workers and
commits suicide.

1615.   Zwisohn, Rose R. The Promised Land. Boston:
Meador, 1955.
Wife of American physician reluctantly emigrates
to Israel with him and becomes enamoured of the
land.

1427, 1441, 1450, 1465, 1539, 1554, 1566, 1577, 1595, 1602

Akiba
282, 496, 653, 1005, 1076, 1333, 1404

Alexander Yannai
1293

Amos
1562

Anthologies
30, 39, 103, 129, 171, 183, 234, 257, 259, 263, 645, 646, 647, 648, 649, 837, 865, 898, 945, 1004, 1056, 1138, 1158, 1159, 1160, 1161, 1162, 1180, 1197, 1280, 1309, 1398

Antique Dealers
618, 920, 1547

Anti-Semitism
50, 99, 106, 110, 111, 132, 142, 154, 156, 203, 204, 207, 216, 229, 241, 243, 253, 259, 267, 284, 286, 304, 339, 361, 363, 364, 365, 435, 439, 458, 461, 463, 473, 491, 498, 508, 524, 528, 553, 575, 582, 612, 629, 676, 688, 721, 724, 754, 776, 782, 808, 811, 813, 814, 817, 821, 830, 847, 863, 875, 890, 891, 926, 934, 939, 945, 1007, 1011, 1019, 1112, 1182, 1263, 1274, 1301, 1302, 1305, 1347, 1366, 1402, 1417, 1424, 1450, 1451, 1459, 1465, 1487, 1506, 1508, 1520, 1522

Arab-Jewish Relations
18, 91, 183, 222, 303, 312, 345, 358, 359, 367, 494, 643, 708, 731, 750, 773, 785, 790, 819, 857, 1079, 1090, 1232, 1240, 1241, 1242, 1243, 1245, 1302, 1339, 1395, 1546, 1547, 1590

Archaeologists
27, 311, 424, 706, 1005, 1437, 1452

Artists
175, 338, 473, 554, 581, 709, 903, 940, 1132, 1145, 1393

Australia
142, 920, 1512

Christian-Jewish Relations
    5, 6, 46, 52, 53, 54, 66, 79, 82, 88, 103, 132, 142,
    192, 214, 243, 249, 314, 334, 337, 389, 395, 416,
    433, 446, 458, 463, 509, 525, 526, 543, 545, 548,
    553, 568, 571, 591, 593, 606, 623, 628, 644, 664,
    671, 673, 731, 759, 768, 791, 808, 832, 882, 899,
    911, 912, 926, 931, 932, 935, 940, 947, 949, 960,
    1007, 1011, 1016, 1019, 1033, 1070, 1098, 1128,
    1139, 1157, 1162, 1171, 1181, 1217, 1225, 1226,
    1313, 1361, 1383, 1402, 1414, 1438, 1439, 1441,
    1442, 1446, 1451, 1452, 1459, 1465, 1487, 1501,
    1512, 1516, 1522, 1540, 1541, 1544, 1579, 1604

College
    10, 33, 43, 119, 151, 170, 181, 331, 374, 415, 460,
    462, 525, 599, 659, 690, 740, 821, 827, 839, 851,
    853, 917, 918, 1033, 1035, 1050, 1068, 1134, 1177,
    1190, 1237, 1259, 1394, 1417, 1505, 1527, 1528,
    1539, 1561, 1584, 1595, 1607

Communications Media
    47, 48, 81, 154, 211, 258, 288, 325, 342, 395, 408,
    561, 581, 730, 1100, 1303, 1408, 1597

Concentration Camps
    5, 9, 106, 141, 153, 176, 196, 198, 202, 232, 237,
    301, 394, 482, 514, 533, 597, 684, 700, 707, 718,
    734, 781, 849, 855, 858, 921, 922, 924, 973, 1025,
    1046, 1073, 1135, 1153, 1188, 1216, 1258, 1274,
    1283, 1286, 1335, 1367, 1370, 1410, 1455, 1465,
    1482, 1507, 1522, 1534, 1550, 1554, 1556, 1580

Conversion
    746, 864, 869, 935, 1070, 1082, 1261, 1338

Czechoslovakia
    159, 196, 466, 565, 684, 687, 901, 921, 922, 923,
    924, 1217, 1234, 1370, 1412, 1514

David
    96, 171, 273, 308, 335, 584, 621, 663, 670, 679,
    1005, 1292, 1513

Dead Sea Scrolls
    1530

Death
    51, 120, 147, 152, 175, 341, 485, 564, 650, 760, 885,

Nineteenth Century
  364, 365
Pre-World War II
  147, 454, 803, 819, 1143, 1342, 1386, 1411, 1537
World War II
  73, 88, 92, 99, 100, 101, 102, 106, 146, 184, 199,
  202, 226, 251, 287, 363, 433, 454, 467, 499, 500,
  502, 530, 612, 613, 660, 687, 688, 759, 762, 794,
  795, 796, 870, 894, 897, 953, 954, 1142, 1224, 1342,
  1456
Post-World War II
  135, 146, 147, 148, 150, 184, 258, 313, 370, 474,
  593, 1060, 1168, 1524

Entertainment Industry
  49, 173, 224, 410, 476, 477, 512, 588, 684, 707,
  881, 966, 1123

Esther
  297, 464, 905, 971, 1531

Family Relationships
  52, 75, 76, 100, 118, 130, 139, 147, 148, 165, 167,
  187, 213, 247, 250, 266, 279, 303, 320, 321, 341,
  353, 369, 381, 385, 390, 393, 440, 454, 465, 468,
  488, 493, 506, 507, 515, 517, 521, 532, 622, 634,
  645, 650, 658, 671, 685, 709, 710, 783, 791, 792,
  804, 833, 846, 851, 879, 893, 918, 1002, 1009, 1017,
  1037, 1048, 1054, 1067, 1072, 1078, 1080, 1122,
  1125, 1132, 1144, 1161, 1184, 1193, 1209, 1219,
  1228, 1269, 1279, 1304, 1336, 1380, 1399, 1403,
  1407, 1413, 1430, 1434, 1462, 1474, 1495, 1496,
  1502, 1517, 1561, 1568, 1579, 1582, 1583, 1594,
  1607, 1613
Father
  90, 175, 493, 692, 712, 741, 810, 946, 1055, 1088,
  1150, 1523
Husband/Wife
  120, 161, 197, 226, 268, 323, 373, 382, 386, 426,
  435, 507, 522, 556, 560, 696, 699, 703, 730, 731,
  829, 1019, 1090, 1099, 1109, 1195, 1203, 1222,
  1227, 1273, 1276, 1300, 1330, 1377, 1453, 1468,
  1495, 1613
Mother/Child
  94, 221, 227, 329, 331, 332, 342, 428, 460, 635,
  724, 726, 728, 730, 737, 739, 777, 843, 881, 919,
  1015, 1062, 1164, 1185, 1191, 1213, 1214, 1519

1118, 1146, 1153, 1154, 1180, 1181, 1225, 1254, 1264,
1274, 1306, 1307, 1396, 1420, 1469, 1470, 1472,
1476, 1478, 1488, 1492, 1499, 1507, 1525, 1553,
1570, 1580, 1581, 1586, 1600, 1612, 1614
Post-World War II
9, 19, 25, 27, 28, 57, 59, 106, 133, 169, 203, 251,
275, 309, 310, 317, 324, 356, 453, 457, 463, 548,
567, 568, 570, 657, 686, 824, 861, 864, 897, 960,
983, 1036, 1128, 1169, 1208, 1257, 1264, 1470, 1472,
1494

Gompers, Samuel
656

Greece
173, 189, 1073

Hadrian
1333

Haganah
106, 269, 494, 495, 785, 1388, 1467, 1480, 1491,
1552

Hagar
1074

Hasidism
13, 14, 39, 233, 234, 264, 277, 803, 862, 884, 1053,
1075, 1093, 1113, 1132, 1133, 1134, 1137, 1158,
1211, 1385, 1474

Herod
124, 190, 396, 786, 1005, 1331

Herod Agrippa
396, 786

Herzl, Theodor
87, 801

Hillel
396, 786

Holland
597, 837, 930, 962, 1014, 1135, 1234, 1263, 1412,
1488, 1535

Holocaust
24, 27, 28, 29, 89, 109, 110, 111, 112, 113, 114,
121, 130, 143, 153, 159, 169, 188, 198, 242, 252,
275, 277, 310, 319, 320, 345, 356, 375, 376, 377,
379, 388, 404, 419, 431, 466, 481, 497, 503, 505,
513, 524, 529, 533, 546, 565, 604, 607, 619, 625,
661, 662, 684, 687, 700, 720, 736, 746, 771, 781,
797, 822, 823, 841, 847, 849, 854, 857, 880, 883,
921, 922, 923, 924, 925, 943, 962, 985, 997, 1013,
1030, 1066, 1070, 1071, 1105, 1122, 1135, 1140,
1141, 1146, 1151, 1153, 1169, 1187, 1188, 1229,
1230, 1235, 1246, 1247, 1254, 1258, 1267, 1274,
1283, 1286, 1306, 1307, 1335, 1337, 1348, 1356,
1360, 1370, 1379, 1396, 1400, 1420, 1425, 1440,
1448, 1466, 1470, 1480, 1482, 1494, 1499, 1507,
1525, 1534, 1542, 1550, 1551, 1553, 1554, 1555,
1556, 1569, 1586, 1600, 1611

Homosexuality
114, 462, 484, 804

Hosea
950, 1085, 1104

Hotel Proprietors
508, 705, 1068, 1498, 1505, 1578

Hungary
252, 375, 376, 583, 687, 693, 701, 746, 771, 1024,
1235, 1343, 1477, 1553, 1556

Ibn Gabirol
1339

Identity Crisis
28, 31, 75, 79, 109, 123, 127, 128, 129, 131, 132,
223, 230, 246, 276, 314, 370, 381, 384, 385, 423,
426, 428, 507, 509, 520, 556, 635, 642, 665, 680,
692, 707, 716, 740, 776, 791, 809, 811, 827, 863,
868, 878, 899, 906, 908, 926, 929, 931, 941, 945,
951, 976, 992, 1006, 1011, 1014, 1027, 1041, 1046,
1064, 1101, 1110, 1133, 1142, 1148, 1159, 1161,
1162, 1200, 1201, 1204, 1210, 1214, 1255, 1259,
1270, 1271, 1281, 1345, 1354, 1363, 1404, 1407,
1408, 1415, 1454, 1473, 1474, 1510, 1516, 1520,
1521, 1537, 1541, 1569, 1574, 1596, 1601

Immigrants, East European in the U.S.
  33, 34, 35, 36, 39, 42, 43, 52, 66, 69, 75, 187,
  246, 353, 385, 393, 455, 480, 491, 504, 506, 641,
  647, 685, 691, 692, 729, 791, 812, 863, 892, 945,
  976, 1047, 1049, 1078, 1082, 1116, 1160, 1164, 1205,
  1206, 1269, 1294, 1316, 1323, 1325, 1336, 1345,
  1347, 1363, 1369, 1378, 1407, 1416, 1426, 1427,
  1464, 1502, 1517, 1519, 1568, 1591, 1593

India
  698, 699

Inter-Dating
  4, 10, 230, 525, 740, 743, 762, 777, 814, 897, 961,
  998, 999, 1186, 1190, 1451

Intermarriage
  46, 49, 54, 58, 66, 78, 88, 92, 97, 122, 133, 142,
  151, 182, 189, 204, 205, 216, 224, 231, 235, 260,
  276, 285, 300, 304, 307, 314, 326, 332, 340, 358,
  400, 404, 416, 422, 428, 432, 445, 454, 456, 469,
  491, 495, 512, 539, 556, 564, 574, 627, 655, 662,
  728, 774, 789, 819, 821, 830, 832, 844, 845, 846,
  851, 869, 885, 933, 990, 991, 1042, 1082, 1087,
  1143, 1158, 1167, 1170, 1181, 1198, 1210, 1212,
  1224, 1227, 1244, 1265, 1278, 1285, 1348, 1354,
  1363, 1372, 1386, 1390, 1411, 1415, 1422, 1424,
  1512, 1516, 1581, 1591

Ireland
  961, 1241

Isaac
  437, 1406

Isaiah
  70

Ishmael
  316

Israel, State of
  1948 War
    399, 452, 624, 708, 717, 874, 901, 914, 1005, 1040,
    1046, 1089, 1127, 1138, 1309, 1367, 1397, 1490,
    1491

IV. APPLYING THE THEMATIC INDEX
TO ADULT JEWISH PROGRAMMING

A Guide to Jewish Themes in American Fiction 1940-1980 includes the only comprehensive bibliography of works relating to Jews and Judaism. The Thematic Index is a unique and necessary guide for anyone who seeks to utilize such fiction for many different purposes. The pulpit book review is a popular means by which rabbis comment upon contemporary fiction and its delineation of significant themes. The Thematic Index will be helpful in the preparation of such reviews, comparisons of the treatment of similar themes by other authors, and discussion of the possible special meaning of the new work. In many congregational schools, high school students are encouraged to write essays on significant Jewish themes. The Thematic Index can be utilized as a resource for that purpose. Literary critics will have a handy tool to assist them in studies of currents in literary thought and the resolutions by writers of the dilemmas faced by human beings. Historians can employ the Thematic Index to help in understanding specific epochs and events in the drama of the Jewish people. Instructors of courses in American literature will find the Thematic Index and the Annotated Bibliography invaluable aids in their academic programs.

The major purpose, however, of the Thematic Index is in its application to adult education. The several illustrations that follow are based upon courses that have been offered at various Jewish institutions. In place of the non-fiction books that were recommended as readings, works of fiction were listed after referring to the Thematic Index.

A.   "Dramatic Moments in Jewish History"

   1.   The Temple Burns

      Feuchtwanger, Lion.   Josephus and the Emperor. Translated by Eithne Wilkins and Ernst Kaiser. New York: Putnam, 1958.

      Gavron, Daniel.   The End of Days.   Philadelphia: Jewish Publication Society, 1970.

   2.   Akiba and Bar Kochba Resist

      Gilner, Elias.   Prince of Israel: A Novel on Bar-Kokba's Uprising Against Rome.   New York: Ex-position, 1952.

      Opatoshu, Joseph.   The Last Revolt: The Story of Rabbi Akiba.   Translated by Moishe Spiegel.   Phil-adelphia: Jewish Publication Society, 1952.

   3.   Torquemada Makes Spain Judenrein

      Andrzejewski, Jerzy.   The Inquisitors.   Translated by Conrad Syrop.   New York: Knopf, 1960.

      Fast, Howard.   Torquemada.   New York: Doubleday, 1966.

   4.   Master of the Good Name Appears

      Buber, Martin.   Tales of the Hasidim.   New York: Schocken, 1947.

      Snitzer, J. L.   The Story of the Baal Shem.   Trans-lated by Samuel Rosenblatt.   New York: Pardes, 1946.

   5.   The Third Jewish State Is Born

      Gillon, Diana and Meir.   Vanquish the Angel.   New York: Day, 1956.

      Uris, Leon.   Exodus.   New York: Doubleday, 1958.

B. "Judaism and the Origins of Christianity"

Asch, Sholem. The Apostle. Translated by Maurice
Samuel. New York: Putnam, 1943.

Brod, Max. The Master. New York: Philosophical
Library, 1951.

Buckmaster, Henriette. And Walk In Love. New
York: Random House, 1956.

Heard, Gerald. The Gospel According to Gamaliel.
New York: Harper, 1945.

Samuel, Maurice. The Second Crucifixion. New York:
Knopf, 1960.

C. "Prophetic Personalities--The Message of Amos, Hosea,
Isaiah, Jeremiah for Our Time."

Asch, Sholem. The Prophet. Translated by Arthur
Saul Super. New York: Putnam, 1955.

Patai, Irene S. The Valley of God. New York: Random House, 1956.

Weinreb, Nathaniel. The Babylonians. New York:
Doubleday, 1953.

Wilson, Dorothy Clarke. The Herdsman. Philadelphia: Westminster, 1946.

D. "Crisis for the American Jew"

1. The American Jewish Family

Gold, Herbert. Fathers. New York: Random House,
1967.

Roth, Philip. Portnoy's Complaint. New York: Random House, 1969.

2. Anti-Semitism

Bellow, Saul. The Victim. New York: Vanguard,
1947.

Miller, Arthur. Focus. New York: Reynal and
Hitchcock, 1945.

3. Intermarriage

Cohen, Arthur. The Carpenter Years. New York:
New American Library, 1967.

Graham, Gwenthalyne. Earth and High Heaven. New
York: Lippincott, 1944.

4. The Negro and the Jew

Kastle, Herbert D. Koptic Court. New York: Simon
& Schuster, 1958.

Sinclair, Jo. The Changelings. New York: McGraw-
Hill, 1955.

E. "Life in the Ghetto: Our Debt to Our Grandfather's
Way of Life"

Agnon, S. Y. A Guest for the Night. Translated by
Misha Louvish. New York: Schocken, 1968.

Asch, Sholem. Salvation. Translated by Willa and
Edwin Muir. New York: Putnam, 1951.

Davis, Saul. The Adventures of Shlomele. New York:
Yoseloff, 1956.

Gaer, Joseph. Heart upon the Rock. New York:
Dodd, Mead, 1950.

Sholom Aleichem. The Old Country. Translated by
Julius and Frances Butwin. New York: Crown,
1946.

_____. Old Country Tales. Translated by Curt
Leviant. New York: Putnam, 1966.

Singer, Isaac Bashevis. The Isaac Bashevis Singer
Reader. New York: Farrar, Straus and Giroux,
1971.

F. "History of Jewish Civilization"

1. Foundations of Judaism

Blacker, Irwin I. and Ethel H.   The Book of Books:
A Treasury of Great Bible Fiction.   New York:
Holt, Rinehart and Winston, 1965.

Hubler, Richard G.   The Soldier and the Sage.   New
York: Crown, 1966.

Steinberg, Milton.   As a Driven Leaf.   Indianapolis:
Bobbs-Merrill, 1940.

2. Medieval Jewish Heritage

Michener, James.   The Source.   New York: Random
House, 1965.

Morrison, Lester M., and Hubler, Richard G.   Trial
and Triumph.   New York: Crown, 1965.

Singer, Isaac Bashevis.   Satan in Goray.   Translated
by Jacob Sloan.   New York: Noonday, 1955.

3. Rise of Modern Judaism

Feierberg, Mordecai Zeeb.   Whither.   Translated by
Ira Eisenstein.   New York: Abelard-Schuman,
1959.

Morgenstern, Soma.   The Testament of the Lost Son.
Translated by Jacob Sloan and Maurice Samuel.
Philadelphia: Jewish Publication Society, 1950.

Wiesel, Elie.   A Beggar in Jerusalem.   Translated
by Lily Edelman and Elie Wiesel.   New York: Random House, 1970.

4. The World of Our Grandfathers

Buber, Martin.   For the Sake of Heaven.   Translated
by Ludwig Lewisohn.   Philadelphia: Jewish Publication Society, 1945.

Ikor, Roger.   The Sons of Avrom.   Translated by

Leonard M. Friedman and Maxwell Singer. New
York: Putnam, 1958.

Singer, I. J. The Family Carnovsky. Translated by
Joseph Singer. New York: Vanguard, 1969.

5. Development of American Judaism

Lewisohn, Ludwig. The Island Within. Philadelphia:
Jewish Publication Society, 1968.

Longstreet, Stephen. Pedlock Saint: Pedlock Sinner.
New York: Delacorte, 1969.

Ribalow, Harold U., ed. These Your Children. New
York: Beechhurst, 1950.

G. "Three Centuries of Jewish Life in America"

1. Jews in Colonial Society, 1654-1750

Barker, Shirley Frances. Strange Wives. New York:
Crown, 1953.

Zara, Louis. Blessed Is the Land. New York:
Crown, 1954.

2. American Jews in a New Nation, 1750-1820

Fast, Howard. The Proud and the Free. Boston:
Little, Brown, 1950.

Gessner, Robert. Treason. New York: Scribner's,
1944.

Zara, Louis. This Land Is Ours. Boston: Houghton
Mifflin, 1940.

3. Jews in an Expanding Culture, 1820-1870

Delmar, Vina. Beloved. New York: Harcourt, Brace,
1956.

Longstreet, Stephen. The Pedlocks: A Family. New
York: Simon & Schuster, 1951.

Warren, Robert Penn. Wilderness: A Tale of the Civil War. New York: Random House, 1961.

4. Jews in Industrial America, 1870-1920

Cahan, Abraham. The Rise of David Levinsky. Revised Edition. New York: Harper & Row 1960.

Frank, Waldo D. Island in the Atlantic. New York: Duell, Sloan and Pearce, 1946.

Roth, Henry. Call It Sleep. New York: Pageant, 1960.

5. Jews and the Strains of a Free Society, 1920-1940

Angoff, Charles. Journey to the Dawn. New York: Beechhurst, 1951.

Bellow, Saul. Herzog. New York: Viking, 1964.

Kaufman, Myron S. Remember Me to God. Philadelphia: Lippincott, 1957.

6. Jews in the World at War, 1940-1954

Hersey, John. The Wall. New York: Knopf, 1950.

Shaw, Irwin. The Young Lions. New York: Random House, 1948.

Uris, Leon. Exodus. New York: Doubleday, 1958.

247